MODERNITY AND EXCLUSION

ONE WEEK LOAN

Theory, Culture & Society

Theory, Culture & Society caters for the resurgence of interest in culture within contemporary social science and the humanities. Building on the heritage of classical social theory, the book series examines ways in which this tradition has been reshaped by a new generation of theorists. It also publishes theoretically informed analyses of everyday life, popular culture, and new intellectual movements.

EDITOR: Mike Featherstone, *Nottingham Trent University*

THE TCS CENTRE
The Theory, Culture & Society book series, the journals *Theory, Culture & Society* and *Body & Society*, and related conference, seminar and postgraduate programmes operate from the TCS Centre at Nottingham Trent University. For further details of the TCS Centre's activities please contact:

Centre Administrator
The TCS Centre, Room 175
Faculty of Humanities
Nottingham Trent University
Clifton Lane, Nottingham, NG11 8NS, UK
e-mail: tcs@ntu.ac.uk
web: http://tcs@ntu.ac.uk

Recent volumes include:

Feminist Imagination
Genealogies in Feminist Theory
Vicki Bell

Michel de Certeau
Cultural Theorist
Ian Buchanan

The Cultural Economy of Cities
Allen J. Scott

Body Modification
edited by Mike Featherstone

Paul Virilio
From Modernism to Hypermodernism
edited by John Armitage

Subject, Society and Culture
Roy Boyne

Norbert Elias and Modern Social Theory
Dennis Smith

Development Theory
Deconstructions/Reconstructions
Jan Nederveen Pieterse

Occidentalism
Modernity and Subjectivity
Couze Venn

Simulation and Social Theory
Sean Cubitt

The Contradictions of Culture
Cities: Culture: Women
Elizabeth Wilson

The Tarantinian Ethics
Fred Botting and Scott Wilson

Society and Culture
Principles of Scarcity and Solidarity
Bryan S. Turner and Chris Rojek

MODERNITY AND EXCLUSION

JOEL S. KAHN

SAGE Publications
London • Thousand Oaks • New Delhi

First published 2001

Published in association with *Theory, Culture & Society*,
Nottingham Trent University

 SAGE Publications Ltd
6 Bonhill Street
London EC2A 4PU

SAGE Publications Inc
2455 Teller Road
Thousand Oaks, California 91320

SAGE Publications India Pvt Ltd
32, M-Block Market
Greater Kailash – I
New Delhi 110 048

British Library Cataloguing in Publication data

A catalogue record for this book is available
from the British Library

ISBN 0 7619 6656 0
ISBN 0 7619 6657 9 (pbk)

Library of Congress catalog card number 00–136290

Typeset by Mayhew Typesetting, Rhayader, Powys
Printed and bound in Great Britain by Athenaeum Press,
Gateshead

FOR JESSICA

CONTENTS

PREFACE

What should we make of the rediscovery of the modern? The evidence of a re-dedication to what Habermas calls the 'project of modernity' is all around us, not just in the writings of intellectuals and academics with an interest in social theory, but in political speeches and advertising copy world wide. All this testifies not just to a renewed enthusiasm for the material benefits of modernisation but to a culture of yearning in North America, Europe and Asia for the clean lines of pure functionality, an abhorrence of clutter and baggage of all kinds, a dissatisfaction with a politics of identity – of anything in short that would constitute a drag on one's freedom to be whatever one wants to be. And this turn of century pursuit of the modern is a broad-based phenomenon informing a large variety of projects. It involves groups like intellectual and aesthetic elites in the West, those we most closely associate with the modernist movements that have their roots in the last years of the nineteenth century. But perhaps unlike early manifestations of modernism, here the appeal appears to be far more widespread, captivating popular culture as well as that of modernism's traditional *avant garde*, emerging in both East and West. But is all this modern, in other words does the dedication to something called modernity mean anything more than a shared dedication to affluent new lifestyles and a generalised impatience with all constraints on our freedom to pursue them? What does it have to do with what earlier generations of intellectuals and artists have called modernity, modernism, modernisation? And what about the argument that modernisation has been the cause not just of all that is good about 'the West' – unparalleled scientific and technological advance, world wide democratisation, a deepening of the modern emancipatory project; but also all that is bad – environmental degradation, turbulence, exploitation, oppression, colonialism, racism, patriarchy, violence and even genocide? We have become quite used to hearing the argument that among other things all the grand narratives of modernisation are implicated in racist belief and practice.

Much of the debate over both the contours and historical implications of modernity has taken place at such a high level of abstraction as to be almost meaningless. Here the multicultural and postcolonial critics of modernity seem to have been in substantial agreement with their modernist foes. Both seem to believe that insights into the nature of modern society can be generated by philosophical debate over the presence, or absence, of exclusionary assumptions in the texts of the high priests of aesthetic and philosophical modernism. But what can defending, or exposing, the exclusionary assumptions present in the novels of Joseph Conrad, or the philosophy of Hegel, tell us either about actual historical practice unless we assume that either of them speaks for the mass of their compatriots? Is modernism best understood as an abstract set of aesthetic or philosophical principles that, once laid down by exemplary modernists like Hegel or Conrad, remain unchanged for all time? If not, then can there ever be a single answer to the question of modernity's exclusions that is valid for all time?

This book is an attempt to understand the nature and consequences of modernity, but one with a different starting point, perhaps partly a consequence of the fact that it is written by an anthropologist in search of an 'ethnographic' – by which I mean embedded and popular – understanding of both modernity and modernism. I argue that there can in fact never be an abstract theory of modernity that is not 'contaminated' by the cultural and historical contexts within which processes we label modernisation take place. It therefore envisages the possibility of both divergent modernisms and, hence, of multiple modernities. One consequence is that it becomes possible to see modernity as open to change over time such that what was once exclusive may become more inclusive, and vice versa. This also has consequences for the way we think about theoretical or analytic discourse itself. The analysis of modernity and racism in very different historical and cultural contexts must itself reflect the embeddedness of the (modernist) conceptual apparatus through which such analysis takes place. It is perhaps only through such a concept of a contingent, diverse and embedded modernity, one moreover within which we as analysts are just as implicated as are our 'objects' of analysis, that we as intellectuals can even begin to think about making a contribution towards a decoupling of the intimate connection that exists between racism and modernity.

In the research for and writing of the book I have received a great deal of assistance along the way. I am extremely grateful to the Australian Research Council once again for providing that most precious of resources, time, without which I could not have completed the writing. I am also grateful to colleagues at both La Trobe University and the University of Sussex for their interest and support. I was able to make valuable use of collections at the New York Public Library, the British Library and the State Library of Victoria, as well as University Libraries at La Trobe, Sussex and Cornell. I spent a useful and productive time at Cornell University's Southeast Asia programme while working on some of the Malaysian materials, and appreciated the facilities they made available,

Large numbers of individuals offered suggestions, references, advice, encouragement and criticisms that helped to sharpen the argument. Of all of them, I would particularly like to thank Francesco Formosa, Maila Stivens, Jon Mitchell, Filippo Osella, Steve Nugent, Beryl Langer, John Goldlust, Sophie Kahn, Adam Possamai, Alberto Gomes, Kean Wong, Matthias Gomes, Estelle Farrar, Robin Jeffrey, Peter Beilharz, Johann Arnason,

Timothy Harper, Mukilika Banerjee, Josep Llobera, K. Shivaramakrish-nan, Albert Schrauwers and Chris Fuller, as well as others who heard and commented on drafts of different chapters in seminars at University College London, the London School of Economics, the University of Sussex, La Trobe University, Cornell University and Johns Hopkins University. I would also like to thank the postgraduate students with whom I worked while this project was being completed. I often felt I was learning more from them than they were from me. Thanks, then, to Chris Houston, Ju Lan Thung, Wendy Mee and Yekti Maunati. I also want to express my gratitude to Richard Fardon, who read the manuscript for Sage, and provided me with an extremely insightful and helpful reader's report. This helped me immensely in focusing the writing and resulted, I hope, in a much clearer statement of the argument.

Finally, I would like once again to acknowledge the support and encouragement offered by Chris Rojek at Sage.

1

MODERNITY AND ITS OTHERS: UNIVERSAL IDEALS AND PARTICULAR OUTCOMES

I

[O]ne can hardly imagine a Scout being such an idiot as to class the Soloman Islanders, the Eskimo, the Laplanders, the American Redskins, the Zulus, the Malay Islanders, the Thibetans, the Hindoos, the Japs, the Maoris, and all the other wonderful peoples of the world as 'wild Indians – and tosh!' From all these people we may learn the art of Scoutcraft. (Hargrave, 1918: 24)

For this is a Law of Nature – ANYTHING UNNATURAL BECOMES WEAK, AND IN THE END DIES OUT. (Hargrave, 1918: 95)

We deplore the depravity of the heathen, their painted faces and their false gods. But are you aware that before civilisation found them they were sound in body and limb? . . . Do we ever consider that man in a state of nature existed for a million years under conditions which would snuff out the greater part of our populations in a week? (Hargrave, 1919a: 23)

II

Many an immortal tune has been born in the stable or the cotton-field. 'Turkey in the Straw' is a magic melody; anyone should be proud of having written it, but, for musical high brows, I suppose the thing is déclassé. It came not from a European composer but from an unknown negro minstrel. (Sousa, 1928: 341)

An attempt to place a melody within geographical limits is bound to fail. Rhythmic qualities are imitated in all popular forms, but music, although it has many dialects, is, after all, a universal language. (Sousa, 1928: 354)

III

The Malay-language film version of *The Thief of Baghdad* is essentially about a budding romance between a commoner, Abu Hassan, and a princess, Tengku Faridah. Having fallen in love from afar, Abu sneaks into Faridah's secluded garden in the palace of her father the King (Raja) and confesses his love. When Faridah replies that she must have nothing to do with him because of the huge difference in status between them, Abu says: 'But you are a girl (*gadis* = maiden or virgin) just like any other girl.' Faridah seems interested, but informs Abu that it is her father who insists that she cannot marry a commoner (*manusia biasa*). Abu replies: 'But the difference is not [as important as] you think. Although we may have different destinies (*nasib*) we are otherwise just the same . . . our limbs, blood and muscles are the same.'

In a later scene Faridah confronts her father, who announces that he has called together the princes of all neighbouring kingdoms, so that Faridah may choose one for her husband:

Faridah: And if there is not one of them I like, then what?

Raja: Don't worry. Surely there will be one who interests you.

Faridah: But if there isn't a single one, can I look for someone else?

Raja: Not possible, you will have to pick one of them.

Faridah: If it's like that, then it is a question of force (*paksaan*) . . . I don't agree with this . . . It's a question of *my* future happiness and well being. Why can't you invite everyone from these kingdoms, whether prince or ordinary citizen (*rakyat*)?

Raja: But don't forget, you are a princess. You can't marry a *rakyat* and have him come to live here in the palace . . .

Faridah: If I marry an ordinary *rakyat*, can't he become a member of the family? We must remember. Everyone has an equal chance at fate/destiny (*nasib*).

(From *Abu Hassan Pencuri*, 1955, produced by MFP/Shaw Brothers, directed by B.N. Rao, starring P. Ramlee)

IV

'Human nature exists, and it is both deep and highly structured,' writes Edward O. Wilson, the biologist and writer whom Tom Wolfe calls 'a new Darwin'. If it did not exist, let us be clear, then the idea of universals – human rights, moral principles, international law – would have no legitimacy.

It is the fact of our common humanity that allows most of us to forgive Bill Clinton his faults, that will not allow us to agree that bombing innocent Iraqis is the right way to punish Saddam, and that makes us want to see Pinochet brought to justice. A world that hounded Clinton but turned a blind eye to Pinochet would indeed be a world turned upside-down. (Rushdie, 1998)

It is notable that in anchoring his political judgements in the notion of a universal human nature, Salman Rushdie chose to resurrect at the end of the twentieth century a form of argument first laid down by European philosophers at least two centuries earlier. Rushdie's words have the very real advantage of demonstrating the continued influence of modern universalism, a particular view of a relation between science and ethics that was first propounded by eighteenth century philosophers, and has since that time been characterised by the proposition that human social arrangements can be judged according to whether they are, or are not, compatible with a universal human nature. The Enlightenment origins of this argument are described succinctly by Geoffrey Hawthorn:

To the ancient equation between the good, the right and the true they [the *philosophes*] added the natural and subtracted the divine. If, they implied, the good was the right, the right the true, and, as scientific inquiry was demonstrating, the right was also the natural (since nature manifestly conformed to reason), so the natural must be the good. If this was so, then it seemed clear that what was evil was what was unnatural. Use reason to distinguish the natural from the unnatural, they argued, and you will have at once distinguished good from evil. (Hawthorn, 1976: 13)

There is little doubt that Rushdie's embrace of modern universalism was no isolated act of mind. The examples cited above, pursued in far greater detail in subsequent chapters, point to the widespread influence of ideas about the basic equality of human beings as a consequence of a shared natural makeup earlier in the cultural history of the modern world. John Hargrave, a leading light in Britain's scouting movement in the years around the First World War, called on 'civilised' Britons not just to appreciate contemporary 'primitives' as being more in touch with nature but in fact to emulate them. The main activities of scouting, according to Hargrave, would bring modern men and women back into that natural relationship with themselves and their surroundings currently enjoyed by peoples in other parts of the globe. The American composer of patriotic marches John Philip Sousa articulated a somewhat earlier critique of European (musical) civilisation, criticising it among other things for its narrow nationalism and lack of contact with 'the people'. Sousa saw his music as more natural and hence universal than the artificial art musics emanating from a decadent Europe. And later on, when Malaya was on the brink of achieving political independence from its British masters, films for Malay audiences engaged almost to the point of obsession with the injustice of aristocratic privilege as an affront to the basic (physiological) unity of humankind.

The turn of the twentieth to the twenty-first century looks then like being another time when intellectuals in many different parts of the globe seemed to be re-dedicating themselves *en masse* to one version or another of a nature-based ethical universalism. Evidence of this re-dedication to this particular modernist project is all around us. It is certainly a significant trend among a western intelligentsia bent on reversing what Habermas among others has called 'nihilistic' postmodernism and deconstructionism precisely because, in his view, these have relativised human values and thereby undermined our capacity for moral judgement. Similarly, in the burgeoning literature on human rights it is not uncommon to find the perception that cultural 'relativism' has been responsible for undermining a global commitment to universal human rights:

> Although the universality of human rights is still widely accepted by many nations, the influence of cultural relativism and multiculturalist and postmodern ideas is slowly undermining the entire system of human rights treaties. (Zechenter, 1997: 319–347)

Or consider the more nuanced but equally damning critique of relativism offered by the anthropologist Terrence Turner. Turner, also concerned to defend a notion of universal human rights against the criticisms of 'cultural relativists', wants to suggest that classical liberal arguments for universal rights were flawed but that it is possible to build into a universalist human rights agenda a right to cultural difference, while still opposing 'essential-ism' which suppresses the universal right of individuals to create/construct their own cultural identities:

> [In a proper regime of human rights, difference is] an invalid basis for denying rights . . . [But it] is [also] inconsistent with claims by an individual or group to have the right to realize its identity at the expense of other, different groups of individuals or to present their realization of themselves in ways different from its own . . . people have the right not only to the different identities they have produced for themselves in the past, but also to those they might produce in the future . . . (Turner, 1997: 286f.)

In a similar vein, numerous writers on the growth of anti-immigrant sentiment in western Europe wish both to attribute it to the retreat from universalism, and also to implicate relativisers in the whole process. One of the best known of such analysts is Pierre Taguieff, in France who has written:

> il est temps que le mouvement antiraciste . . . prenne conscience de la rupture qui s'est opérée dans les représentations et les argumentations racistes elaborées, à savoir le *déplacement de l'inégalité biologique vers l'absolutisation de la différence culturelle*, et en tire les conséquences pour le type ou le style du combat à venir. (Taguieff, 1992: 15; emphasis added)

That the problem is cultural relativism, and that the cultural 'left' is in part responsible for this attack on universalism now appropriated by the politi-cal right in France, is explicitly argued by commentators like Guillaumin, who writes:

> The cultural Right . . . which has made use of a Gramscian approach to culture, has occupied a rather special position in intellectual and political life during the last twenty years . . . It is the self-proclaimed advocate of the right of 'difference', of culture and roots . . . The right to be different is also inherited from left-wing discourse. In fact, the 'droit à la différence' was a priority during the 1970s for the anti-racist movements. This new approach was extremely fortuitous for the Right which promptly appropriated the crucial term difference . . . as the backbone for a 'cultural' rather than racial argument. (Guillaumin, 1991: 9)

Calls in France for resurrection of the idea of a universal citizenship implied in the ideals of the Republic are echoed in other parts of Europe where 'progressive' intellectuals decry the Germanic or organicist claims to national identity based on shared ties of blood and/or *volksgeist*, advo-cating instead what Habermas calls a civic nationalism (in America the preferred term is patriotism) based on values that are universal to all cultures, rather than specific only to some (Appadurai, 1993; Habermas, 1995; Llobera, 1996).

Meanwhile in Great Britain, no word is more publicly associated with the current political regime than 'modern'. Whatever else the 'Third Way' may, or may not, aim to be, one thing is certain: it is modern, and to be modern implies commitment to a universal understanding of citizenship – free of the 'traditional' trappings of Englishness whether racial or cultural. This

understanding of what constitutes modern identity is of supreme importance to Tony Blair, as he explained in a speech on 'Modern Patriotism'
given on the occasion of the *Daily Mirror*'s 'Pride of Britain Awards' in
May 1999. Adopting the terms of an American distinction between patriotism and nationalism, Blair told his audience:

> Ours is a modern patriotism not a narrow nationalism. It is about how we can
> build a great future not just look back to past glories. We never forget the past.
> We salute it. But that does not mean we damn the present and bemoan today's
> young people . . . And my aim as Prime Minister is to galvanise this great nation
> into producing more successes, building a more modern and confident country.

The rediscovery of the seductions of modern universalism has not been
limited to the West. Malaysia, a country long known for the particularistic
nationalisms of its constituent 'racial' groupings, and particularly of its
politically dominant Malay community, is a case in point. In the early 1990s,
the Prime Minister and arch-moderniser Dr Mahathir Mohamed gave a
speech which he called 'Vision 2020' (*Wawasan* 2020), a speech that stimu-
lated widespread discussion of the meaning and implications of modernity,
especially for Malaysia's majority, Malay population. The speech prompted
one of Malaysia's more astute social commentators to ask about its
implications (Rustam, 1993). What does this commitment to the culture of
modernity, based on science and technology, modern organisation and the
modern nation state (*Negara-bangsa*) mean for the Malays? Can Malays,
Rustam asks, enter the modern world as members of a distinctively Malay
society that has experienced modernisation, or must they in order to do so
abandon all elements of 'Malayness'? In the process of social modernisation,
elements of traditional culture must be preserved, he argues, but it would be
neither possible nor desirable to retain them in their original form. They
must be transformed so they are suitable to new circumstances (Rustam,
1993: 2). The traditions associated with the monarchy cannot and should not
simply be preserved. They must be made compatible with the system of
modern democracy based on the equality of all citizens. Culture, social
relations, religion, Malay political forms, everything needs to be modernised
in the drive to develop the Malaysian economy.

Rustam's call for Malays to modernise, and hence abandon ideas of a
unique and irreducibly non-modern Malay identity, was echoed widely in
the Malaysian press. In a 1993 newspaper article Asma Abdullah wrote:

> Whether we like it or not, we have to learn the rules of the business jungle –
> 'survival of the fittest' which sometimes mean [*sic*] being more assertive than our
> culture condones. Such self-determination, competitiveness and assertiveness, for
> example, which are often associated with an individualistic society, are necessary
> for survival in the business environment. . . .

> Gone are the days when Malays will be given special handouts, special privileges
> and attention – the future Melayu [Malay] must be able to survive in this era of
> change, of great transformation, not because of birthright but because he has
> attained competence equal to the people around him. (Asma Abdullah, 1993)

In a nation known for its internal racial antagonisms, and for a government bent on ensuring the dominance of a particular race, the Malays, the
1990s saw an apparent easing of racial tensions. The Prime Minister began
dismantling the system of racial preferences that non-Malays saw as
exclusive, even calling at one point for a new understanding of Malaysian
citizenship that would include all Malaysians – Chinese, Malays and
Indians – on an equal footing, a vision of a pan-Malayan citizenship, be it
said, advanced earlier, and immediately rejected by Malay nationalists, by
the British in the final years of colonial rule. Influential intellectuals called
for an 'intercivilisational' dialogue, and there was even an emergent discourse on human rights, previously discouraged by Mahathir's insistence
on the distinctiveness of Asian values.

What are we to make of this universalising impulse that seems to have
swept through at least some parts of the globe somewhat more than two
centuries after modernist philosophy established a firm link between ethics,
science and human social and political arrangements? This is the issue with
which I am centrally concerned in subsequent chapters. Specifically I will be
concerned with a particular question to which any attempt to assess
modern universalism gives rise, namely: what are the implications of universalising beliefs and practices for the ways in which modern societies cope
with human diversity?

One might suggest that answers to this question fall into one of two
broad categories. On the one hand, as much of the material cited above
suggests, there are those who maintain that modernity broadly understood
constitutes an antidote to racism as well as other regimes of domination
based on colour, gender, sexuality, culture and the like. For such advocates
of modern universalism exclusionary ideas and practices such as racism are
a sign of incomplete modernisation and hence of pre- or non-modern
people, groups, beliefs or institutions within the modernising nation, or
elsewhere on the globe. At one level it is this critique of tradition more than
anything else that characterises what we call modern thought.

On the other hand, critics of modernity have tended to see particularising
impulses such as racism as arising out of the very processes of universal-
isation that we associate with modernisation, as intimately bound up, in
other words, with modernity itself. For such critics the current wave of
universalising discourses and practices sweeping the globe do not bode well
since they are as likely to be associated with new projects of colonialism
and/or racial and cultural domination and/or genocide as they have apparently been in the past. In the last decades of the twentieth century, for
example, we became used to hearing the argument, associated with the
emergence of poststructural, postmodern, postcolonial and multicultural
currents in critical theory, that exclusionary phenomena like racism, sexism,
even genocide were the inescapable byproducts of all the universalising/
totalising 'grand narratives' of social modernisation. Just one of many such
is the analysis of the Holocaust provided by the social theorist Zygmunt
Bauman. In his *Modernity and the Holocaust* (1989) Bauman argues that

the genocidal actions of the Nazi regime cannot be dismissed as an aberration in the history of the modern state, but were on the contrary a direct consequence of its innermost tendencies to produce a culture-free, for which read culturally homogeneous, citizenry.

Bauman's assessment of the link between modernism, universalism and the Holocaust finds its parallel in a veritable flood of writing on the links between modernism and European colonialism. The political scientist Uday Mehta, for example, assessing the links between liberalism with its ideas about universal freedom and emancipation on the one hand and the denial of freedom to colonial subjects by liberal regimes on the other, remarks:

> The universality of freedom and derivative political institutions identified with the provenance of liberalism is denied in the protracted history with which liberalism is similarly linked. Perhaps liberal theory and liberal history are ships passing in the night spurred on by unrelated imperatives and destinations. Perhaps reality and, as such, history always betrays the pristine motives of theory. Putting aside such possibilities, something about the inclusionary pretensions of liberal theory and the exclusionary effects of liberal practices needs to be explained. ([1990] 1997: 59)

Mehta himself goes on to provide an answer that, given his allegiance to the postcolonial paradigm, is not altogether unexpected. In the piece from which the above was extracted he argues that modern narratives of emancipation, in this case in their liberal guise, are, in spite of their pretension to universality, so inextricably inflected by particular cultural assumptions about the nature of mature human reason, that they become inevitably exclusionary. Examining the underlying conceptualisation of human reason present in the works of classical British liberals, Mehta finds it so imbued with the very particular values of middle class, white and, one might add, male Englishmen of the time that it would have inevitably found Britain's colonial subjects in India incompletely rational, hence justifying their exclusion from processes of political emancipation, perhaps indefinitely. His answer, then, is that at least in the case of the association between universalising liberalism and racial exclusion, 'inclusionary pretensions' and 'exclusionary effects' are neither a result of historical accident ('ships passing in the night spurred on by unrelated imperatives'), nor of the betrayal of good intention by history. Instead, Mehta's analysis leads him to the conclusion that in fact 'liberal history projects with greater focus and onto a larger canvas the theoretically veiled and qualified truth of liberal universalism [itself] . . .' (pp. 59–60).

Does then the advocacy of universalism have a broader resonance within western, or indeed global culture at certain times and in particular places? Does the current wave of universalising discourses signify a meaningful shift away from a postmodern politics of difference, and if so will it, as its advocates so firmly believe, provide more effective ways of dealing with racism in the modern world? Or is this renewal of modern universalism, as an earlier critique would have it, likely in fact to be associated with an intensification of the kinds of exclusionary beliefs and practices associated earlier on in the twentieth century with racism, colonialism and violence? What, in other words, is the relationship between modernity and its others likely to be in the new millennium? Will it be genuinely inclusive or grossly exclusionary? Will the 'new modernism' really be able to play a part in overcoming the racial violence that has been our legacy from the twentieth century or will it even bring forth new exclusions and expose new fault lines within and between nations?

This book is intended to be a further contribution to these debates over the connections between universalising modernism, racism and violence. But any argument about the links between racism and modernity is in danger of foundering at the outset because of the highly abstract terms in which it is often posed. Perhaps betraying the author's own personal and disciplinary background, I will not engage here in yet another abstract exercise either to defend or 'deconstruct' modern thought. Nor will I claim to occupy a privileged terrain from outside modernity, whether in temporal (as in *post*colonial and *post*modern theories) or in cultural space (as in traditional anthropology) where such a deconstruction might conceivably be grounded. Instead, by arguing that the intellectual, cultural, political and economic constitution of radical alterity is best understood in the context of both modern thought and culture and of processes of modernisation, I tackle the issue of universalism's exclusions in a rather different way and in so doing hope to take the debate in a rather different direction.

Central to the analysis that follows, in other words, is the assumption that while at a general abstract level we can understand modernity as an epochal attack on tradition by 'self-creating' human subjects based on some notion of universal human reason, in most respects the modern must be understood to be embedded in particular cultural and historical circumstances, and that we as analysts are just as bound up in context as are the modern objects of our enquiries. To see that this is so requires a brief detour into the meaning of the term modern.

Meanings of Modernity

The approach adopted here emerges in reaction to the problematic way in which modernist theorists speak of modernisation, modernity and modernism as pure abstract processes, 'uncontaminated' by culture and history. Very roughly, one might say that recent theorists of modernity – to borrow Wagner's description of social theorists in the twentieth century who build on 'the double notion of autonomy and rationality' (Wagner, 1999) – attempt an understanding based on a broadly shared Hegel/Marx/Weber tradition that sees modernity as an identifiable socio-historical process of transformation out there in the world, one that began in either sixteenth or the eighteenth century western Europe. Here modernity is used in an objective sense to refer to the result of a process of modernization, by which the social world comes under the domination of asceticism, secularization, the universalistic claims of instrumental rationality, the differentiation of the various spheres of the lifeworld, the bureaucratization of economic, political and military practices, and the growing monetarization of values. Modernity therefore [is seen to arise] with the spread of western imperialism in the sixteenth century; the dominance of capitalism in northern Europe . . . in the early seventeenth century; the acceptance of scientific procedures . . .; and pre-eminently with the institutionalization of Calvinistic practices and beliefs in the dominant classes of northern Europe. We can follow this process further through the separation of the family from the wider kinship group, the separation of the household and the economy, and the creation of the institution of motherhood in the nineteenth century. Although the idea of the citizen can be traced back to Greek times via the independent cities of the Italian states . . ., the citizen as the abstract carrier of universal rights is a distinctly modern idea. (Turner, 1990: 6)

Building on this heritage, revisionary modernists like Habermas see modernisation as the outcome of processes of social differentiation and cultural autonomisation which reached their fullest extent at the end of the nineteenth century, a view broadly accepted also by Anthony Giddens, Scott Lash and other critical theorists (see Lash, 1990).

There are of course differences. On the issue of periodisation, for example, some prefer an Enlightenment rather than sixteenth century point of origin (see Smart, 1990: 16), while others are more inclined to trace its origins farther back to 'classical civilization' (see Castoriadis, 1991). There are further disagreements about whether or not the modern has come to an end, and hence over whether so-called postmodernity describes a new historical epoch or refers instead to a critique of modernity from within as it were. But these debates do not threaten in any significant way a broadly shared abstract-objectivist understanding of the meaning of the modern.

The term modern*ism* is somewhat more problematic. It is typically used to refer to an aesthetic sensibility, and hence movement within the arts. Scott Lash's use of the term modernism to refer to both a particular historical period of aesthetic development and an interrelated complex of aesthetic sensibilities is fairly typical of critical theory:

Modernism, for its part, rejects history in order to embrace movement and change. Modernism in Vienna, Paris, Berlin and a number of other European cities, as the nineteenth century drew to a close, was ushered in by a series of effective 'succession' movements. These movements consisted of a rejection of 'academic' standards by artists and architects. This was at the same time a rejection of state sponsored art . . . French Impressionism (and realism), Viennese Art Nouveau . . . and German Expressionism, all took from the institutional context of the reaction against historical art. In each case the rejection was in favour of a modernist or proto-modernist aesthetic of working through the possibilities of aesthetic materials. (Lash, 1990: 66)

In such usages there is the general implication that, following Habermas, modernism refers to a cultural sensibility to which modernity gives rise.

A somewhat different account of this link is suggested by Castoriadis who prefers to restrict the use of the term modernity precisely to refer to the development of a modern aesthetic sensibility or what might be called a particular aesthetic discourse on the modern, suggesting a rather different relationship between the 'objective' and 'subjective' dimensions of the modern. Castoriadis writes for example:

> What has been called modernity is something which reached its climax between 1900 and 1930, and which ended after World War II . . . In music, Schönberg, Webern, and Berg had invented atonal and serial music . . . Dada and surrealism were in existence by 1920. And if I were to begin the following list, Proust, Kafka, Joyce . . . would you please tell me how you would continue? (Castoriadis, 1991: 225)

That modernism might in fact constitute modernity rather than the other way around is a possibility to which I shall return.

In any case, from this common baseline in the Hegel–Marx–Weber tradition a more recent generation of critical theorists have attempted in various ways to revise this classical narrative. On the face of things, these revised notions of modernity that we have received from more recent critical theory are at least potentially more satisfactory than classical conceptualisations. Various attempts have been made, for example, to go beyond uni-dimensional understandings of modernity, attention now focussing on 'differentiation' as a multidimensional process of separation both within and between separate spheres of modern existence. This also produces a less unilineal and teleological reading of the history of the West (cf Arnason, 1987; Heller, 1990; Luhmann, 1982). Indeed in part as a consequence of the challenge of modernising processes outside the West, and in part as a result of the critiques of postcolonial and multicultural theory, at least some revisionary modernists are no longer as quick to see modernity as always and inevitably a western phenomenon, hence opening the way for a more inclusive understanding of modernisation. As a consequence some social theorists are now calling for a notion of 'multiple modernities' (cf Eisenstadt, 2000, Wittrock, 2000), echoing earlier discussions in anthropology itself. Summarising these somewhat diverse revisionary trends, Johann Arnason writes that social theorists have been led to:

> a new understanding of modernity as a loosely structured constellation rather than a system, and . . . a stronger emphasis on the role of cultural premises and orientations in the formation of different versions [of modernity] within a flexible but not amorphous framework. (Arnason, 2000: 65)

Of particular interest here is the emphasis on the distinctiveness of modern 'cultural premises and orienations' found in more recent critical theory. This sense of modernity as specifiable cultural processes is captured by Peter Wagner who has described the modern*ist* social theorists in the twentieth century as those who build on 'the double notion of autonomy and rationality' (Wagner, 1999). To quote Arnason once again:

> One of the most important – but not yet fully explored – implications of this culturalist and pluralist view has to do with the recognition of conflict as inherent and essential to modernity . . . the most sustained and interesting variation on this

theme – pioneered by Max Weber and developed most recently by Cornelius Castoriadis and Alain Touraine – stresses the conflict between two equally basic cultural premises: on the one hand, the vision of infinitely expanding rational mastery; on the other hand, the individual and collective aspiration to autonomy and creativity . . . On this view, the cultural orientations characteristic of modernity are embodied in institutions, but not reducible to them . . . [they] are mutable enough to translate into different institutional patterns, and at the same time sufficiently autonomous to transcend all existing institutions and allow the construction of critical alternatives as well as utopian projections. (Arnason, 2000: 65)

The 'discovery' of culture in recent modernist theory has two very significant implications for the understanding of modernity. Firstly, and partly in response to anti-positivist trends in social theory more broadly it shifts from an objective to a subjective emphasis. The consequence is a view that puts modern subjectivity at the core of our understanding of what it is to be modern so that modernity becomes as much a state of mind as a set of objective historical processes. Modernity is now seen as inseparable from the modern imaginaries that make it possible. Modernity in other words, and *contra* Habermas, cannot now in any simple sense be said to pre-exist modernism. Modernism constructs modernity as much as modernity provides the conditions for modernism's emergence. Modernity can never be unambiguously defined except in the context of how it is constructed in an ambivalent/interrogating modernism.

Secondly, as Arnason argues, modernity should be seen as a product of contradictory or conflicting cultural processes, which heralds a significant break with classical narratives of modernisation. Most such narratives construct modernity instead as a single cultural movement – of rationalisation, instrumentalisation, alienation, commodification or such like. Single logic notions of cultural modernisation are, however, extremely problematic. They are completely unable to produce a theory of modern culture, understood as the meanings and performative values of actual people living under modern conditions. Surely reducing modern subjectivity to any single logic cannot then account for the cultural lives of modern peoples. At the same time single logic notions of cultural modernisation fail to provide for the possibility of modernist theory itself. How is it possible for the theorist to see modernisation as a loss of meaning, when everyone else is a slave precisely to a culture of rationalisation? Only by rejecting single logic notions of modernisation as rationalisation, commodification, abstraction or whatever can a genuinely reflexive modernism ever be achieved. Only in this way can modernism – as a culture of ambivalence – ever be understood.

The immediate sources for this critical understanding of modernisation as rationalisation are, as Arnason suggests, the writings of Weber and, following him, the theorists of the so-called Frankfurt school. But its roots are much deeper, indeed it could be said that the core of the culturalist model of modernity stems from what can be called the first critical intellectual encounter with modernisation, namely what is usually called the romantic critique of Enlightenment philosophy, and particularly of its instrumentalist notions of human reason. More particularly I have in mind what Charles Taylor calls the 'expressivist' conception of human life that develops as a reaction and hence alternative to an Enlightenment vision of man that is based upon an 'associationist psychology, utilitarian ethics, atomistic politics of social engineering, and ultimately a mechanistic science of man' (Taylor, 1975: 539). The instrumental code of evaluation, inherited from the Enlightenment, and against which expressivism develops, has, argues Taylor, become endemic to modern society.

> [In it t]he major common institutions reflect . . . the Enlightenment conception in their defining ideas. This is obviously true of the economic institutions. But it is as true of the growing, rationalized bureaucracies, and it is not much less so of the political structures, which are organized largely to produce a collective decision out of the concatenation of individual decisions (through voting) and/or negotiation between groups. (1975: 541)

At the same time the Enlightenment vision has also informed 'many . . . conceptions of society which have been invoked to mitigate the harsher consequences of the capitalist economy . . . [such as] notions of equality, of redistribution among individuals, of humanitarian defence of the weak'. The expressivist critique, however, takes a view of human life quite different from that implied by Enlightenment anthropology. Rather than seeing human life and activity as essentially without any meaning, expressivism sees them as 'expressions', as realisations of a purpose or an idea. This notion differed from premodern ideas of expression in two main ways. Firstly, for the premoderns the meaning or purpose of human life was pre-given, that is it was already established outside human subjectivity. In modern expressivism on the other hand meaning is seen to unfold within human subjectivity – hence the modern/Enlightenment notion of a self-defining subject is retained. Secondly, that meaning is not necessarily known in advance, that is humans may grasp it or recognise it as their own only once it has been realised.

Expressivism therefore represents simultaneously an embrace and a critique of an Englightenment anthropology (in the philosophical sense of the term). It posits a self-creating modern subject, but locates it in a modern world that is objectified and potentially without meaning. More than epistemological critique – expressivism is also a heartfelt despair at the world view propounded by 18th century philosophy. To quote Taylor once again:

> The Enlightenment developed a conception of nature, including human nature, as a set of objectified facts with which the subject had to deal in acquiring knowledge and acting. [It created a] rift . . . between nature, whether as plan or instrument, and the will which acted on this plan.
>   It was this rift which the originators of expressivist theory . . . could not tolerate. They experienced this vision of things as a tearing apart of the unity of life in which nature should be at once the inspiration and motive force of thought and will. It was not enough that nature provide the blueprint for the will, the voice of nature must speak through the will. (1975: 22f.)

The rift between humans and nature was not the only rift declaimed by expressivists. As Taylor's discussion of Herder shows, expressivism also decried the rift among humans created by the Enlightenment vision of human nature. As Taylor points out,

> what has been said of communion with nature applies with the same force to communion with other men. Here too, the expressivist view responds with dismay and horror to the Enlightenment vision of society made up of atomistic, morally self-sufficient subjects who enter into external relations with each other, seeking either advantage or the defence of individual rights. They seek for a deeper bond of felt unity which will unite sympathy between men with their highest self-feeling, in which men's highest concerns are shared and woven into community life rather than remaining the preserve of individuals. (1975: 27f.)

The very notion of freedom espoused by Enlightenment philosophers and the French revolutionaries was, according to expressivism, only negative, and hence meaningless. For the former freedom meant only that unshackling of the individual free to pursue his/her own private ends. But where did these ends come from if not from the communities/languages in which they were embedded? And if so then unshackling all human bonds in the name of freedom is to create a new kind of slavery in which humans are now left only with their natural desires and inclinations, pursuing these goals and these goals alone in purely instrumental fashion. This is what is left by Enlightenment reason and the emancipation promised by the French revolution. Expressivism thus represents a critique of an Enlightenment anthropology in which the world is objectified and subjected to human reasoning and manipulation.

This is not the place to trace the varied manifestations of expressivism in the history of modern social theory (cf. Kahn, 1995). It is clearly present, as Taylor so convincingly argues, in Hegel's critique of civil society, a critique taken up within the more radical rejections of 'bourgeois' rationality by the Young Hegelians, and thence into Marx's own writings on human alienation under capitalism. It appears also in nineteenth century German critiques of first British political economy and then neoclassical economics, from where it first posed the problem of the historical specificities of capitalist rationality to a young Max Weber (Kahn, 1990). Most importantly for the genesis of a critical theory of modernity in the twentieth century, an expressivist sensibility is clearly articulated in the work of the so-called Frankfurt school, which sprung as much from the concerns of Weber as the vision of Marx, and explains the obsessions of writers like Adorno with the cultural degradation effected by the modern culture industries.

But for our purposes what is most significant is that expressivism serves to define the ambivalence to modern rationalism, and rationalisation, that informs the project of contemporary modernist social theory. Here, in the words of Habermas, modernisation (understood as rationalisation) is not so much rejected as counterbalanced by an expressive (communicative) rationality in the unfinished 'project' of modernity. In a distinctive, although parallel, argument Castoriadis sees in the search for autonomy a virtuous counter to the West's concurrent obsession with rational mastery. What critical theorists therefore share is what Bauman describes as a profound ambivalence towards the modern, a deep unease when confronted by its claims to a superior/abstract rationality. This is coupled with some idea of how it also generates the possibilities for forms of human community not characterised by the continual search for advantage and personal gain (cf. Bauman, 1991).

Embedding Modernity

But in spite of the greater theoretical rigour that has been brought to bear on clarifying the concept there are areas where even such apparently rigorous critical theory is so ambiguous and problematic as to make one question the coherence of any theory of modernity. This is manifest in our ultimate inability on the basis of an objectivist theory of modernity to provide definitive answers to such basic questions as: When did modernity start (and when did it/will it end)? Is it an analytic concept, a characteristic of particular institutional arrangements or simply a state of mind? Is it something uniquely western? Or should we rather ask is it something unique to Protestant, urban, northwestern, middle class, male Europe? If so, is the appearance of elements of modern organisation and culture elsewhere to be attributed merely to the imperial expansion of Europe, as suggested in the characterisation offered by Turner and cited above?

These problems spring from what might be called the continued inattention in most attempts to theorise modernity to issues related to its social, historical and cultural context. This problematic aspect of modernist theory has recently been nicely exposed by the sociologist Peter Wagner (Wagner, 1999). Wagner's specific theme is the image of America in European social theory, in particular in what he calls modernist social theory that revolves around the 'double notion of autonomy and rationality'. Modernist theory tends, Wagner argues, to represent America as the sphere of a 'pure modernity'. This treatment of America as the terrain of a modernity 'uncontaminated' by history and tradition, leads to a judgement of America as superior to Europe in a technical-economic and socio-political sense, but at the same time as inferior in a moral and philosophical sense.

Wagner's focus on America is important to what follows in a number of ways, but here I am especially concerned with the way he exposes the critical flaw in modernist theory thrown up by its encounter with America. Wagner writes that all such approaches:

> . . . have in common . . . a double intellectual move. They first withdraw from the treacherous wealth of sensations that come from the socio-historical world to establish what they hold to be those very few indubitable assumptions from which theorizing can safely proceed. And subsequently, they reconstruct an entire world

from these very few assumptions. Their proponents tend to think that the first move *decontaminates understanding*, any arbitrary and contingent aspects being removed. And that the second move creates a *pure image* of the world, of scientific and/or philosophical validity from which then further conclusions, including practical ones, can be drawn. (Whatever dissonance there may be between sensations and this image will then be treated as the secondary problem of the relation between theory and empirical observation.) (Wagner, 1999: 43; emphasis in original)

But such an operation is bound to fail, Wagner argues, because concepts like autonomy and rationality, so central to the modernist interpretation of the world

are never pure, or merely procedural and formal, never devoid of substance. As a consequence, they cannot mark any unquestionable beginning, and doubts can be raised about any world that is erected on their foundations, that is, about the consequent second move. (1999: 43)

But paying attention to context does not end all our problems. For if modernity is always and everywhere embedded, then this opens the door to the pluralisation of modernity. If modernity can only ever be embedded in particular historical, social, and cultural contexts, if in other words there can be no such thing as a pure 'procedural' modernism, then unless we are prepared to argue that one such context is the only possible locus of modernity, we are forced to consider the possibility of alternative modernities, a possibility indeed entertained by a number of contemporary critical theorists. Some have been led to consider this possibility by the apparent 'spread' of the modern outside the West. Is this to be understood as a consequence of economic or political or cultural globalisation? Is then the appearance of multiple modernities a consequence of modernity's subsequent 'indigenisation' outside the West?

One problem with such a view is that it is not always certain that at least elements of modernity did really appear first in the West, only then to be transported and indigenised elsewhere. Finding evidence for the contemporary modernisation of the West and the non-West – in Russia, Japan, the Islamic world, China – evidence not of a single modernity subsequently indigenised as a consequence of 'westernisation', but instead of parallel modernities, some observers as we have seen have been led to consider the possibility of plural or multiple modernities.

But what are the implications of a relativised and pluralised modernity? If modernity, as Wagner so convincingly argues, can never be dis-embedded from particular historical contexts, then how can it ever be conceptualised in the singular at all without retreating to the formalistic and procedural notion of a pure modernity? If the modern cannot be abstracted from context and singularised, then is there any use in speaking of modernity at all? This strikes at least this observer as an apparently fatal contradiction at the heart of any attempt to produce an abstract general – if pluralised – theory of modernity as some kind of objective description of particular types of society or specific historical processes.

This further reinforces the view that the modern is always more than an objective social process (call it modernisation), and/or a specific constellation of social forces (call it modernity). It is always also a particular state of human consciousness (call it modernism) without which we could never speak of ourselves as moderns. And this as we shall see has significant implications for the way we approach the problem of the exclusionary dimensions of modernity. But before returning to the question, it is important to see how it is that theorists of modernity have tackled this issue of what is sometimes called the reflexive dimension of modernity since it is the overwhelming tendency to handle the issue of reflexivity by means of a theory of exemplary modernism that makes current attempts to theorise modern reflexivity particularly problematic.

Reflexivity: Exemplary and Popular Modernisms

How is modernity's reflexive dimension to be understood? What, in other words, is modern culture or modern subjectivity? To this question, I want to argue, revisionary modernism can offer only very unsatisfactory answers. There are two sources of a theory of modern subjectivity on which most theorists draw. First there is a notion of rationalisation, derived largely from a tradition of analysis that is most clearly represented by the work of Max Weber. Secondly, there is the model of an exemplary modern sensibility provided by aesthetic and/or philosophical cultural elites.

As is well known, Weber, elaborating on his early interest in the specific origins of the calculus of capitalist economic rationality (see Kahn, 1990), came to see in the onward march of instrumental and bureaucratic rationality both a central feature in the formation of modern society, and also the main factor leading to the loss of meaning, the production of the 'iron cage' of modern society. It is tempting to see in Weber's discussion of rationalisation a theory of the formation of a modern (rational) subjectivity, and hence the basis for a theory of an instrumentalised modern culture. Following Weber, for example, theorists of the Frankfurt school, and particularly Habermas, see the triumph of instrumental rationality in both economic and political spheres, and its spread from there into the 'lifeworld', modernity's poisoned gift to modern culture. Similarly, Castoriadis maintains that it is the cultural dominance of the idea 'rational mastery' that is the cause of modernity's dark side, while Zygmunt Bauman attributes the violence of the Holocaust to the 'rationalising' discourse of the functionaries of the 'garden' state who are therefore prompted to control and cleanse the nation of untidy elements (Bauman, 1989). Of course this critique of the modern cult of instrumentalism has a longer history as we have seen.

But Weber's theory of rationalisation is on its own an unsuitable basis for a theory of modern culture, if that is understood as the existing meaningful and performative values of human beings living under the conditions of modernity. It is unsuitable because for Weber rationalisation is precisely about the loss of meaning. The idea of a culture of rationalisation is, therefore, oxymoronic, and it is not surprising that at least for Weber, only tradition can provide a source of modern culture for those facing such a loss of meaning. At best, then, Weber's theory of rationalisation of modern life can provide justification for a view that there is no culture of/in modernity, a view which as we shall see cannot be empirically substantiated.

In part because they recognise the futility of denying meaning in modernity, Habermas, Castoriadis, Bauman and other revisionary modernists are not satisfied to leave it there, since they also want to argue that Weber was wrong to see the complete triumph of instrumental rationality as inevitable. Unlike Weber who was pessimistic about the future of a fully 'rational' modern society in which life is at the same time completely without meaning, late twentieth century critical theorists have argued in different ways that countervailing emancipatory, and hence meaningful, tendencies exist within modernity itself. Hence for Habermas, the project of the Enlightenment can still be accomplished, not by the further colonisation of the lifeworld by instrumental reason, but instead by pushing back the boundaries of instrumentalisation through what he calls communicative action based on at least a formal search for meaning informed by a communicative rationality. For Castoriadis the true potential of modern life is achieved by the project of autonomy. It is through the pursuit of autonomy, and the rejection of heteronomy that for Castoriadis constitutes the emancipatory dimension of modern existence.

And it is here that the exemplars of aesthetic and philosophical modernism come in.

In this context the theory of exemplary modernism becomes a normative description of a culture or discourse of modern critique, a critical interrogation of the modern condition. What makes modern artists or modern philosophers, modern*ist*, it is maintained, is that they are the first to see the ambiguities of the modern condition, as well as its contingent and fleeting qualities. In short, modernism, in this sense, is the recognition that the modern condition is not natural and given for all time. Modernism is then a special way of interrogating modernity, from a perspective that is able at least to imagine that there are alternatives to it.

The exemplary status of modernist discourse is assured because modernists are able to see both the instrumental and expressive sides of the 'project' of modernity, both its potential for exploitation/oppression/even genocide, and its emancipatory possibilities. It is precisely this ability to think its way out of modernity as it were, and hence the ambivalence to modernity of modernism in the aesthetic/philosophical sense, that provides critical theorists with their exemplar. By exemplary modernism, therefore, I mean the tendency to describe as modern or modernist only those prominent artists and intellectuals whose work interrogates the modern but, in recognising its contingent status, also draws on positive trends within modernity in ways admired to a greater or lesser extent by critical theorists. Exemplary modernism provides for critical theorists the only source of an authentic modern subjectivity, and hence the underpinning in modernity itself for their own critical discourse on the modern.

The philosophies of Kant and Hegel have both been proposed as early versions of such exemplary modernism, but 'it is the work of Baudelaire which is frequently considered to provide the turning point in the development of an understanding of modernity'. It was Baudelaire's ambivalent recognition of the good and bad sides of the modern condition, his discussion of its 'transient, fleeting and contingent character' (Habermas's terms), and his critique of 'bourgeois' visions of a triumphal modernity (see Smart, 1990: 17) that so often make him a candidate for the role of pioneer of exemplary modernism. Presumably other visions or understandings of modernity, including the 'bourgeois' vision mentioned by Smart, are not exemplary because unlike those of modernism they are in one way or another infected or, to use Habermas's term, 'colonised by' instrumental reason. Only authentic, that is, exemplary, modernism pursues the emancipatory project of modernity through communicative rationality, the pursuit of autonomy, etc., all because it is able to recognise that the modern condition is contingent. It is clear then that exemplary modernism is a description of the subjectivity of an aesthetic and philosophical *avant garde*. Exemplary modernists are modern *avant la lettre* as it were – only when everyone else catches up with them will the project of modernity, presumably, be complete.

Yet exemplary modernism is very far from providing us with a true theory of modern subjectivity except in the normative sense. It is in no way a theory of the subjectivity of people living in modern society. Those outside the narrow circles of the aesthetic and philosophical elite are, one must assume, incapable of interrogating the modern condition. They presumably are either culturally traditional (premodern) in Weber's sense, or else captives of the rationalising tendencies of modern instrumentalism, unable to see that these are anything but the natural and inevitable givens of human existence. They are, in other words, without culture and reflexivity altogether. They can become culturally modernist only through the advanced thought of the vanguard. Like the Marxian notion of false consciousness, exemplary modernism provides us with no insights into the subjective and hence reflexive dimensions of modernity at all, except insofar as the culture of the modern masses is thought to be spoken by exemplary moderns like Kant, Hegel or Baudelaire.

A tendency to interrogate, criticise and build upon the modern, whenever it manifests itself outside the circles of high or *avant garde* modernism, therefore, can be neither explained nor even recognised as authentically modern at all within modernist social theory, even though it must be recognised as part of a project of constituting meaning, and a meaningful basis for the performance of a self-consciously modern life, by people who live their lives under conditions of social differentiation and cultural autonomisation. Nor can or should it be merely dismissed without further investigation for the absence of 'theoretical rigour' in its understanding of the modern condition.

Popular modernism cannot and should not be seen prima facie as merely traditional, meaningless or lacking a critical edge, nor as a substandard version of the more sophisticated modernism of aesthetic and intellectual elites. Whether we like it or not, popular modernism is as likely to interrogate modernity, to recognise its fleeting and contingent nature, as is high modernism. The three examples cited above, taken from the modern popular culture industries or modern social movements, all show quite clearly that popular critiques of modernity are not just possible, but in fact have been extremely pervasive, often precisely during periods that also witnessed the flowering of high modernism in the arts and philosophy. There is no reason to presume either that these popular discourses were merely the result of a 'trickle down' of ideas from the contemporary modernist *avant garde* in Britain, America or Malaya, or that these *avant garde* were merely acting as spokepersons for an inarticulate mass, no matter that this may be the fond hope of contemporary artists and intellectuals.

It needs to be stressed here that in advocating a focus on popular modernism, I am not arguing for some form of subalternism, that is for the conceit, prevalent in recent years among critics of modernity, that they have privileged access to mass consciousness. When I speak here of the popular modernism constituted through the modern entertainment industry, or though modern social movements, I do not assume that it somehow merely reflects the deep subjective pre-existing cultural meanings of 'the masses'. Modern social movements and the media are instead what might be called middle level discursive formations. They are the arenas in which popular meanings and performances of the modern condition, together with a popular tendency to interrogate modernity, have been constructed and reconstructed since the time of the establishment of mature modernity.

It is ironic that modernist theory has chosen to focus on the period of high modernism associated with the emergence of an aesthetic and intellectual *avant garde*, when as we shall see this was precisely the time when far more widespread popular modernisms were also taking root thanks to the changes wrought by social and cultural modernisation – that is, the creation of modern empires and nations, advances in communication technologies and the birth of the modern culture industries. Here understandings of the modern were created by individuals and groups who were in general neither members of the philosophical, aesthetic or political elites, nor members of the new proletariat or underclasses. Their role in reworking the modernist meanings and texts of the elites on the one hand, and constructing meanings for the masses on the other was, as we shall see, of pivotal importance in the emergence of the broad modernist sensibility that I have called popular modernism.

Reconstituting Modernity

An argument about the inevitable historical and cultural 'embeddedness' of modernity need not lead to a denial of the concept altogether, nor to a rejection of popular modernism as no more than a collective delusion. I say this because to do so is to assume that the contextual imperative demands that all our analyses focus on socio-historical processes that take place entirely within the boundaries of individual nation states. But it is now evident that a crucial, even constitutive feature of the modern world is precisely its 'globality' (see Featherstone et al., 1995). In other words, the processes – economic, political, social, cultural – that one might say formed the modern world do not, and have not since the inception of modernisation taken place solely or even largely within the boundaries of individual states. To speak of global modernity does not mean that modernisation is a simultaneous process everywhere in the world. But it does mean that it would be misleading to treat simultaneous modernisation in different parts of the globe as though this were necessarily a consequence of parallel but essentially separate processes. To do so would be to succumb to the fetishism of the modern nation state.

This particular appreciation of context – of the specific historical processes in which modernity is embedded, but also of the possibility that these circumstances escape present day national boundaries – explains in part the scope of this book. The geographical scope of this study is defined by a focus on three social spaces, namely Great Britain, the United States and Malaya both during and after colonial rule. The choice is to some extent dictated by the exigencies of familiarity: Malaysia has for some time constituted one of my main fields of anthropological research, Britain and America the loci of my intellectual training in the discipline. But the three are more closely linked than this suggests, or perhaps I should say my own trajectory from one to another is a result of a great deal more than pure historical accident.

One can speak for example of the more or less contemporaneous appearance of modernising ideologies in all three. From around the turn of the nineteenth century certain intellectuals in these different corners of the globe were espousing views about progress, the failings of traditional religious and political institutions, and the possibility of epochal change brought about by the application of human reason (even to religion itself) that bore family resemblances to each other, and that shared a commitment to projects of autonomy and rationalisation that Wagner sees as definitive of modernism.

This simultaneous emergence of a family of modernist ideas, broadly understood, must be explained in a variety of ways. It can of course be partially accounted for by referring to reciprocal intellectual flows given the spread of ideas from Britain itself, and partly by economic and political conditions linked to the formation of a modern British empire. Both the United States and Malaya were at different times important sites of British colonialism, and hence were both at the receiving end of a significant British intellectual and cultural legacy if for no other reason than Britain's acknowledged cultural supremacy in the Anglophone world, a supremacy which increased in the nineteenth century. In the twentieth century the balance of the relation, at least between the United States and Britain, was reversed, while the United States has replaced Britain as the dominant external economic, political and cultural force in the lives of most Southeast Asians. It is no accident, for example, that as an American reaching the age of the military draft in the late 1960s, I found Southeast Asia first appearing on my own horizons as the site of a 'war against communism', although I was lucky enough to escape that call on my services.

And beginning late in the nineteenth century the deepening of market relations, the rise of modern social and political movements, and the emergence of the modern culture industries coincided with the growth of the popular modernisms in all three places that are the main concern of this book. I refer here to broader-based universalising cultural sensibilities that simultaneously embraced and criticised what were perceived to be the dominant tendencies of modern social transformation. Towards the end of the nineteenth century popular notions of Americanism emerged that were highly disparaging of 'decadent' European civilisation. This is also the time of the beginnings of the Malay nationalist movement, which was critical of both Malay 'feudalism' and, increasingly, of British paternalism. And in Britain itself, what I am calling popular modernism increasingly took on primitivist overtones, attacking the 'unnaturalness' of modern British civilisation. Broader technological, economic, political and cultural influences were at work again. But again it is better to see these as diverse if more or less simultaneous processes of culture and nation building then as all flowing from a single (European or western) source.

To describe the parallel development of modernising ideologies in the three places as merely an offshoot of British (and subsequently American) imperialism, or as a simple reaction (whether positive or negative) to it would be misleading. Early emancipatory and anti-traditionalist intellectual and political currents, for example, spread to the United States as much from France as Britain, while early Malay intellectuals were influenced just as much by ideas coming from other parts of the Islamic world. There is no reason to think of the Malay peninsula as any more, or less, external to this discursive arena than the United States or Britain itself.

These cultural transformations, as I have suggested, produced shared popular sensibilities across all three regions. I have been particularly inclined to describe these as modernist for a further reason – in all three cases popular modernism was characterised by universalising aspirations, based as it was on some notion of universal human reason and hence of a principle of the (potential) unity of mankind. This is perhaps clearest in the example of British liberalism, as well as its primitivist critique. Unlike notions of Englishness, Scottishness, Irishness etc., liberal visions of Britishness have by and large been self-consciously culturally neutral, resting on liberal notions of reasonableness, decency and civility that were constituted as a possible universal endpoint of human social evolution. The notion of civilisation so central to nineteenth century British social evolutionism is generally taken to apply to all human beings regardless of race, culture or gender – the only thing supposedly distinctive about the British (or more accurately the middle class British) is that they are presumed to have arrived at the end of universal history before anyone else. Never mind that others may never achieve the liberal utopia in practice. In this sense liberal notions of Britishness are not nationalist, at least in the self-consciously racially or culturally particularist ('blood and territory') understandings of that term that have prevailed, for example, in the German tradition.

But this universalising aspiration also applies in the case of most republican versions of Americanism, as we shall see. Amercanism from at least the time of Jefferson has generally been envisaged to be at least a potential way of life for all, republican institutions being presumed by their advocates also to be neutral with respect to culture and, especially important to the Founding Fathers, religious belief. This is not to say more organicist understandings of the nation have not emerged from time to time in American history, nor that republicans have not expressed concerns that certain peoples might have tremendous difficulties adapting to the American way of life. On the contrary, as we shall see, Americanism has proved at times just as exclusive as has, say, German nationalism. But the difference is that the former is perceived by its advocates to be potentially inclusive of all of humanity, while the latter is not.

The case of Malay nationalism appears at first sight to be an exception to this modern attachment to universalism rather than national particularism. And yet, as I shall argue, it has not been without its universalising tendencies. Most importantly its link with so-called Islamic modernism makes its appeal rather different from that of a narrow nationalism based on the particular traits of a unitary Malay 'race'. Many advocates of an Islamic state in places like Malaysia do not presume an end to religious diversity, arguing instead for a distinction between public and private, civil society and the state that, while it differs markedly from the one presumed to operate in the West, none the less distinguishes between principles of governance appropriate for all religious believers, and other particularistic principles that apply only to the Muslim citizenry (cf. Hussin Mutalib, 1993). At the same time, as the extract cited at the beginning of this chapter so clearly shows, as important to Malay nationalism as its concern with Malay distinctiveness was a critique of aristocratic privilege that has parallels in Europe, in both cases being limited to arguments about the (biological) unity of humankind.

Yet in spite of this attachment to universal ideals, none of these places can be described as genuinely inclusive of humanity in all its diversity at any time in history. So-called 'native stock' Americans battled physically to exclude immigrants, and subjected African Americans to a long history of oppression and exploitation, witnessing at the same time widespread physical or cultural extermination of its native peoples. As we shall in the case of the Sousa-phenomenon, popular forms of Americanism towards the end of the nineteenth century excluded both African Americans and recent immigrants, although on different grounds.

Britain too has a long history of opposition to 'uncivilised' immigrants from overseas, indeed from other parts of the British Isles, to say nothing of a legacy of oppressive colonial rule, at the same time often denying members of even the English working class the same rights enjoyed by its middle class citizens at home. Primitivism may rest on supposedly universalist assumptions about what social evolutionists called the 'psychic unity of mankind', but even admirers of the primitive condition like Hargrave showed very little concern for the actual historical fate of other races, preferring instead to draw on their admirable qualities in the generation of a superior British race.

The Malaysian government enshrined preferential treatment of so-called *bumiputera* ('sons of the soil') in legislation, also pursuing policies against indigenous groups like the *orang asli* and the tribal people of East Malaysia that are anything but inclusive; and, like Britain and the United States, denied, and in some cases continues to deny, legal equality to certain categories of human beings – women, gays, children, refugees, those judged mentally incapable and a whole range of 'criminal' types. All in different ways are involved in hostile relations with the peoples and leaders of particular foreign states.

While some of these exclusions may be defensible on a variety of grounds, the point is that all contradict the commitment to human universalism if that is understood as encompassing actually existing humanity in all its diversity. Put another way, 'universalism' is not, and can never be as inclusive as it pretends to be. And there is a very good reason why this should be so, and this has to do with the embeddedness of modernity and modernism within particular historical circumstances and sets of cultural understandings, in this case of what it is to be a complete human being. Once we begin to examine what Mehta calls modernism's 'exclusionary effects' we find that they are almost inevitably a consequence of particular cultural assumptions about what constitutes human nature, human reason and the like. Paradoxically, then, universalism always has its others and this is unavoidable, a fact that the ideal of cultural neutrality cannot easily conceal. In this sense universalism is a culture like any other, differing only in that it always fails to recognise itself as such.

But recognising the embeddedness of modern commitments to universalism can lead to conclusions rather different from those of modernity's recent critics. For if exclusionary practices are the outcome of particularistic cultural assumptions, then it is also conceivable that they can be overcome, not necessarily through pure intellectual critique and debate, but instead as a consequence of the way 'culture' is always being transformed, through competition and conflict over the power to define who is and who is not a Briton, an American, a Malaysian. Once one moves away from the disembedded, avant guardist notion of modernity as a set of unchanging philosophical or aesthetic principles – a notion, be it said, often shared by modernist and anti-modernist alike – into the realm of what I am calling popular modernism, one can then see that all such principles are the subject of ongoing debate and even conflict. As a consequence it is possible to envisage that what was once exclusive can through time become more inclusive (as well as the other way around). This is the subject of the final chapter in which I trace the fate of popular modernisms in America, Britain and Malaysia into the latter part of the twentieth century, and argue that although each retains certain distinctive features, each has also been substantially transformed out of a contest between those seeking to maintain the exclusions, and those seeking to be included in new understandings of the modern.

This book, then, is indeed about an encounter. But it is not an encounter in the salons of the high priests of modernity over the aesthetic and philosophical principles that define modernity; nor is the encounter between moderns and non-moderns. Instead, it is about what is better seen as a contest or often a conflict between self-appointed moderns on the one hand and on the other a diversity of peoples and groups formed within processes of modernisation, seeking also to be recognised as moderns and striving against their histories of exclusion from the prizes offered by modernity itself.

2

NATURALISING DIFFERENCE: CIVILISATION AND THE PRIMITIVE IN THE BRITISH IMAGINATION

> [T]he Redman can do a greater service now and in the future. He can teach us the ways of the outdoor life, the nobility of courage, the joy of beauty, the blessedness of enough, the glory of service, the power of kindness, the super-excellence of peace of mind and the scorn of death. (Ernest Thompson Seton, 1912: 8)

In 1916 John Hargrave, one of the original members of the Baden-Powell Boy Scouts, advised his readers that it would be of interest 'to learn something from the stoic Red Indians of North America' (1916: 15). Among their admirable qualities, Hargrave drew the attention of his readers particularly to their endurance, silence, honesty and kindness as well as their supreme expertise in woodcraft and scouting. Indians, he wrote, attribute their endurance to 'the cold dip in the river every morning' as well as the tests of endurance to which every Indian boy submitted himself. Indians were always taught to keep silence, to truly know the 'folly of words'. A man who could keep his silence was one who 'could also control his whole body'. Experience of their dealings with whites shows that 'they never once broke a treaty or went back on their word'. Reports to the contrary, the Indian never indulged in cruelty except when 'driven to desperation'. The practice of scalping, often used to support allegations of barbarism, was restricted to enemies already killed in battle, the tortures they did inflict in any case having been learned from the white man. Instead 'his whole teaching and his religion was one of kindness to man and beast. His children and squaws were happy and well treated.' Summing up the aptness of Red Indians as models for the scouting movement, Hargrave maintained:

> Among all the races of the world the Red Man stands out as the finest type of man – the real Scout. In intelligence and cleverness his mind was as . . . nimble as his supple and powerful limbs. He could not only run and swim, ride and shoot, he could think clearly and keep his wits about him in a tight corner . . . He will be noted for his exceptional tracking powers. . . . His eagle eye, his unerring judgement in following up a trail, his silent footfall, his graceful carriage of body, his silent tongue, his listening ear, his sniffing nose, his splendid pluck . . . These, and many more attributes too numerous to mention . . . made the Red Indians the finest and most magnificent type of scouthood upon the face of the earth. (Hargrave, 1916: 16–18)

The pamphlet in which the above comments on 'Red Indians' appeared was one of several collections of short 'talks' prepared by Hargrave, who had recently been appointed 'Commissioner for Woodcraft and Camping to the Boy Scouts, Headquarters Staff'. Many had appeared in one form or another in *The Trail*, the official magazine of the Baden-Powell scouts, and by the time of their publication Hargrave already had a devoted following within the scouting movement that was to form the basis of the breakaway Kibbo Kift movement.

The Wigwam Papers (1916), *The Totem Talks* (1918) and *Tribal Training* (1919) all take this form, combining general philosophising on the benefits of scouting, detailed instruction on setting up scouting organizations along 'totemic' principles of 'tribal' governance, and very concrete tips on activities to be pursued by scouting troops, many of which draw on 'tribal' activities of song, dance and 'woodcraft'.

As the titles of the published collections indicate, the whole is shot through with such imagery of Native American peoples with a liberal admixture of 'information' on contemporary peoples elsewhere in the world, examples from European prehistory, and material from more overtly fictional sources: Robinson Crusoe (described by Hargrave as the Lone Scout), 'The Bushmen of Australia', 'the men who lived in prehistoric ages', 'Soloman Islanders [*sic*]', Eskimos, Laplanders, Zulus, Malay Islanders, Thibetans [*sic*], 'Hindoos', 'the Japs', Maoris and 'all the other wonderful peoples of the earth', from all of whom 'we may learn the art of Scoutcraft' (1918: 24).

There are three reasons why I have chosen to begin this discussion of the encounters between modernity and its others with an account of the ideas of the now rather obscure John Hargrave, and the Kibbo Kift Kindred that he headed from its beginnings in the early 1920s. First, I am concerned in one way with issues debated extensively over the past decade or so in both anthropology and cultural/postcolonial studies about modernism's exclusions and the problems of representation. Hargrave's modernist 'anthropology' of Native Americans – here understanding the term in a very broad sense to refer not just to those located within the discipline, but that broader group of modern intellectuals who take on the job of producing 'knowledge' about human cultural diversity – appeared at just about the time that the 'modern' discipline of social anthropology was taking shape in Britain, when its twin culture heroes – Malinowski and Radcliffe-Brown – were developing their own particular contributions to the new discipline, the one methodological, the other theoretical. I want to use this example of popular or non-professional modernist anthropology to begin an exploration of the historical and intellectual context of this formative period in the history of British professional anthropology and, more generally, of what seem to be certain specifically British modernist modes of constituting otherness, particularly in the twentieth century.

Secondly, and more specifically, Hargrave's 'construction' of an idealised 'Red Indian', and of a generalised savage or primitive human condition, fits into a category of modern discourse on otherness that can be labelled *primitivist*, by which is meant the assumption that at least particular forms of cultural otherness can be understood to be a consequence of their *anteriority* to modernity. Primitivism in this sense is not separable from the particular form of evolutionary liberalism that emerged particularly in Britain in the wake of the Darwinian revolution. The critical deconstruction of various basic assumptions of primitivism has been one of the central projects of postmodern and postcolonial intellectuals for some time now, so much so that we have now all come to judge it as invariably and inevitably implicated in western practices of racial and sexual exclusion and oppression both at home and overseas. It has been widely argued that the representation, however sympathetic, of others – children, women, the insane, the criminal, the savage, the occupants of distant lands – as incompletely civilised has been responsible, variously, for the impetus to dominate them as part of a civilising mission, or, at the very least, for justifying such actions in the eyes of the general populace 'back home'.

But, thirdly, whether this critique of primitivism is justified, or not, what is of particular significance about Hargrave's version of the primitivist narrative is that it provides us with the opportunity to assess a rather particular form of popular modernism, here a critical interrogation of the modern condition from the terrain of an imaginary primitive other. Despite Hargrave's extensive interest in the lives of indigenous North Americans, there is no doubt that he saw his task primarily as not just a reflection on the problems of modernity, but as a means of overcoming them.

Most importantly, Hargrave's thoughts on civilisation and the primitive provide us with a kind of ethnographic picture of what appears to be an extremely pervasive British discourse on the nature of modern British-ness. In its different guises this discourse seems to set out the parameters by which Britons, at least in the twentieth century, defined who was, and who was not British. As such it has served among other things to shape the pattern of race relations in modern Britain in rather distinctive ways.

A Popular Primitivism

John Hargrave was no intellectual in the normal modern sense of the term. He was not part of, had no interest in seeing himself as a member of, and has not with historical hindsight been included within the British aesthetic and literary *avant garde* of his time. But neither was he of course a typical Englishman,[1] speaking the subaltern voice of the English working class, although especially during the 1930s through the Social Credit-inspired Green Shirts, he sought to mobilise and speak on behalf of urban workers. His critique of modernity is of that 'middling' sort that we are accustomed to calling 'popular'.

The son of artists and Quakers, Hargrave left school at the age of 15 to pursue a career as an illustrator, working for the publisher Thomas Nelson and their most popular novelist John Buchan before two years as chief cartoonist with London's *Evening Times*. This was to be his last job before becoming a member and employee of Baden-Powell's Boy Scouts in its foundation year, 1908. He concentrated on the outdoor camping and nature study aspects of the scouting movement, contributing to the development of these activities within the movement, and writing for scouting magazines. His first book, *Lonecraft* published in 1914, attracted the interest of Baden-Powell, and his experience as an illustrator led to his appointment as official artist at the Staff Headquarters.

Hargrave never fitted easily into a movement the ethos of which was imperial and militaristic, dominated as it was by public-school educated ex-army officers, many with experience of imperial campaigns. A pacificist, Hargrave none the less volunteered for duty during the First World War as a Field Officer with the Army Medical Corps, and served at Sulva Bay and Gallipoli. Like many of his generation, and unlike both the officers he met on the battlefield, and the leadership of the scouting movement, he was appalled by the destructiveness of modern warfare, especially after witnessing the deaths of up to 20,000 soldiers at Sulva Bay. The impact of his experience of the war explains, as we shall see, a good deal about his views on modern civilisation. As he was to write in one of his most widely read books:

> Organised death – Civilised, Mechanical Death sprang upon the world and swept away the flower of our manhood . . . If it does nothing else . . . [the war] will have brought home to the great mass of the people in these islands, not merely the horrors of modern warfare, . . . it has brought home to them the fact that we were on the wrong track; that in spite of all our Christianity, in spite of all our Scientific Research, and in spite of our commerce – we had somehow lost something, something most vital. (1919b: 50)

Hargrave continued to write from the battlefield under the 'tribal' name of 'White Fox' for *The Trail* and other official scouting publications, and when he was invalided back home, though considered something of a hothead by Baden-Powell, he was promoted to the position of Commissioner for Camping and Woodcraft in an ultimately fruitless attempt to harness his considerable talent and energies to the movement. Fruitless, because he was now beginning to develop his own distinctive constituency inside the movement that was to form the basis of a breakaway group, a constituency enthused by his ideas for 'woodcraft training':

> Woodcraft training combined romance and education. It was to be picturesque. It was to have a language of its own, to emphasise natural health, a harmony of physical and mental alertness and an unembarrassed celebration of the human body. (Drakeford, 1997: 18)

Being of a younger generation, lacking a public school background, and with his pacifist views, together with the fact that he seemed to be developing an independent base within the scouting movement, Hargrave was almost inevitably increasingly seen by the leadership as a problem. Baden-Powell branded him a bolshevik, and expressed grave reservations about his 'Red Indianism'. Hargrave did nothing to reassure Baden-Powell, among other things publishing in 1920 a provocative article in the left wing magazine *Foreign Affairs* that denounced the Scouts for their imperialism and militarism. After a period of heightened tensions, Hargrave was duly expelled from the Baden-Powell scouts.

The Kibbo Kift Kindred,[2] an alternative scouting movement, was born out of this split, first meeting under the sponsorship of Mrs Pethick Lawrence, an important supporter of progressive causes. Its second Althing or Folk Moot, as its annual meetings were called, brought together 200 individuals, and 14 organised sections, mostly from London and the Home Counties, but also supporters from the North, as well as the Netherlands and Bavaria. By 1922 Kibbo Kift had its own magazine, *The Mark*, later re-named *The Nomad*, an increasingly organised leadership, and a wide range of contacts with other organisations promoting progressive causes such as English folk dancing, criminal and child welfare, eurythmic dance, Esperanto, vegetarian and health food diets and naturism (Drakeford, 1997: 50ff.). It also attracted some influential patrons, the following included in a list of members of the 'Advisory Council' published in the June 1922 edition of *The Mark*: Norman Angell, Havelock Ellis, Julian Huxley, Mary Neal, Rabindranath Tagore, Prof. J. Arthur Thomson and H.G. Wells. According to a Hargrave biographer:

> The Kibbo Kift was to be not merely a youth organisation but was to involve old and young, male and female. Hargrave called for Outdoor Education, Physical Training, the learning of hand crafts, the reintroduction of Ritual into modern life, World Peace and the regeneration of urban man through the open air life. The new movement was to be nothing less than the 'human instrument' that would create a new World Civilisation. (Smith, 1995, n.p.)

Of the Kibbo Kift, Hargrave himself wrote:

> It must be an idea clothed with flesh and blood. It must show itself healthful, dynamic, capable . . . It must inspire and direct. It must be mobile and rapid in action; able to respond and resist . . . It must take its inspiration from a thousand sources and leap to life as one resolute effort . . . It must look to the young first and implant its message in words of one syllable. It must develop a technique of life in the midst of a chaotic civilisation . . . It must have an epic quality of thought and action . . . It must fire the imagination, hold the attention and liberate the will. It cannot look back for a historical counterpart, it is a new thing. It cannot be amusingly mystical in the half-shades; it must stand four-square in the full white light of the morning. We have need of this instrument – this living thing – now . . . We have need of it, however feeble and halting its embryonic emergence may be . . . because it already exists dumbly, incoherently, within the hearts of millions of human beings . . . Because of this dire need such an instrument will take shape. (cited in Smith, 1995, n.p.)

Equally significant was the close alliance forged in the early years between Kibbo Kift and the cooperative movement, particularly the Royal Arsenal Co-operative Society. The RACS, founded in 1877, had a long-standing interest in progressive education, launching a series of its own initiatives. But many of its educationalists were attracted by Hargrave's ideas about 'woodcraft' and his vision of 'a new society based on craft guilds and woodland communities, rejecting the old world of slums and smoky towns, [preaching] love of neighbour and community' (Attfield, 1981: 107). Speaking at a conference of cooperators in 1923, Joseph Reeves, a RACS education officer, told his audience:

> Kibbo Kift would give to the co-operative movement a new vitalising force, which would have the effect of re-energising it in all its phases. First of all an appeal was made to the individual boy and girl to develop the mind and body to their utmost capacity in the interest of the individual and community. Kibbo Kift, being based on true evolutionary principles, recognised that progress could be achieved only by the elimination of anti-social tendencies in human nature, with the simultaneous encouragement of social and altruistic tendencies. (cited in Attfield, 1981: 108)

Consequently, the RACS sponsored several Kibbo Kift 'Tribes'as the local organisations were known, made contributions to the organisation, and helped spread the word through its own publications, in meetings with co-operators from elsewhere, and at festivals and exhibitions involving co-operative societies. Leaders of the Co-operative Society assumed leadership positions within Kibbo Kift, most notable among them being Leslie Paul (tribal name 'Little Otter') (see also Paul, 1929). Although not itself an explicitly socialist organization, Kibbo Kift did therefore have close connections with, and many sympathisers among members of, the working class movement in the early 1920s.

This was to change over the years, however. After disagreements over Hargrave's leadership style, and what was seen as his excessively 'mystical' views, Leslie Paul and others from the Co-operative Society decided to break away from Kibbo Kift and founded their own woodcraft movement, the so-called Woodcraft Folk, an organization that to this day remains a highly successful alternative to the Boy and Girl Scouts, retaining much of the spirit of Hargrave's Kibbo Kift, but with a greater emphasis on world peace, internationalism and socialism.

In the 1920s after a meeting with Major C.H. Douglas, Hargrave discovered a new cause. Douglas was the author of a number of books that advanced the argument, unorthodox from the perspective of both left and right of the time, that economic crisis was a consequence of the inadequate purchasing power of workers, and advocating a solution based on state provision of funds for this gap between earned and unearned income, a solution that came to be called 'social credit'. Hargrave was attracted to Social Credit as a way of spreading the message of Kibbo Kift beyond its rather narrow base, in particular to the mass of workers and the unemployed who, without an improvement in their economic circumstances, would be unable to afford to participate in the leisure activities so necessary to their uplift out of the degenerate condition imposed on them by civilization. The result was the foundation of a socio-political movement with a radically different constituency, the urban-based working class. This lost Hargrave some of his middle class supporters, but as leader of a socio-political movement called the Green Shirts that clashed with both communists and fascists, he managed for a few years in the 1930s to broaden considerably the movement's base.

Hargrave established links with the one social credit electoral success, the government of the Canadian province of Alberta, before witnessing the decline first of social credit in Britain after 1935, and then of his own influence altogether. Hargrave died in 1982, although it could be argued that the woodcraft movement he played a major role in initiating lives on in diverse ways – through the ultimately more successful Woodcraft Folk, but perhaps more ambiguously in the so-called 'deep ecology' movement, and in the late twentieth century social credit movement which at least in some parts of the world has forged links not with the left but with the far right. That said, I want to return to the subject of Hargrave's primitivism.

In the above-cited passages from his work, John Hargrave's representation of Native Americans is clearly a popular version of a form of modern discourse called primitivism. Primitivism, as the term is being used here, refers to more than a positive attitude towards the primitive. It refers also to a series of related assumptions and concepts about particular groups or individuals through which these others are understood as not just outside what in Hargrave's time was called civilisation, but in some sense *prior* to it. Central to the discourse I am labelling primitivist is a notion of history that found its first full expression in nineteenth century western ideas about the laws of historical development. The transition from primitive to civilised in primitivism is seen to be a universal process governed by unconscious laws of development, whether of the human psyche or human sociality. A primitive can only become civilised when the time is ripe, that is when historical conditions permit it. Primitivist discourse is therefore clearly exclusionary, but it is potentially inclusive at the same time. If someone is in a state prior to the modern, then he or she may through some law-like process of transformation *become* modern over a more or less prolonged period of time and by various means such as education, evolution, or what is sometimes called assimilation. We shall return to an assessment of the exclusionary effects of primitivism shortly. But I want first to show why examining the example of John Hargrave and the Kibbo Kift movement may shed some light on some especially thorny problems in the existing debates over primitivism in particular, and the exclusions of modernity more generally.

Much of the discussion of primitivism has taken place in the context of analysis of the thought, and particularly the texts, of the high priests of modernist thought. In the British context we can find traces of primitivism in the realms of aesthetic, and particularly literary modernism, for example in the writings of W.B. Yeats, D.H. Lawrence, Joseph Conrad, T.S.Eliot, and even James Joyce. As we shall see, a primitivist impulse is also detectable in contemporary British social anthropology. The rejection of the civilising narratives of nineteenth century anthropologists like Tylor and Frazer by the first generation of British social anthropologists can be seen as part of the modernist discovery of the primitive in the Anglophone world in the years just after the First World War.

But there are good reasons to suppose that such analyses are insufficient to produce an account of the relationship between primitivism and more concrete modernising practices and cultural presuppositions in early twentieth century Britain. While the philosophical debate over the exclusionary potential of high modernism is interesting, there is every reason to suppose that modern primitivist discourse is likely to appear in a variety of historical and political contexts. To find primitivist sentiments expressed by particular colonial officials, for example, is clearly on its own insufficient to demonstrate an inevitable logical link between primitivist ideology and imperial practice.

Before attributing to any particular formulation of an idea like primitivism the power to generate particular exclusionary practices, we would need to establish the extent to which, say, actual practices of racial or colonial exclusion were informed by the same version of primitivism articulated in the texts under analysis. The more popular ideas of someone like Hargrave are not generally assumed to be modernist at all to the extent that modern*ism* is assumed to be a discourse of a small, and misunderstood, *avant garde*. And yet, as we shall see, Hargrave's ideas are just as modernist as those of someone like D.H. Lawrence if by that we understand a desire to 'de-naturalise' the assumptions upon which appeals to rational mastery and instrumental reason are founded.

In question, therefore, are the pervasiveness, or representativeness, for example, of an aesthetic or philosophical doctrine like primitivism, the way that doctrine is read or interpreted by whichever group of historical actors we might find responsible for racial and/or colonial exclusions, and equally importantly, the degree to which it is really confined to a supposedly elevated circle of artists and intellectuals. Apparently no one wants to argue that Conrad or Malinowski were themselves directly involved in or primarily responsible for twentieth century British colonial policy in India or Africa. At issue here presumably is the extent to which their ideas either reflected views more widely shared by the active agents of empire, or served to justify colonialism by convincing a wider public of its desirability. But to know whether or not this was the case, one must establish both that these views were pervasive in Britain at that time, and that those who held them read or interpreted them in this particular way. We face, in other words, a problem identified by contemporary cultural theorists, that ideas, images, and texts can be read very differently by different consumers who as a consequence construct meanings quite different from those intended by their authors, to say nothing of those we construct as readers of these texts almost a century later. Although it certainly does not provide a once and for all solution to this problem, the investigation of middle level discursive formations such as those manifest in popular culture and/or social movements such as the Kibbo Kift and Green Shirts movements, at least makes the problem explicit.

Examining Hargrave's thoughts on civilisation and primitivism at one level amounts therefore to a kind of audience research. Here is someone who constructed his own brand of British primitivism from a wide variety of sources – including the writings of the committed rationalist and populiser of Victorian scientific and anthropological thinking Edward Clodd,[3] the American children's writer, pioneer of scouting and 'expert' on Native American life Edward Thompson Seton (cited above), and evolutionary anthropologists E.B. Tylor and James Frazer, as well as popular writers of 'adventure' fiction like Robert Louis Stevenson, John Buchan and Rudyard Kipling. Although he may not have had much in the way of a formal anthropological education, Hargrave read all of the above, and his own writings are in a certain sense merely part of a rather broad stream of primitivist ideas that have been central to British thought and culture, not just to high modernism, at least from the time of Darwin. Looking at Hargrave provides some clues then as to the wider influence of these better-known thinkers, and how the works of nineteenth century high intellectuals and novelists were in fact interpreted or read by people outside the modernist *avant garde* at the beginning of the twentieth century and in a country where a form of social evolutionism had survived perhaps more strongly than anywhere else.[4]

But a figure like Hargrave is also interesting not just for how he interpreted or read the high texts of primitivist thought, but because he was himself a constructor of meaning for others, and as such might also be thought of as a kind of organic intellectual in the Gramscian sense, a broker acting between the intellectual high culture and others whose knowledge of that culture would only have come from the influence of people like Hargrave himself. Moreover, as we have seen, Hargrave's primitivism was more than a purely intellectual phenomenon, it was practice. In a literal sense the activities of Kibbo Kift scouting – camping, tests of strength, the shedding of clothing, swimming in cold water, sun bathing – were modern primitivist performance *par excellence*.[5]

This focus on a concrete case of primitivist belief and performance also addresses itself to a third problem with much of the existing focus on the exclusionary features of high modern thought, and that is its tendency to exaggerate the degree of discursive coherence in patterns of belief and historical practice. Recent work not just on imperial formations, but on the constitution of culture and society more broadly, has done much to undermine the kinds of homogenising assumptions behind the existing critiques of primitivism, orientalism and the like. Writing this time not of texts but of international exhibitions – another oft analysed expression of nineteenth century imperial ideologies – the historian Paul Kramer reminds us:

> The fairs themselves were as fractured and cobbled together as the empires that participated in them. Unlike many scholars of exposition, I am not convinced that a given exhibition should be examined historically as a centrally coordinated 'event' at all. Planners and sponsors labored mightily to give such events an air of aesthetic and political coherence, and put this vivid but deceptive impression

before the public in the form of abundant promotional literature and celebratory in-house histories. But in fact, turn-of-the-century expositions, one of the cultural forms most characteristic of the period's public life, were shot through with irresolvable contradictions . . . It was the task of exhibitors, including imperial ones, to position themselves carefully, profitably and imperfectly within what amounted to a welter of chaotic and contradictory formats and messages. (1999: 79)

The same could equally be said of the 'texts' of someone like John Hargrave, and certainly of the scouting activities associated with the organisation he led. In both cases an attempt may be made to impose a sense of coherence on the activity, the texts playing the role played by promotional literature for the exhibitions. But of course, as Drakeford's interviews with participants in Kibbo Kift indicate (1997), these could not completely disguise the diversity of motivations and experiences of the participants, to say nothing of the contradictions within Hargrave's own accounts of a supposedly coherent underlying philosophy. At a more general level it seems that any attempt to suggest that the mobilisation of primitivist imagery from a variety of sources at any period in time had a single origin and a single consequence, equally fails to recognise the contested and fragmented nature even of British society in the nineteenth century. Once again, therefore, the focus on a particular expression of primitivism, itself internally fragmented, helps to draw attention precisely to the absence of a coherent discourse and practice of primitivism even if we limit ourselves, as I do here, to the case of a particular national tradition, that of Great Britain.

Now it is true to say that recent anthropological, cultural and post-colonial theorists have gone some way towards rectifying the assumption of homogeneous/unified cultures. But without wanting to open out a long diversion into the problems in contemporary cultural theory, it is none the less worth pointing to what can only be called the crudity of the general theoretical apparatus that operates in much of the existing literature on representation and identity. Here I am referring to the shortcomings of the bowdlerised amalgamation of the ideas of Gramsci and Foucault with which many in both anthropology and cultural studies read representations of otherness as examples either of hegemony/knowledge-power or of resistance. This 'discovery' of resistance in particular shows evidence of an overabundance of wishful thinking on the part of analysts keen to find their own voice spoken by subalterns.[6]

This over-saturation of our analyses with power is in some cases equivalent to an earlier over-saturation with economics, and certainly in a case such as that of Hargrave and Kibbo Kift, neither treating them as a simple case of hegemony nor as some kind of expression of a subaltern resistance gets us much further than do earlier culturally essentialist approaches to the same phenomenon.[7]

That said, there are two features of Hargrave's 'discourse on the primitive' that deserve particular attention. First, there is the fact that Hargrave's own reading of history produces a vision of the primitive condition that is in a very real sense precisely the inverse of the primitivism of the better known Victorian social theorists. While the latter might be called primitive-phobes, Hargrave manifests a form of primitive-mania. Secondly, from what has already been said, British primitivism is commonly thought to be best understood as deeply embedded in the project of empire, and linked to both beliefs and practices of colonial/racial othering, Hargrave's primitivism stems from a set of debates about the British worker as the primitive other. These rather distinctive features of turn of the century popular primitivism in Britain can be usefully explored through Hargrave's own writings.

Primitive-phobia: Primitive-mania

What, if any, is the significance of the, in one sense quite different, normative evaluations of the primitive expressed in primitivist discourse? The question is prompted by an interesting re-analysis of European representations of India undertaken by Thomas Trautmann, whose central contention is that when applied in the Indian context, Said's redefinition of the term 'orientalism' has led to some serious analytic muddles, precisely because it lumps together two quite different phenomena: first, orientalism in the earlier sense of the term (which Trautmann characterises as 'Indo-mania'), and secondly the 'orientalism' of nineteenth century British 'evangelical liberals' such as John Mill and John Stuart Mill, whom Trautmann labels 'Indophobes'. Certainly the links between these two quite distinctive versions of orientalism and the project of empire will be quite different, the former clearly not a very suitable justification for colonialism of the 'civilising' variety.[8] Trautmann explains the importance of making the distinction following the much broader definition of orientalism offered by Said, Inden *et alia* in these terms:

> There is nothing wrong with such inflationary redefinition of a familiar word, which happens all the time. But it creates the problem that new and older senses of this word trip up one another in discussions of India . . . In India, the British Orientalists [in the traditional sense of the term] were by no means a unitary group, but Orientalists constituted the core of a distinct policy group who . . . had been dominant since the time of Hastings and who had devised the Orientalizing policy . . . these 'Orientalists' were in opposition to the 'Anglicists', Evangelicals and others who promoted English as a medium of instruction. The Anglicists were also involved in the production of knowledge of a kind Said calls Orientalism . . . the Saidian expansion of Orientalism, applied in this context, tends to sow confusion where there once was clarity. (1997: 23)

A similar inversion operates between the 'primitive-phobia' of British social evolutionists like Tylor and Frazer, and the 'primitive-mania' of someone like John Hargrave.

Primitive-phobia, it can be argued, does provide an underpinning for accounts of civilisation's triumph over, or mastery of nature. But in itself adopting a primitivist frame of reference does not commit one to this kind of Victorian triumphalism, since it can equally be mobilised by those deeply critical of the artificiality, that is, un-naturalism, of modernity. Hargrave's is an example of this use of the language of primitivism to denounce western civilisation for moving too far from its natural beginnings. For Hargrave, it is precisely their 'closeness to nature' that makes Native Americans so admirable in relation to a western civilisation that had lost touch with its natural moorings. One might say that it is precisely this dimension of primitivism that provided the central *raison d'être* of the entire scouting movement.

Hargrave's view of modern life is outlined at the outset of the 1919 pamphlet *Tribal Training* in a description of the crowds at a London railway station:

> What a crowd! What a crowd! And this terrible mass of struggling humanity, what is it that drives them? The poor and the well-to-do struggle alike – a wild mad struggle for existence. It is neither a gang of galley slaves nor a crowd of Egyptian peasants building a Pharaoh's tomb under the whips of their task-master. They struggle of their own free-will, and they call it the struggle for existence – the struggle for life . . . It is a bitter struggle. (1919a: 15)

Hargrave questions the purpose behind all this struggle, and the assumption that it produces the 'survival of the fittest':

> This is the . . . only explanation I receive to my enquiry. But it leaves me in the same muddle. I am bewildered. The survival of the fittest! – *Which of them is fit?* I saw this worrying hurrying crowd. Not one of them is fit – physically fit – not one in a hundred! Nevertheless they *survive* . . . *How long* will this go on? Strenuous body labour is less and less needed. Everything nowadays is done by machine. Probably we can go on forever. (1919a: 16; emphasis in original)

Taking up his critique of prevailing notions of progress, he goes on:

> Something has gone wrong. As a race we are not 'up to the mark' – slums and drink, luxury and comfort, poverty and profligacy, inherited degeneracy . . . The fact is we are *over-civilised* . . . In former ages civilisation after civilisation was overwhelmed by a horde of barbarians . . . This we say can never happen again . . . [We] are protected [by] . . . the terrible inventions of modern warfare . . . Our physical deterioration is always counter-balanced by the greater expansion of our inventive facility . . . The machine is our god . . . But in all classes the appetite for more is never satisfied . . . So the machine goes on and this is civilisation . . . (1919a: 17–20 *passim*)

That these are rhetorical questions becomes evident when Hargrave turns to the contrast with 'natural man' with 'simple wants'. 'We deplore', he writes

> the depravity of the heathen, their painted faces and their false gods. But are you aware that before civilisation found them they were sound in body and limb? . . . Do we ever consider that man in a state of nature existed for a million years under conditions which would snuff out the greater part of our population in a week? . . . the effect of civilisation has been to produce the *un*natural man, a man padded and propped up by unnatural comfort and effeminacy; who resorts to

unnatural expedients because he leads an unnatural life, with no inherited tribal instinct [and] no tribal custom to restrain him . . . It is impossible to lead an artificial life – you are only leading an artificial existence at the expense of life. Life cannot be artificially produced . . . (1919a: 23–24)

[W]e have blindly shut ourselves up in towns and cities, workshops and factories, offices . . . mansions and slums; we have turned away from Nature . . . the body and soul of the race is degenerating at an . . . alarming rate – and no National Missions or Religious Revivals can ever 'kindle the spark' . . . (p. 25)

Somehow or other we *must* get out . . . Civilisation is strangling us, wrapping round us like ivy round a tree trunk until it chokes us. Cost what it will, we must cut away the ivy and give the branches a chance to live. (p. 31)

For this is a Law of Nature – ANYTHING UNNATURAL BECOMES WEAK, AND IN THE END DIES OUT. (1918: 95)

That all this provides a justification for the activities associated with scouting should by now be fairly obvious, since scouting understood as 'training the children of to-day on a Primitive Tribal System' provides for Hargrave the only way to escape the artificiality of modern civilisation:

This Natural Reconstruction by means of the primitive tribal training is not only a natural necessity, it is an individual duty which each one of us must try to carry out. It is the only way out of our tangled civilised system . . . (1919a: 28)

And this training, which he advocates for all boys and girls, derives from the image of the primitive utopia of tribal peoples. Taking up another theme common to primitivist discourse, the theory that the development of the individual recapitulates the evolution of civilisation, Hargrave argues that 'tribal training' for boys is based on 'the fact that in his habits, instincts, and desires *the boy is a primitive man*' (1919a: 39). And everything he proposes – from an organisation of troops based on the totemic principles of primitive government, to the importance of daily scouting activities like swimming in cold water, exposing the body to the sun, physical training, bathing of the 'racial organs in cold water night and morning' (p. 80), sleeping outdoors, tests and initiations to advance to higher stages of scouthood and the like are all designed to bring both children and adults in touch with nature, and, hence, their own primitive natures.

The benefits of the natural life are, for Hargrave, self-evident. Consider how he justifies tribal training as an antidote to the ills of adolescent sexuality, of broad concern in Britain at the time:

The boy is now entering on youthhood and early manhood and the attraction of sex is growing stronger and stronger . . . [But] [b]rought up from birth upon open-air woodcraft methods sex will not come suddenly and overwhelmingly upon him. He will know something of reproduction and fertilisation in animals, plants and insects . . . In the Tribal Training the totemic laws – 'emu may not marry emu, snake may not marry snake' – have been explained . . . And he thus has an elementary knowledge of eugenics; in the health instruction he has learned the dangers of self-abuse . . . Moreover, his eye and mind is used to the naked body, he is not ashamed of it . . . A boy so trained will not find the primitive sex instinct

so unhealthily intense either in body or mind; and . . . he will have developed
more self-control than those brought up on a less Spartan system . . . Given girls
trained upon the same primitive principles there is no danger; but unless the girls
of the race are given a training based upon some idea of health and hardihood we
shall find that all the training given to the boys is of no avail. (1919a: 116)

This transformation of British liberalism at the turn of the century is not,
of course, unique to Hargrave. Much better-known examples can be taken
from the world of imaginative literature influenced by the work of James
Frazer. Frazer, a committed rationalist, civilisationist and, hence, primitive-
phobe, was paradoxically one of the most widely read of turn of the century
primitivists. Although his influence on the discipline of anthropology has
been surprisingly slight, Frazer was, and remains, one of the most widely
read anthropologists outside it (cf. Strathern, 1990). A recent collection of
essays emphasises the extremely wide-ranging influence of Frazer's work on
the British literary imagination. Throughout, the point is made that in
contrast to contemporary anthropologists, literary figures consistently read
Frazer against Frazer, as it were. Writers as otherwise diverse as Yeats,
Synge, Conrad, Eliot, Wyndham Lewis, D.H. Lawrence, Freud and John
Buchan used him as basis for a highly un-Frazerian romantic vision of the
primitive past (Fraser, ed., 1990).

Many of these literary Frazerians drew heaviliy on Frazer's own accounts
of the 'primitive' beliefs and rituals both of contemporary 'savages' and
European peasantries, both historical and contemporary, while largely
ignoring Frazer's own 'scientific' view that these were inferior versions of
western scientific rationalism. In this sense Hargrave was more explicit
about his own break with primitive-phobia, for example, taking direct issue
with E.B. Tylor, that other well-known evolutionary anthropologist, in the
following terms:

[Tylor] is able to show that civilisation improves. He is unable to show that
civilised man improves. . . [Civilisation] creates and fosters the unfit, the
degenerate, the lunatics, and the diseased. (1919b: 16)

In fact, of course, the literary celebration of the primitive condition –
whether Hargrave's, or that of 'higher' literary figures like Yeats and D.H.
Lawrence – was part of a general re-assessment of rationalism, progress,
civilisation, and social evolution that began as early as the 1890s in Britain,
a re-assessment that was manifest in many different areas of British cultural
life. The growing critique of civilisation, and particularly of liberal/
Spencerian visions of evolutionary progress, took many different forms,
and was, when politicised, embedded in highly diverse political projects
from left to right. It may well have been strengthened by economic
depression in the 1890s, by a growing disillusion with the empire, or by
particular cases of imperial excess including the Boer War. As the title of
his 1919 book *The Great War Brings it Home* indicates, in the case of
Hargrave and many others, this wave of civilisational disillusion was most
certainly solidified by the horrors of the First World War.

To cite only a few examples, one might point to the re-emergence of spiritualist beliefs and practices from the 1890s, often among precisely those figures who were most closely associated with radical and free thought at the height of social Darwinism. One such figure was Annie Bessant – leading radical and free thinker and campaigner for women's rights and sexual liberation who went on to become a noted spiritualist and then head of the theosophical society (Assayag et al., 1997; Dinnage, 1986). Spiritualism was also very widely practised among the Victorian working classes (Barrow, 1986).

Another example is provided by the renewed popularity of astrology. During the seventeenth and eighteenth centuries astrology was very popular in Britain, but by the beginning of the nineteenth century it had gone very much into decline. From the late nineteenth century, however, it experienced immense renaissance, so much so that one London newspaper in 1910 spoke of London as 'a confusion of prophets'. According to a recent observer, astrology was in this period 'overwhelmingly a metropolitan phenomenon' (Curry, 1992: 11). By the early decades of the twentieth century, astrology

> was the universal and tolerated fixture it is today. In fact, as a going concern it has outlasted many of its occult contemporaries. For Victorian and Edwardian England also saw a boom in mediumship, phrenology and spiritualism, as well as the founding of the Society for Psychical Research and the Theosophical Society. Magic and the supernatural also appeared in the most popular novels of the day . . . Both the astrologers and their clients came, broadly speaking, from the urban middle classes . . . Although otherwise unexceptional, such a social background for the reappearance of astrology is striking, given the overwhelmingly rural and uneducated character of astrology's previous constituency. (1992: 11–12)

Along with this developing Victorian counter-rationalism went a re-assessment of the evangelical liberal attitudes towards other societies. The field of orientalist discourse, for example, went through a different, but parallel transformation from the late nineteenth century – following Trautmann one could argue that Indo-phobia gave way again to a transformed Indo-mania, this time as part of a more generalised search for the source of a universal spirituality with its source in India, and also other parts of the 'orient'. Perhaps far from being primitive or barbarian 'survivals' as Tylor would have it, these places had something to teach us. The emergence and development of the theosophical movement already mentioned is perhaps the best example of a version of Indo-mania that succeeded the Indo-phobia of earlier evangelical liberalism. But it was not just Indo-mania that was on the rise, but rather a more general quest for a universal spirituality that could be found in a form, even a purer form, outside the West. Typical of this were the ideas of one J.S.M. Ward, fellow of the Royal Anthropological Institute and author of numerous books on spiritualism and freemasonry (Ward, 1917, 1921) who co-authored a two volume study of rituals of the Chinese Hung Society, with William Stirling, formerly of the Malayan Civil Service employed by the Chinese

Protectorate in Singapore (Ward and Stirling, 1925–6). Seeing parallels between ancient Chinese beliefs and western freemasonry and spiritualism, Ward wrote:

> I have never seen a greater ritual, or one more perfect in all its parts, than that of the Triad Society. It bears every evidence of an immemorial antiquity and it still has a great work to do for the aspiring soul. (Ward and Stirling, 1925–6, vol. 1: iii)

That Ward's quest for a universal spirituality through the investigation of 'the mysteries of backward peoples, or those of ancient Egypt, Mesopotamia, Syria, Greece, and Rome, or the modern possible survivals of them' was not considered mere quackery by leading scientists of his day, can be demonstrated simply by pointing out that this citation is taken from the preface to the Ward and Stirling volume written by none other than A.C. Haddon, the eminent psychologist and respected precursor of modern social anthropology.

While theosophists, universal spiritualists like Ward, and those prone to 'diffusionist' speculations about the common origins of human spirituality like Haddon and G. Eliot Smith, Hargrave sought a more 'anthropological' foundation of a universal human religion in the primitive 'oneness with nature'. Like Tylor and Frazer, Hargrave saw in primitive man's closeness to nature the source of his supernatural beliefs. Unlike them, however, he valued this nature worship above both western religion and science, advocating the universal desirability of synthetic natural religion because we are all primitives on the inside as it were. 'Long ago,' he writes,

> primitive man began to think about things. It was when he began to think that he began to be quite different from the animals – because he began to *wonder* about everything. (1919a: 93)

Because he could not understand, he began to worship all these wonders, 'he began to set up wooden "gods" as symbols of the Great Life Force which he realised must be "behind it all" . . . Worshipping spirits – he could only account for things by saying they were . . . MAGIC!' (1919a: 94). But, unlike the progressivists, Hargrave did not see in science a replacement for all this:

> Science has taught us a great deal about things . . . But still one thing we don't know . . . what this Great Life Force or Power is . . . It is still a Great Mystery. It is still wonderful . . . We must not become unnatural . . . because if we do we shall not belong to the Great Mystery of Nature – we shall not be a part of It All. It is the duty of the Scout, therefore, to realise that life is full of the wonder and mystery of the Great Power . . . (1919a: 94)

It may be that academic disciplines like anthropology were able to escape some of the less sophisticated forms of primitive-mania or Indo-mania that swept through at least the popular middle class consciousness from the end of the nineteenth century, if only because as it became increasingly disciplinised and institutionalised in the interwar years, British social anthropology would have been increasingly subject to its own internal dynamics.

And yet the development of the academic discipline of social anthropology in Britain in the years after the First World War shared in some of the discursive features of turn of the century primitivism as outlined here.

George W. Stocking, the foremost authority on the history of anthropology in both Britain and the United States, while inclined to avoid issues to do with the broader historical cum political influences on the discipline, has none the less drawn attention to such parallels. Of E.B. Tylor, probably the pre-eminent Victorian anthropologist, he writes:

> Tylor's conception of anthropology as a liberal 'reformer's science' purging Victorian culture of the unexamined 'survivals' of traditional 'superstition' took for granted its own unexamined utilitarian assumption that conservatism, political or cultural, could have no positive 'social function' (though were the issue posed to him, Tylor might have acknowledged its utility in preserving 'respectability') . . . (1995: xiv)

In this context the emerging postwar doctrine that came to be labelled structural functionalism in British social anthropology can be seen first, and in spite of considerable protestations to the contrary, to have retained a good deal of the primitivist/evolutionist project intact, at least until the end of the 1950s if not beyond. Adam Kuper, writing of the 'invention' of primitive society, has maintained for example that this idea, 'which crystallised, with anthropology itself, in the 1860s and 1870s . . . persisted very recently (indeed still survives, if no longer within mainstream anthropology)' (Kuper, 1988: 1). He maintains that this 'illusion' of social primitivity was based on a relatively simple 'elementary conception', itself based on the idea of an original social-organic whole that split into 'two or more identical building blocks – exogamous corporate descent groups', with marriage taking 'the form of regular exchanges between them', and with each practising 'the worship of ancestral spirits'. Evidence of this primitive society could be found, it was assumed, among contemporary 'savages' in whose languages (particularly in whose kinship terminologies) and ceremonies these original forms were preserved. The evolution of 'civilisation' was seen as a long process, over many generations, of the development of the 'family, private property and, eventually the state'. It is Kuper's contention that 'for the past 130 years, social anthropology [from the writings of Maine, Morgan, McLennan and Tylor through those of W.H.R. Rivers and Radcliffe-Brown] has been engaged in the manipulation of this elementary conception' (1988: 231). This supports a general impression that somewhat in contrast with the situation in the United States, classical British Social Anthropology has not broken, except perhaps rather recently, with the basic primitivist problematic of its nineteenth century intellectual ancestors.[9] This probably also goes some way towards explaining why it was that while early modern anthropology in the United States took as its central task the deconstruction of racial theorising, the critique of race came a good deal later in Britain and 'did not play the same role in the development of anthropological theory' (Stocking, 1995: xvi). Indeed, one might go further to suggest that the carryover of certain basic elements of nineteenth century social evolutionist doctrine, if inverted through the lens of primitivism, has been far stronger in twentieth century British political and intellectual life than it has in the United States.

The work of Malinowski and his students may well be considered to mark a more radical break with nineteenth century social evolutionism in twentieth century social anthropology, although this did not prevent Malinowski from declaring himself 'a faithful disciple of the Golden Bough' or as 'bound to the service of Frazerian anthropology' (cited in Stocking, 1995: 235). But here one is forced to question the extent to which that break was with primitivism *tout court* or whether it was in fact with the primitive-phobia of classic social evolutionism.[10] Since the publication of his diaries, Malinowski cannot be accused of romanticising the primitive condition. And yet there are at least echoes of the more popular primitive mania of contemporaries such as John Hargrave in the 'Malinowskian revolution'.

Consider, for example, that constant theme in Malinowski's writings, the rejection of the Tylorian doctrine of survivals. We have already had occasion to remark on the link between Tylor's concept and the central project of Victorian liberal progressivism. It follows that Malinowski's 'functionalist' account of survivals, and his frequent dismissal of the view that certain 'primitive' practices and customs exist only due to the, unhealthy, weight of tradition to be a kind of reverse primitive-phobia. Similarly Malinowski's own brand of physiological/psychological functionalism, his use of the study of 'savages' to shed light on his central interest in the 'biological and instinctual bases of human behaviour' (Stocking, 1995: 278) at the very least gives the impression of the existence of a Hargravian assumption about the greater closeness-to-nature of contemporary savages. Stocking supports this reading of the 'naturalising' aims of Malinowski's anthropological project, pointing out that his psychologising 'had a universalistic thread' and therefore in his view the study of contemporary 'savages' like the Trobrianders gave us access to 'human nature in its "savage" – that is "essentially human" – state' (1995: 276).

Another central theme in Malinowski's writings, that 'savages' were as capable of practical reason as modern westerners, represents similarly an attack on the progressivist assumption of the superiority of a scientifically based society over one in which religious, or magical thinking prevails.

By the 1930s at any rate Malinowski had taken to expressing a full-blown primitivist critique of 'our ultra efficient modern culture . . . a Frankenstein monster with which we are unable to cope', arguing elsewhere that rather than extending 'the benefits of Western civilization as the ultimate goal of all humanity,' we should be thinking of how 'to prevent the spread of our own troubles and cultural diseases to those who are not yet afflicted by them' (cited in Stocking, 1995: 415).

All this supports the view that, filtering out the significant influence of developments internal to the discipline, British Social Anthropology from the time of its formation was also characterised by a primitive-mania of the kind already discussed in the case of the non-professional, John Hargrave.

In typically cautious terms, Stocking himself echoes such a view when he suggests an alternative to more common opinion that structural functionalism emerged as a defence of a particular colonial objective:

> What has sometimes been understood in terms of a compatibility of theoretical orientation ('functionalism') and administrative policy ('indirect rule') in the mature colonialism of the interwar period might also (if not alternately) be seen in relation to an earlier moment of *domestic* political and cultural crisis. (Stocking, 1995: xiv; emphasis added)

Far from being in a vanguard of modernism, academic anthropologists, and modern literary figures in postwar Britain were in a significant way only part of a far broader modernist movement seeking to interrogate modernity from the terrain of a primitive other somehow closer to nature and, as a consequence, also more authentic.

Naturalising Difference

I have taken some care to sketch in the parameters of a discourse I have been calling primitivism more or less as a prelude to considering the ways in which this uniquely modern mode of constituting otherness has been involved in the exclusionary practices of modern history. We all know, or think we know, what is wrong with such classical western narratives of human difference, particularly in the nineteenth century – they were (eurocentric, androcentric, racist and) primitivist. In casting human social and cultural variation in a racial mould, and in reading the record of contemporary human variation on a temporal axis which consigned the other to the status of primitive ancestor of civilised European men, nineteenth century historians, ethnologists and sociologists not only produced a misleadingly hierarchical view of human groups, but provided the justification, even the impetus, for racial and sexual oppression both at home and overseas.[11] If others were incompletely civilised, then it was 'our' mission to civilise them. In so far as it represents various others – children, women, the insane, the criminal, the savage, the occupants of distant lands – as in some sense *not yet* fully civilised, the modern aspiration to universality has been exposed as deeply parochial, since what universalists fail to appreciate is the extent to which their own understanding of the universal human condition is inflected by the particular cultural values of white, western, middle class males.

It needs to be pointed out that, far from being a perversion of Enlightenment universalism, primitivism is an extension of it. If for Enlightenment philosophers, all 'that intervened between the essential rationality of basic human needs and the potential rationality of social institutions to satisfy them was superstition and error' (Stocking, 1987: 19), nineteenth century theorists added the intervening variable of time. Now superstition and error were not necessarily to be overcome merely by the application of reason, but by the unfolding of the unconscious 'laws' of history and social structure. In spite of this historical (and social) relativisation of human difference, however, nineteenth century social philosophers did not in general abandon the universalism of the previous century, indeed the assumption of a 'fundamental unity of human mental processes' was a central methodological principle at least of social evolutionism, for it was only on the basis of this presumed 'psychic unity of mankind' that superstition, magic, even religion could be understood as solutions, however imperfect, to precisely the same existential problems with which science was now presumed to be grappling (cf. Stocking, 1987: 313–314).

There is accordingly a sense that primitivism, at least since the mid-nineteenth century came to constitute a quintessential feature of modernism, shaping from that time more than any other conceptual schema the ways in which the modern intellectual, and modern culture more generally, defines the modern condition. And because more often than not it has been the lens of primitivism through which modernists have viewed the evidence of human otherness in their midst, there is the equally compelling sense that primitivism is profoundly implicated in modernity's exclusions. For these critics of modernity, it is precisely this tendency to constitute others as primitive, in other words as in some sense *temporally anterior to* the universal modern condition, that is the key to modern practices of colonialism, genocide, racism and patriarchy.

There is certainly much to be said in support of this sense of primitivism's centrality to the modern sensibility, and its implication in the exclusionary practices of modern societies, as a generation of feminist, postcolonial and postmodern critics have demonstrated. None the less, there are important questions about the nature and consequences of primitivism that have not been satisfactorily addressed, if indeed they have even been asked.

What is the precise relationship between universalising aspirations and primitivising outcomes, since the two appear on the surface at least to be contradictory? Is there really a logical link between universalism/modernism and racism? What of the argument much in vogue recently that it is not universalism, but cultural particularism that is responsible at least for the phenomenon recently identified as 'cultural racism'? Does the exclusion of the other as primitive exhaust the racialising possibilities of modern thought? How then can we account for the rather different racialised images of, for example, Jews in Europe, and overseas Chinese in Southeast Asia, both groups frequently demonised not for their primitive characteristics, but instead for being in some sense too modern or overly civilised? And what are we to make of the developing critique of civilisation and modernity that primitive-mania articulates?

We moderns like to believe that, perhaps with certain modifications, we all share the sentiments so eloquently expressed in the preamble to the American Declaration of Independence about human equality and the universal human right to 'life, liberty and the pursuit of happiness'. In fact, as we have seen, as we draw the curtain on a century which has so manifestly failed to fulfil the emancipatory promises with which it began, there is a sense in which at least modern intellectuals are re-dedicating themselves to the causes of the universal ideals of the European Enlightenment, making one wonder whether – given the events of both late eighteenth and nineteenth centuries – *fins de siècle* may for some mysterious reason have become a regular time for re-dedicating modernism to the project of univeralistic humanism. The words of Salman Rushdie quoted in the previous chapter have the very real advantage of demonstrating clearly a particular view of a relation between nature and ethics that was shared by many eighteenth century philosophers and nineteenth century 'social Darwinists'; and twentieth century primitivists, namely that human social arrangements can be judged according to whether they are, or are not, compatible with human nature.

This 'solution' to the perceived problem of finding a grounding for a universal ethics was not substantially altered by the historicism of nineteenth century social philosophy. Post-Enlightenment philosophers may have seen in the eighteenth century equation of the good and the natural an oversimplification given the tremendous diversity of social, cultural and, hence, ethical systems encountered by ethnologists, folklorists, orientalists and others in the nineteenth.

If, however, this required nineteenth century ethicists to postpone the equation of the good and the natural in the short run, social evolutionism allowed them to resolve it in the long. Primitive social arrangements could now be judged instead according to the ethical standards that would apply once they were fully civilised since the processes of evolution would finally restore the balance between the two.[12] Put crudely, for many nineteenth century thinkers, the maximisation of human happiness could not provide a universal framework for deriving ethical judgements in all historical epochs. But since all societies were moving towards that happy state of affairs, the end of history did provide such a standard. And given the assumptions upon which the comparative method was based, the standards of the more civilised West being far closer than anyone else's to the end of history were best suited to the task of constructing what we might now call an intercultural ethics.[13]

At first sight it strikes one as distinctly odd that anyone should feel the need to re-assert the concept of universal human species-being. Some such idea after all has been a central one in the culture of the West for a considerable period of time. We tend to identify it clearly with the philosophy of the French and British Enlightenments, although it could easily be argued that it goes back to the English Revolution, or to the Renaissance, or to the emergence of Christianity, or even to classical times. One may, however, like to see a break in the seventeenth and eighteenth centuries, when a modern notion of human universalism based on the presumed state of Man in nature was first clearly expressed by John Locke, Jean Jacques Rousseau, Condorcet, Adam Ferguson, Adam Smith, Thomas Jefferson and others. Certainly something very much like the Enlightenment notion of a homogeneous human nature persisted through the nineteenth century as we have seen, finding its way into the elaborated evolutionary historio-graphies of Comte and Spencer, Hegel and Marx, and, in the guise of the presumption of the 'psychic unity of mankind', forming the central assumption of the sociology and anthropology of Victorian Britain.

That this is not the first time that intellectuals have felt the need to formulate and reformulate the ideal of human universalism should warn us, therefore, of the possibility that far from being a solution to the dilemmas of our time, universalism might in fact be part of the problem. Specifically we need to look closely at the paradox that appears to lie at the heart of all agendas based on universalising aspirations at least up until now, namely that they seem to coincide with historical practices of exclusion, more often than not framed in a language of naturalism. After all, as many have pointed out, the author of the stirring phrases which open America's Declaration of Independence was himself a slave owner,[14] the leading figures of nineteenth century liberalism were firm advocates of European colonial expansion, the great emancipator of the slaves in the United States was a staunch racist, and the Frenchmen so dedicated to the rights of men were far less sympathetic to the rights of women.

Is racial and sexual exclusion an inevitable byproduct of the seemingly benign belief in a universal human nature? Or is it possible to espouse a universalism which is genuinely inclusive of humanity in all its diversity? This question at least still needs to be asked, given both the existence from the outset of racial and sexual exclusions within modern social life and the exclusionary arguments buried in the writings of most advocates of human universalism. It needs to be answered if only because for some time now critics of modernism have been suggesting that the co-existence of univer-salism and exclusion is more than mere historical coincidence, that in some sense they are inevitably intertwined. Ignoring this in favour of program-matic statements, while they might make us feel better, will not make the problem go away.

At first glance the idea of human universalism appears straightforward and unproblematic. Humanity, after all, constitutes a species, defined by the *Concise Oxford Dictionary* as a 'group of animals or plants subordinate in classification to genus and having members that can interbreed and that differ only in minor details'. The biological unity of humankind, moreover, is not contradicted by the fact of culture, since as anthropology reminds us the capacity for culture is itself something which unites rather than divides individual human groups. To believe in the possibility of discovering universal attributes or principles of human species-being is not, apparently, to ask very much of us. But if that were all that was required, it would be difficult to see universalism as embattled, and its supposed demise as genuine as recent commentators seem to imagine.

But of course there is much more to human universalism than this. In the first place, to establish the category 'humanity' requires the drawing of boundaries around a particular class of living beings. In the second place, once the category has been produced, further questions need to be answered

– particularly those having to do with its normative implications, and the interpretation of human actions that appear unnatural in the light of the definition.[15]

Take, as an example, the erosion of the sharp dividing line between humans and other animals by the findings of geneticists about how much of our genetic material is actually shared with other forms of life – an erosion which contributes to a growing discomfort with the ways we treat non-human animal life. Or the debates around the effects of scientific and technological development in relatively new fields like informational systems and genetic engineering which affect our understanding of what it means to be human and about the difficulty of drawing boundaries between the human bodies and the machines which increasingly sustain our ways of life at the turn of the twenty first century. Consider the passions generated by different determinations about how long after conception, or even before conception, actual human life can be said to begin, or over whether there are circumstances that justify the taking of human life. And all societies, and one presumes all advocates of universal human rights, have an understanding of what constitutes the human essence that excludes certain members of the species – either temporarily or permanently – from full membership in the human race – children, criminals, the insane, deviants, those on life support machines, etc. All this suggests that even if one believes in the possibility of a strictly objective/biological definition of the human race, the universal ideal involves selective and constitutive processes that can be seen to be cultural or discursive.

But the ambiguities of any notion of human 'species-being' do not end once one has addressed such issues. On the contrary, many more immediately arise. First: what actually is the content of the category human? In other words once we have established that there is such a category, what are its specific attributes? Second: having established what it is to be human, what implications does this have for human interaction and, since this is particularly important for political theorists, for human rights? Third, how do we account for the fact that, once having established the characteristics of the category, some humans and/or groups of humans seem to behave in ways which contradict their very humanity? It is only necessary to note that once again while the questions are inevitable, answering them requires the intervention of human judgement, prejudice, discourse.

Many answers to the first question are minimalist almost to the point that they make the category 'human' a completely empty one. One writer, for example, has maintained only partly facetiously that the endless speculation of eighteenth century philosophers on human nature produced only one firm conclusion, that it is the nature of humans to have no nature (Weyant, 1973). Other answers are patently ideological – such as arguments about the innateness of aggression, or patriarchal attitudes. Although Rushdie seems unaware of it, such has certainly been asserted about the central assumptions in the work of sociobiologists like E.O. Wilson. The very fact that there exist a large variety of answers, and endless debate about the actual content of human nature, suggests that an 'objective' or purely 'rational' answer to the question is difficult if not impossible to achieve.

Secondly, it does not follow that a discovery of what Turner has called universal attributes or principles of human species-being would lead us anywhere else. The normative assumptions about universal rights implied in the work of people like Turner and Rushdie instead requires a further assumption, namely that human social life must somehow be arranged so as to ensure the fullest possible expression of human nature. This is, of course, based on further assumptions about the ethical value of the laws of nature. That that which is 'unnatural' is at the same time morally undesirable was of course the assumption made by advocates of natural law in the eighteenth century as we have seen, but it is no less a theoretical assumption for all that.

This points to what is perhaps the greatest paradox about the assertion of the universal ideal and that is that it seems inevitably to be found in discourses which, far from being accepting of the current state of human affairs, are instead in some sense reformist in intent. I say paradoxical because the assertion of human universalism might well be taken logically to imply that everything humans do and have done, because it is done by humans and therefore expressive of human nature, is compatible with it and, hence, morally acceptable. And yet as we see so clearly for example in the late twentieth century discourse on human rights, human universalism is mobilised precisely to distinguish desirable from undesirable, self-consciously to recapture some capacity for normative judgement, and hence to criticise particular human social arrangements as unjust. If humans are always and everywhere the same, how, then, is it possible to criticise some social arrangements and not others?

Thus, while it may not be always clearly acknowledged by advocates of universalism, it is a very unusual universalist for whom there are not both human individuals and groups who are still excluded from the category human, whether that exclusion is taken to be permanent or temporary. It seems safe to assume that in all definitions of the human essence, there will be some humans – children, criminals, the insane, or those temporarily 'deranged' through the effects of chemicals (drugs, alcohol) on the brain – who will be judged as in some sense incompletely human. Until these incomplete or not-yet humans are fully humanised – through education, civilization, development, psychoanalysis, rehabilitation, detoxification, breeding etc. – they will presumably also be denied the rights that go with a fully human status. The point of these observations is not to suggest that any particular understanding of human essence is necessarily faulty – it is only to point out that universalism, like relativism, involves cultural as well as biological principles in the constitution of human-ness. In other words, universalism, like relativism, is a discursive construction.

And given the centrality of a concept of human *nature* in this construction, it is perhaps not surprising that actual human diversity will be understood in naturalistic terms. What this therefore suggests is that modernism, to the extent that it is based on some underlying assumption about the nature of human species being, tends inevitably towards a naturalised discourse of human diversity. This is not to suggest that it is inevitably racialised in the narrow sense, since definitions of the *not yet* fully human may instead be cast as physical and mental 'immaturity', chemical and psychological 'alteration', and the like. But it does suggest that universalism in general, and primitivism in particular, will be most likely to interpret human diversity by means of a language of biological, or should we say phenotypical differentiation.

There is a second way in which nature enters into primitivism, and that is through the commonly held primitivist assumption that equates historical anteriority with 'closeness to nature'. Regardless of whether the state of nature is valued positively or negatively, here the move from primitive to civilised, premodern to modern, is at the same time a move from nature to culture. This is as true of the positive primitivism of someone like John Hargrave, as it is of the negative primitivism of nineteenth century social evolutionists who, unlike Hargrave, saw in the primitive closeness to nature a stigma.

Given the association between primitivism and naturalism, it is not at all surprising that primitivist discourse, at least in the past, has been closely related to various naturalistic understandings of human difference and that in the most developed systems of primitivist thought – notably for example the 'social Darwinism' of Herbert Spencer – the movement from primitive to modern, nature to culture (or civilization), was at the same time a natural and a cultural process. In Spencer's writings no distinction was made between what we might now see as separate processes of biological and social evolution. This explains once again the apparently intimate relationship between primitivism and the naturalisation both of the universal human condition, and of human difference.

Culture, Biology, Race

Is primitivism, indeed are all forms of modern discourse based on a concept of a uniform human species being, therefore inevitably racist? The main villain has been identified – it is the biological category of 'race'. For some the nineteenth century flirtation with race represented an aberration in modern history, a betrayal of the finer ideals of Enlightenment universalism, a betrayal which in the twentieth century was finally exorcised. For others, it was only in the twentieth century that we finally got on top of racial theories of human difference, and this was made possible by an entirely new (to the twentieth century) way of understanding difference as *cultural* rather than biological. Has or will culture provide an antidote to the racial assumptions of primitivist discourse?

In the published version of his 1992 Sidney W. Mintz memorial lecture, Eric Wolf wrote about what he called the three 'perilous ideas' that have

played a 'guiding and legitimizing role' in the history of modern anthropology. These are: *race, culture* and *people*. He then offered a brief history
of each concept, a history that is long term for race – going back to the
time of the 'great archaic civilizations of the Old and New World[s]';
shorter term for culture (he saw it as basically starting with Franz Boas);
and even shorter term for people – which, since he equated it with the
concept of ethnicity, he traced back only to the 1960s. But clearly Wolf was
interested in more than conceptual genealogy, as the following suggests:

> I will attend especially to the concept of race, because it remains a major source
> of demonology in this country and in the world and anthropology has a major
> obligation to speak reason to unreason. (1994: 1)

> [peoplehood] is unduly voluntaristic . . . [with] too much talk about agency and
> resistance and too little attention to how groups mobilize, shape, and reshape
> cultural repertoires and are shaped by them in turn. (1994: 6)

The latter is clarified when Wolf speaks of the problem of what he,
following Stolcke, called 'cultural fundamentalism', a reified understanding
of culture. So once again the project seems to be to speak reason to
unreason. The reason belongs to anthropology, with its (good) concept of
culture, the unreason to racists and 'cultural fundamentalists'. In fact then,
in this short paper, Wolf was concerned with two 'perilous ideas', race and
people; the third, culture, was characterised as benign, even as something of
an antidote to the first two.

But has the emergence of a concept of culture provided us with a genuine
alternative to the biological models of human diversity so prevalent
especially in the nineteenth century? Has the culturalist critique of race
served to exorcise the primitivist demons in modern culture, or does it
provide an antidote to the exclusionary and genocidal practices so closely
associated with primitivist ideologies in the nineteenth and twentieth
centuries? Are histories of the notions of race, culture and people as easily
distinguishable as Wolf implies? Can cultural anthropology be so easily cut
off from the historical processes of exclusion associated with notions of race
and peoplehood?

A useful entry point into these debates is provided by a look at the
feeling on the part of a growing number of observers that Europe, and the
countries of western Europe in particular, are witnessing the rise of new
forms of exclusionary rhetoric. Suggesting that the developing hostility to
immigrants that has marked recent events in France and Germany takes a
rather different form than earlier racial rhetoric on the continent, observers
in the 1980s began to speak of the rise of a new kind of 'cultural racism'
which, it is argued, inscribes the discourse of cultural difference into
projects that were previously grounded in a biologically based differentiation of the human species.

A case in point is the anthropologist Verena Stolcke who has maintained
that the 'demons of race and eugenics . . . have been politically if not
scientifically excised partly by the work done by UNESCO and other bodies

in defence of human equality'. But she goes on to argue the decline of race
has seen the rise of 'cultural identity and distinctiveness . . . [which] have
come to occupy a central place in the way in which anti-immigration
sentiments and policies are being rationalized . . .' (1995: 2). This culturalist
exclusion Stolcke terms 'cultural fundamentalism'. How are racial and
cultural forms of exclusion to be distinguished? Echoing a fairly standard
twentieth century distinction between race and culture, Stolcke writes:

> Modern Western racism rationalizes claims of national superiority or socio-
> political disqualification and economic exploitation of groups of individuals
> within a polity by attributing to them certain moral, intellectual, or social defects
> supposedly grounded in their 'racial' endowment which, by virtue of being innate,
> are inevitable . . . Cultural fundamentalism, by contrast, assumes a set of
> symmetric counterconcepts, that of the foreigner, the stranger, the alien as
> opposed to the national, the citizen. Humans by their nature are bearers of
> culture. But humanity is composed of a multiplicity of distinct cultures which are
> incommensurable . . . Instead of ordering different cultures hierarchically,
> cultural fundamentalism segregates them spatially, each culture in its place . . . By
> building its case for the exclusion of immigrants on a trait shared by all humans
> alike rather than on an unfitness allegedly intrinsic to extracommunatarians,
> cultural fundamentalism, by contrast with racist theories, has a certain openness
> which leaves room for requiring immigrants, if they wish to live in our midst, to
> assimilate culturally . . . Hostility against extracommunatarian immigrants may
> have racist overtones, and metaphors can certainly be mixed. Yet, as somebody
> remarked to me recently, immigrants carry their foreignness in their faces.
> Phenotype tends now to be employed as a marker of immigrant origin rather than
> 'race's' [sic] being construed as the justification for anti-immigrant sentiment.
> (1995: 7–8)

Is there, as those who talk of new exclusionary discourses based on
culture rather than race assert, a genuine difference between race and
culture, racism and culturalism? If so, what is its basis? A closer look at the
extract from Stolcke cited above reveals a reliance on tautology that is
surprising given the overall commitment to such a distinction. In 'modern
Western *racism*', we are told, social distinctions are 'supposedly grounded
in . . . [people's] "*racial*" endowment which, by virtue of being innate, are
inevitable'. *Cultural* fundamentalists, on the other hand, assume that
'humanity is composed of a multiplicity of distinct *cultures* which are
incommensurable' (emphasis added). The confusion is compounded by her
admission that these 'metaphors can certainly be mixed', followed by a
perfect example of the assertion which is neither clearly racist nor culturalist that 'immigrants carry their foreignness in their faces'.

Can this distinction between race as a quality of phenotype, and culture
ever be upheld?[16] I want to suggest a number of reasons why it cannot, why
in other words it is in many ways misleading to speak of cultural difference,
cultural racism and cultural fundamentalism as new phenomena. In so
doing I also hope to provide a clearer assessment of the racialised dimension of primitivist discourses on human difference.

First, it can be demonstrated that racial and cultural models of human
diversity are both flawed in formally the same way. They rest in other

words on identical logical principles of inclusion and exclusion. *Contra* Stolcke, this seems to me to make the two virtually indistinguishable. To summarise briefly an argument that I have made elsewhere (Kahn, 1995), race has been rejected as a scientifically precise category because, in Boas's terms:

> The term race . . . as here understood . . . applies solely to the biological grouping of human types. On account of a lack of sharpness of demarcation the attempts at classification, based on varying characteristics, have not led to a generally accepted system . . . (1940: 25f.)

The main problem with the notion of race therefore seems to be that while 'as a folk concept in western and non-western societies the concept of race is a powerful and important one' it has 'no scientific validity, since evolutionary theory and physical anthropology have long since demonstrated that there are no fixed or discrete racial groups in human populations . . .' (Seymour-Smith, 1985).

But if the concept of race needs to be disregarded because phenotypical variation among humans is sufficiently continuous and unstable to make the drawing of all racial boundaries impossible, the same must be said about culture. Just as no physical anthropologist has been able to produce a system of racial classification that generates 'fixed or discrete racial groups', so no cultural anthropologist can produce a system of 'fixed or discrete cultural groups' that stands up to critical scrutiny. To define races and cultures is to draw boundaries that are arbitrary from the point of view of phenotypical variation or variation in learned behaviours respectively. We are thus entitled to ask: is one more real than the other? And further, if all such boundaries are products of human classificatory systems, then how does one differ from the other?

A possible resolution to this dilemma might be to argue that the racial difference is itself cultural; in other words, that while neither races nor cultures exist in a scientific sense, the distinction remains important in the world as it were. In other words since some classificatory systems are based on the presumption of the reality of discrete racial phenotypes, and given that this presumption implies something rather different about the mutability of human difference than does a classification based on culture, then the distinction remains an important one. In the above example, therefore, the distinction between the 'old' and 'new' racisms rests not on the greater scientificity of one or the other – both are after all folk models that are themselves scientifically discredited, and discredited for the same reasons. The difference instead is in the content given by racists to their exclusionary categories. And to the extent that that content is 'racial' rather than 'cultural', then it rests on a view of difference that is immutable or, to use Stolcke's term, inevitable. Surely this distinction is an important one?

The difficulty with this attempt to distinguish culture from race on the basis of the implications of so-called folk models is already implied in the ambiguity conveyed by Stolcke's statement that 'immigrants carry their foreignness in their faces'. This captures in a particularly apt way the essence of much nativist discourse, whether in the nineteenth century or the twentieth. It points clearly to the ways in which cultural differences are frequently biologised at least in the popular imaginary. It shows how it is virtually impossible to hold to a mode of human classification that is somehow purely cultural, how discourses of cultural difference almost inevitably slide into a view of the bearers of cultural difference as also physically different. Of course, on reflection a nativist might admit that what are said to be observable differences between immigrant and native are themselves a product of cultural or environmental factors – style of dress, carriage, bearing, even skin tones. But there is something almost inevitable about the way purely cultural differences become naturalised by nativist discourse.

But if the race–culture distinction is eroded in popular discourse because of the tendency of those who use it to slide into external physiological markers, in other words in a certain way to biologise cultural differences, the reverse is also the case. In other words, if we look at the 'old', that is nineteenth century, system of racial classification, here we find the reverse to be the case. What are presumed to be biological categories were almost always culturalised.

There is no doubt that nineteenth century primitivist classifications were overwhelmingly racial in the sense that the word race is used in preference to any other, and there was a curiosity to the point of obsession with the physiological differences among human groups. But to conclude that the differences between racial discourse in the nineteenth century and culturalist discourse in the twentieth are always and everywhere qualitative is greatly to exaggerate the practical differences between the two.

First, ideas about race before the Darwinian revolution did not always imply hereditarian differences among different human groups. Even limiting ourselves to the conceptual arsenal of the 'men of science':

> [I]n general it seems fair to say that the eighteenth-century writers did not conceptualize human diversity in rigidly hereditarian or strictly physical terms, if only because comparative anatomy and physical anthropology were barely beginning to provide the basis for such thinking. Furthermore, developmental speculation was still severely constrained by traditional biblical limits of human time and biological species . . . And although there were several exceptions among the French, the 'evolutionism' of the progressivists was essentially social and not biological . . . Allowing something for the effects of prolonged environmental influences, what separated savage man from civilized man was not a difference in inherent mental makeup so much as the progress of refinement and of civilization itself. (Stocking, 1987: 18)

And while racial rhetoric gathered force in the nineteenth century, it continued to be informed by an intersection of what we would now call racial and cultural assumptions. This was to some extent a result of the continued prevalence of assumptions about the inheritance of acquired characteristics.[17] As long as such a view prevailed, what we now tend to see as rigid and immutable racial characteristics could be viewed by nineteenth century thinkers as just as mutable as cultural ones, that is they could change in a single generation. To quote Stocking again on the first half of the nineteenth century:

> Although the political connotations of the race idea suggest to twentieth-century readers a rigidly biological determinist approach, in 1850 this was far from necessarily the case. The process by which 'race' took on a clearly biological meaning was by no means complete, and contemporary biological assumption in fact justified a confusion of physical and cultural characteristics. The notion that acquired characteristics could be inherited was widely accepted . . . Much of Anglo-Saxon and other forms of 'racial' nationalism, as well as Müller's Aryanism, may best be understood in this context. (1987: 63–64)

The Origin of the Species, and more generally the tremendous expansion of human history associated with developments in archaeology, geology and biology from around mid-century, of course changed many of the assumptions about human diversity prevailing at the time. And yet once again views of race in the English-speaking scientific community did not conform to the twentieth century caricature. Writing of the evolutionists, for example, Stocking argues:

> Although classical evolutionism was not primarily concerned with the physical differentiation of humankind, it nevertheless incorporated a substantial body of racialist assumption – in effect preserving the biological unity of mankind by accepting the substantial differentiation of human races in evolutionary time. At the same time, it was still strongly influenced by the unitarian assumptions of the Christian and Enlightenment traditions and took for granted that the cumulation of mental difference had not destroyed the fundamental unity of human mental processes. But in thus limiting the significance of racial difference, classical evolutionism also reduced the significance of the variety of cultural forms . . . the variety of cultural forms represented flawed or imperfect manifestations of the processes of Western practical cultural rationality, produced by small-brained primitive men – and by their contemporary savage representatives – in the attempt to understand and control the external world. (1987: 313–314)

It is interesting to note, in this regard, that it was more often critics of evolutionism who advocated more rigid notions of racial difference because they felt that evolutionists, overly committed to unitarian assumptions, had precisely failed to capture the true diversity of what we would now call human cultural activity. With hindsight, this critique has a modern feel, but lacking a concept of culture, these critics stressed rather the diversity of human mental capacity and hence race to advance their arguments. One such was Leslie Stephen, who attacked evolutionists for being insensitive to human diversity:

> For Stephen, however, it was not culture but 'race' that was the rubric for 'the influences by which society is moulded through beliefs and customs'. That something other than a rigid hereditarianism was at issue is indicated by the fact that in 1900 Stephen was willing after all to follow Buckle and Mill in excluding organic race from sociology. But he would not exclude 'the influence of the "moral" element in building up the social structure.' In short, he insisted on what an anthropologist today would call 'culture' – although he still spoke of it in

terms of 'moral and social evolution.' The point, of course, is not to belabor Stephen for failing to employ a concept unavailable to him, but by contrast to explicate one that was. Carrying much of the meaning that 'culture' does today, 'race' was a kind of summation of historically accumulated moral differences sustained and slowly modified from generation to generation. Threatened with rigidification by polygenist hereditarianism, this 'cultural' sense of race seemed once again viable within an evolutionary framework in which 'Darwinism' was not incompatible with the inheritance of acquired characteristics. (Stocking, 1987: 138f.)

If, therefore, anyone in the nineteenth century held a view of race that did not in some ways approximate twentieth century notions of culture, it was probably not those social evolutionists motivated first and foremost by scientific developments of the time, but those who took issue with the dominant interpretations of the Bible. In the nineteenth century the assumption of ultimate biological unity was seriously called into question by polygenist racialism, which saw different groups of mankind as 'aboriginally distinct and irreducibly unequal'. Physical anthropologists like Robert Knox, Retzius, Bernard Davis, John Beddoe, Louis Agassiz, Samuel Morton, Paul Broca and others were, much more than evolutionists and primitivists, the advocates of a concept of race that comes closest to the twentieth century stereotype, but everywhere they were motivated more by a strong polygenist and hence religious impulse than by the dominant scientific paradigms of the times.

A final point about nineteenth century notions of human diversity is worth making here. We are frequently told that a significant difference between racialist and culturalist discourses lies in their different effects. If, it is suggested, someone clings to racial categories as opposed to cultural ones an inevitable implication is that for them the differences between human groups become immutable; constructing one's own group on racial rather than cultural grounds therefore is said inevitably to imply exclusionary practice. It remains to be seen, of course, how mutable twentieth century 'cultural' groups really are and there is little evidence that the new 'cultural racism' is particularly open to the possibility of immigrant assimilation. The point I want to make here is that pre-twentieth century racialist discourse was neither more nor less rigid in this regard. There were probably just as many, or perhaps better just as few, believers in assimilationism in the nineteenth century as in the twentieth. In other words, there is no prima facie case to argue that classical racial discourses of national identity were any more exclusionary at least in practice than are twentieth century culturalist ones. This is because given especially non-Darwinian ideas about phenotypic change, racial categories can be as mutable over time as cultural ones. All this suggests that the race–culture distinction so central to the self-understanding of the twentieth century hides what is in fact a significant continuity in the modern debate over how we can account for the tremendous diversity of human belief and practice given the basic unity of humankind, and in the exclusionary consequences of these beliefs and practices.

Naturalising the Worker: A British Primitivist Debate

All this should not be especially surprising – universalism, its nineteenth century offspring social Darwinism, and twentieth century primitivism, are almost by definition at once inclusionary and exclusionary discourses. To the extent that the universal human condition, or the universal endpoint of progressive history, are cultural constructs, then they may well contain the possibility that all humans will ultimately achieve those rights to which their nature entitles them, but only when they become culturally recognisable as fully human. But this is as far as the abstract philosophical evaluation of primitivism can take us. For any attempt to further evaluate primitivism, context becomes all important precisely because primitivism, like other universalising discourses, is inevitably inflected by particularistic cultural values, to say nothing of varying political agendas. Thus, as critics like Uday Mehta have argued, the universal human future proposed in liberal evolutionism in the nineteenth century, and to which the 'laws of history' were thought to be driving all societies, might not be universal at all. Theirs was instead, or so the argument goes, a utopia shot through with the highly particular cultural assumptions of white, middle class, Protestant Victorian males. According to this critique, therefore, this variant of British 'social Darwinism' was highly dependent on a particular cultural and historical context in spite of the protestations of its advocates. But having established the inevitability of the context-dependence of any totalising discourse, nothing further can be concluded about its precise exclusions by logical/philosophical argument alone. The same must be said of twentieth century primitivism. If primitivism is wholly determined by the cultural and political contexts within which it emerges and is deployed, then one cannot argue further that it is logically or necessarily imperial, racist or whatever. That must depend on the exigencies of time, place, class and culture. There is no one primitivism, only primitivism*s* – John Hargrave's being one.

It may well be the case that for anglicist liberals in the first half of the nineteenth century, primitivism was deployed within an overarching discourse on empire, that in other words what we with hindsight labelled racial othering was central in the development of British primitivism. Approaching the problem from a very different direction, Burrow reached a similar conclusion. His account of the origins of British social evolutionism saw it as a modification of utilitarianism made necessary by the experience of radical othernness associated with nineteenth century imperial expansion (Burrow, 1966).

Towards the end of the century, even from the time of Darwin himself, however, one would be hard put to make a similar argument. As Stocking has pointed out, for Darwin and those who came after, what we now call human racial and cultural diversity was not a central concern (see Stocking, 1987: 44, 313–314). This is not to say that Victorian evolutionism did not imply a process of othering. Instead, even for scholars as apparently concerned with human global diversity as E.B. Tylor and James Frazer, primitive-phobia was mainly directed at a threat from within rather than outside their own society.

In a lecture delivered at the University of Liverpool in May 1908, on the occasion of his taking up (if for a very short time) a new Chair in Social Anthropology, James Frazer made it very clear what he thought posed the main threat to civilised society. He began with an unexceptional recapitulation of the main assumptions of evolutionary anthropology, by pointing out that social anthropology by definition 'assumes that civilisation has always and everywhere evolved out of savagery . . .' (1908: 6), making the specialised study of 'savages' a particularly fruitful activity to which to dedicate a discipline since,

> by comparison with civilised man the savage represents an arrested or rather retarded stage of social development, and an examination of his customs and beliefs accordingly supplies the same sort of evidence of the evolution of the human mind that an examination of the embryo supplies of the evolution of the human body. (1908: 7)

Equally important to Frazer, as evidenced by the weight of 'ethnographic' evidence in his books, is the study of folklore, since folklore is the study of superstition 'which means literally survivals . . . the *survivals* of more primitive ideas and practices among peoples who in other respects have risen to a higher plane of culture' (p. 11). Why, he asks, do these practices survive' The answer, he says,

> is to be found in the natural, universal, and ineradicable inequality of man. Not only are different races differently endowed in respect of intelligence, courage, industry, and so forth, but within the same nation men of the same generation differ enormously in inborn capacity and worth. No abstract doctrine is more false and mischievous than that of the natural equality of man . . . (pp. 11–12)

It now begins to become clear where, for Frazer, the important boundary between savagery and civilisation should be drawn:

> On the whole the men of keenest and strongest character lead the rest . . . The dull-witted majority in the end follows a keener-witted majority . . . The true rulers of men are [not statesmen or legislators but] the thinkers who advance knowledge. (pp. 11–13)

Superstitions therefore survive because 'the better ideas, which are constantly forming in the upper stratum, have not yet filtered through from the highest to the lowest minds' (p. 14). These minds are

> as different as if the two belonged to two different species . . . [these others may be moulded by their betters] into an appearance of civilisation, [but they] remain barbarians or savages at best. (p. 14)

As the Brothers Grimm have revealed, Frazer continued, 'a mass, if not the majority, of people in every civilised country is still living in a state of intellectual savagery . . . We appear to be standing on a volcano which may at any moment break out in smoke and fire to spread ruin and devastation . . .' (p. 15).

Some have seen in Victorian social theory a smug apology for the superiority of Victorian Britain, taking it to be the pinnacle of civilisation and, as such, an exemplary path of progress for all other peoples of the world to follow. Casting his eye over the landscape of late Victorian Britain, James Frazer on the contrary saw evidence only of chaos and confusion. Perhaps inadvertently Frazer speaks of impending 'ruin and devastation', showing an ominous prescience regarding the events which were to overtake a civilised Europe within just six years from the date of his Liverpool inaugural. The evidence was there for all to see – drunkenness, vice and poverty, as well as the growth of 'superstitious' beliefs as in spiritualism, astrology and theosophy discussed above. This was taking place not in the farthest reaches of the British Empire, but on the contrary in the heartland of civilisation, giving the lie to Victorian optimism about Britain's superior place in the world of nations.

But what is important to note is that far from calling into question Frazer's supreme faith in rationalism and the civilising process, this evidence of Britain's dark side is read in a particular way, a way that merely confirms Frazer's 'progressive' vision. As for Tylor before him, Frazer saw in all this proof of 'survivals', the survivals of primitivity into a civilised age. Perhaps more for Frazer than for his evolutionist predecessors, modern civilisation is taken to be a thin veneer which hides a nation teaming with primitive superstition. Most particularly, the survival is strongest among the lower orders who themselves seem to have survived almost untouched from a time before culture and civilisation were brought to them by their betters. And given the nexus between the primitive and nature that we have traced above, we can see clearly why it is that for Frazer, as for many of his contemporaries, vice was seen to be a primitive indulgence of natural desires and physical wants – this, after all, is what characterises the behaviour of uncultured savages.[18]

Reading the published version of Frazer's Liverpool speech, one is left in no doubt where he perceived the threat to civilisation lay. It lay in the working class, more particularly in that large segment of the British urban population which had not (yet) cast off its superstitions, its quest for the satisfaction of base desires. The 'unrespectable' poor made up the base of that 'volcano' on which 'we' (Frazer's academic audience) were standing.

In this Frazer's views were not all that unusual for his time, although he may more than most have forced them into an anthropological discourse of primitivism, and although Frazer may have been far less optimistic about the prospects of further progress than more radical turn of the century British liberals. Spurred on by a similar view of the un-respectable British working classes[19] similar to that articulated by Frazer, more reform- and radical-minded liberals were already dedicating themselves to the civilisation of the primitive within British society, in contrast to Frazer, who appears to have seen the situation as an inevitable one.

This is not the place to trace out the well-documented history of efforts on the part of, first, reform and radical liberalism and, then, the growing labour movement to eradicate primitivism from the British national landscape by civilising the working classes. Others are in any case far more qualified than this writer to do so.[20] Nor is this the place to look in any detail at the diversity of solutions proposed – from active non-intervention, to private charity, to mobilising the resources of the state. Instead, two points about the rise of British welfarism from the turn of the century might suffice to link these developments to the issue at hand. First, while there were many differences – moral, practical and political – among advocates of welfare reform, most reformers from 'left' to 'right' clung to the primitivist vision of the British worker.[21] Secondly, and not surprisingly given that they were operating a primitivist discourse in which naturalising and culturalising trends were closely intertwined, in which, in other words, the belief was that biological and social progress were inextricably linked, most reformers directed their efforts at both the physical as well as the cultural make up of the British population. Welfare and eugenics almost inevitably went hand-in-hand in the quest for a means of civilising the British worker.

All this allows us more clearly to see the radical nature of Hargrave's new version of primitivism. But let us be clear. Hargrave's primitive-mania was no 'subaltern' discourse rising up to resist the hegemonising primitive-phobia of people like Frazer. Although anti-imperialist, Hargrave could in no way be taken to be a spokesman for Britain's colonised peoples. Although entirely critical of Frazerian attribution of the problems of Britain to the primitiveness of the working classes, Hargrave's was no unmediated working class voice of resistance. Hargrave as I have already suggested is best seen himself as one of many new-generation 'organic' intellectuals, seeking a following to challenge the intelligentsia entrenched at the turn of the century. In Hargrave's case the generation he sought to challenge was that of Baden-Powell and the public school-educated, militarist, imperialist leadership of the scouting movement.[22] As such, he constructed himself, and was constructed by others, as a leader of a new generation seeking new solutions to the problems of civilisation.

This new diagnosis of the problems of the age we have already sketched out. Rather than the survival of the primitive being the problem, the problem for Hargrave was civilisation itself. Vice, warfare, imperialism, misery and deprivation were all, for Hargrave and those like him, not caused by an atavistic eruption of natural man into the world of civilisation, but precisely the opposite. They were a consequence not of naturalness, but of artificiality, and the only solution was a return to the nature from which we all originally came. Hargrave's obviously was no lone voice as we have already noted. Nor was the 'woodcraft' solution the only one around. Indeed, Hargrave's own vision for scouting is best considered in the context of a more general movement that saw in things like urban reform, garden cities, fresh air, physical fitness, naturism, sea water bathing, sending urban children into the country, Esperanto, eastern religion, public access to the countryside, as well as nature preservation, environmentalism, population control and so on solutions to the ills of contemporary civilisation.

And it is equally significant in this regard, that after Kibbo Kift, it is the Social Credit movement organized through the Green Shirts for which Hargrave is best remembered. This movement indeed reached out to the British workers, and addressed their economic problems, but only as a first step for rescuing them from the unnaturalness of modern life.

This, finally, allows us to look at the potential for very specific exclusions effected not so much by primitivism in general as an abstract philosophical system, but by the particular culturally and politically inflected primitive-mania spoken by John Hargrave and his contemporaries. Without suggesting that these exclusions were practised either by Hargrave himself, or the organisations he was directly associated with – Kibbo Kift and, later, the Green Shirts – one might point to two kinds of exclusion that modern primitivism has effected, at least in certain times and specific places. First, although Hargrave himself was not directly concerned with contacts with actual 'primitive' peoples,[23] primitivism particularly in colonial situations has often been associated with the colonial exclusions not so much of people classified as authentically 'primitive', but of peoples who have somehow been categorised as 'inauthentic' or 'corrupted' primitives. Thus, in white dealings with Native Americans in the history of the United States, primitivism has been found alongside the denial of rights to people adjudged to be impure Indians. My own survey, for example, of turn of the century American popular literature, the so-called 'dime novels', shows very few negative stereotypes of Indians, but a consistent demonisation of what were commonly called 'breeds' or 'half-breeds' – that is, Native Americans classified as not conforming to the primitivist stereotype. Similarly, writing of the situation in Australia, the historian and anthropologist Patrick Wolfe has argued convincingly that a form of primitive-mania which elevated the 'pure-blood' Aborigine to a position of admiration, severely discriminated against, and continues to discriminate against so-called 'non-traditional' Aborigines – those who for one reason or another appear to have abandoned the 'traditional' life (see Wolfe, 1991).

Yet the main thrust of primitivism is in fact not to demonise the primitive at all, but on the contrary to use the primitive as a weapon in the fight against civilisation. It follows, therefore, that primitivism of the Hargrave-variety may, at least under certain circumstances, be turned not just against civilisation itself, but against individuals and groups who are taken to be 'over-civilised' in one way or another. It is primitive-mania, rather than primitive-phobia, that makes most sense, for example, of the demonisation of Jews in Europe, particularly in the twentieth century. Quite unlike colonial images of blacks, anti-semitic discourse in twentieth century Europe has depicted Jews as 'too modern', too committed to the principles of instrumentality and civilisation in general in contrast with 'real' Germans, Frenchmen, Englishmen etc., who, on the contrary, are said to be concerned with historical (primitive) attachments to family, community, blood and soil. This is not to suggest that Hargrave or his contemporaries were necessarily anti-semitic in spite of their anti-civilisationalism.

Hargrave himself, particularly after founding the Green Shirts, clearly subscribed to a more generalised attack on banking and financial institutions, but does not appear to have associated them with Jews, or any other religious or cultural group.

But in the hands of others in the 1930s there is little question that primitivism and its corresponding naturalising critique of civilisation were closely bound up in the renewed wave of anti-semitism and fascism sweeping Europe at that time.

In this there are strong parallels between primitive-mania in interwar Europe, and various Southeast Asian nationalisms in which this time it is the overseas Chinese who are depicted as overly instrumental and modern, so much so that they are seen to pose a threat to the economic survival of 'indigenous' groups – the *primbumi* in Indonesia, the *bumiputera* in Malaysia etc. I shall return to the parallels and differences between Southeast Asian and British modernism in Chapter 4.

Primitivist discourse, by projecting modernity's cultural diversity onto a temporal axis that begins with a (naturalised) primitive and ends with a (culturalised) bearer of universal civilisation represents in a significant sense the nineteenth century culmination of Enlightenment universalism. And like the latter, it aspired to include the whole of humankind within a single framework. At the same time it made possible an exclusion of particular human individuals and groups on the grounds that, while contemporary they were paradoxically adjudged *not yet* modern. The impression to which a generation of critics of modernity has given rise, namely that universalism and primitivism are to be largely understood in the context of the growth, consolidation and decline of the British Empire, that primitivism was mobilised as a defense of empire, and indeed even provided the compelling reason for colonial expansion is too simplistic. The contextual history of primitivism is in fact far more complex. It could be, and was mobilised by both advocates and critics of empire. Indeed at certain times it was not primarily to do with empire at all, but about the internal divisions inside Britain itself, most notably between the working classes and everyone else, or between the respectable and unrespectable members of British society.

While it cannot be reduced to a particular political perspective or historical context, however, primitivism did tend to generate and set limits on a particular set of debates and conflicts between what I have termed, following Trautmann, primitive-phobes and those manifesting instead a primitive-mania, each with its own capacity for a politics that was simultaneously inclusive and exclusive.

Of course primitivism was not the only conceptual schema for reading the relationship between modernity and its others in turn of the century Britain. But it did seem to be a very important one, setting down a mode of debating and dealing with otherness in Britain that in some sense continues to this day as we shall see. But I want now to turn to another set of debates and conflicts over modern self-identity and otherness that has had quite different effects, and, given that these debates were more pronounced in the United States than Britain, my next example will be an American one.

Notes

1 The material on John Hargrave is taken from Drakeford's (1997) analysis of the Green Shirts movement that he founded, various electronic publications put out by the Woodcraft Folk (an organisation that has its origins in the Kibbo Kift Kindred), and Hargrave's own published books and articles, many of which appeared in scouting magazines. Hargrave was an influential writer in the Baden-Powell scouting magazine *The Trail*, and then, after the establishment of the Kibbo Kift Kindred, its magazine *The Nomad*. The Kibbo Kift archive is currently stored at the London School of Economics.

2 The term is derived from an archaic Kentish dialect phrase meaning 'a proof of great strength'.

3 See Clodd, 1895.

4 In the 1920s and to the mid-1930s, when most of Hargrave's work appeared, the kinds of primitivist narratives which characterised his writings were falling out of favour in the United States, especially among professional anthropologists, as a consequence of the Boasian revolution. In British anthropology, however, the break with social evolutionism was never so sharp.

5 I use the term performance here to draw attention to two things: first, the fact that cultural meanings are not just for contemplation as it were, but that they underlie concrete social practices; secondly, that such meanings are manifest not just in highly ritualised occasions, but in more mundane spheres of everyday life (see, for example, Herzfeld, 1985).

6 One might cite the particular example of the single incidence of mass hysteria among female factory workers in Malaysia leading to what amounted almost to an industry of studies of 'resistance' on their part to global capitalism and/or patriarchy. I have discussed this tendency to place modern critiques of capitalist instrumentalism into the mouths of third world peasants elsewhere (Kahn, 1995). A similar argument about the anthropological obsession with resistance has been made recently by John Morton in an, as yet, unpublished paper delivered at a conference at La Trobe University in August 1999, entitled 'Anthropology and Cultural Studies: Whose Cult?'.

7 For a sympathetic treatment of Foucault that none the less draws out the difficulties in his tendency to read everything as a manifestation of 'power', see Kögler, 1996. For a critique particularly of subalternist intellectuals for their essentialising reading of cultures of resistance, see Sivaramakrishnan, 1995.

8 Indeed the link between the orientalism and imperialism has itself been called into question, at least in the Indian context. Assayag, for example, like Trautmann, has drawn attention to the diversity of views conflated under the term 'orientalism' in the Indian context, drawing attention in particular to two distinct types: the 'real orientalists' such as Max Muller and the 'civilisers' such as the Mills. The former may have defended empire but were most definitely not 'cultural imperialists', the latter definitely were. Moreover certain 'real orientalists' such as Annie Bessant were implacably anti-empire, theosophy's first principle being non-discrimination. Bessant and the theosophists were prime movers in the formation of the Congress Party and in the independence movement before Gandhi (see Assayag, Lardinois and Vidal, 1997).

9 Kuper would clearly take issue with this statement both because he wants to argue that in the United States the very clear break with social evolutionism marked by the work and influence of Franz Boas was overturned in the post-Second World War period by the re-assertion of evolutionary perspectives in the work of Murdoch, Steward and White; and because he sees in the contribution of that other 'founding father' of British anthropology, Malinowski, a far more original twentieth century project. I do not wish to overemphasise the differences between the two national traditions here. It remains, however, that among the most

prominent of later twentieth century American anthropologists are figures like Clifford Geertz, Marshall Sahlins and their students whose project is far closer to that of Boas than of the evolutionists singled out by Kuper. Malinowski's work, on the other hand, for all its originality, and while it may be seen as marking a more radical break with the progressivism of Tylor and Frazer, also manifests certain assumptions of what I have termed twentieth century primitive-mania.

10 In speaking of the primitivism of the Malinowskian influences on British anthropology, one might note that perhaps the best-known contemporary example of anthropological celebration of the primitive condition was, in fact, American and not British. I am referring to the work of Margaret Mead, whose first book in particular, Coming of Age in Samoa, should be read in my view as a primitivist text. Perhaps surprisingly given that Mead was a student of Boas, it remains that Coming of Age in Samoa is not a classic culturalist text at all. Of course it makes the case for the mutability of human cultural life, but culture here is being used in the Tylorian sense of the universal human capacity for culture. The distinct impression one gets from Mead's analysis of Samoan adolescence is that it is in some sense more 'natural' than adolescence in the United States – Samoa thus being more primitive than America (and this is what makes Samoan customs more desirable in Mead's eyes).

11 From a potentially very long list of references, see, for example, Fabian, 1983; JanMohammed, 1985; McGrane, 1989; Mehta, 1997; Said, 1978.

12 The obvious difference between scholarly versions of primitivism in the latter part of the nineteenth century, and earlier Enlightenment accounts of the same peoples, is captured by the different meanings of the terms 'savage' and 'primitive'. As some have observed, primitivism strictu sensu emerged as much in reaction to, as in continuation of, the Enlightenment classification of non-western peoples as savage by dint of their ignorance of, rather than their historical priority to, western 'civilization' (cf. McGrane, 1989). In the case of the former, human diversity was understood mainly as divergence from the standard set by civilisation. Because of their belief in a universal human nature, Enlightenment philosophers saw in savages and barbarians peoples ignorant of the 'progress' of the West, a state that they could therefore only explain in terms of chance or contingency. The primitive, however, was different for a reason, a reason moreover that was itself capable of scientific reflection. And as we know, nineteenth century social philosophers, from Comte to Marx, Hegel to Spencer in different ways offered explanations based on the new notions about the laws of society and history (Jacques, 1997). Primitives were thought to be different not merely because they lacked knowledge of the ways of civilisation, but because of their social and historical circumstances. Curiously, then, and contrary to most assumptions about the post-Enlightenment critiques of eighteenth century social philosophy, it was the theorists of the nineteenth century who were the more relativist, who gave more credence to the profundity of the differences between cultures and societies. Of course, with the hindsight provided by twentieth century relativism, we may find that of the nineteenth century still deeply 'ethnocentric' and superior. But we should not forget that the main 'advances' made by twentieth century social theory in some basic sense only take the nineteenth century relativisation of difference one step further. It is therefore curious to find towards the end of the twentieth century an increase in the number of nostalgists for the universalism of the Enlightenment.

13 That such continuities with, particularly, utilitarianism are to be found in British social evolutionary thought is a central contention in Burrow's work (1966). Stocking (1987) has criticised Burrow's contentions, arguing that he failed to take into account what happened in the intermediate half century. This does not in my view, however, negate the fact of the political similarities between utilitarianism and, particularly, Spencerian liberalism to which Burrow first drew attention.

14 Thomas Jefferson is considered to have been unusually 'liberal' in his attitudes towards slavery and people of African descent – and yet he shared in a general view of the time that blacks had no future in American society, saying that he suspected that 'the blacks, whether originally a distinct race, or made distinct by time and circumstances, are inferior to the whites in endowments both of body and mind. It is not against experience to suppose, that the

different species of the same genus, or the varieties of the same species, may possess different qualifications' (from *Notes on the State of Virginia*, quoted in Horsman, 1981: 101).

15 For useful discussion of the issues involved in the construction of a singular human 'species being', together with a consideration of the cultural underpinnings involved in the rejection of notions of human sub-species (i.e. races), see Hirschfeld, 1998 and Hull, 1998.

16 For another version of this argument about the culturalisation of nature evident in racial discourse, see Wade, 1993.

17 Assumptions typically associated with the evolutionism of Lamarck, but present (though underemphasised) also in Darwin's work (see Hawkins, 1997).

18 Once again it is worth drawing attention to the ways in which Malinowski's theory that culture can almost universally be explained as a response to universal psychological and physiological needs – a clear undermining of the view of primitive-phobes like Frazer who maintain that while true of savages, civilized humans have gone beyond that. Malinowski's understanding of culture was the precise inverse of Frazer's.

19 Victorian notions of 'respectability', about which a great deal has been written, were intimately connected with primitivising discourse, like much late nineteenth century primitive-phobia deriving also from anglicist cultural assumptions. To quote a recent observer, 'to be respectable in Victorian times was to come up to that most real, though very indefinite standard of goodness, the attainment of which is exacted of everyone as a condition of being allowed to associate upon terms of ostensible equality with the rest of the human race' (Bailey, 1998: 32). Respectability thus entailed moral rectitude, economic continence and self-sufficiency, in short a distillation of evangelical disciplines, 'a secular version of election – minus the uncertainties – and in so far as it demanded appropriate faith and conduct, it both incorporated an ideology and defined a life-style' (1998: 33).

20 For an extremely thorough documentation of the decline of the Liberals and the rise of Labour as the main political opposition to the Tories from the turn of the century, which among other things also presents a detailed account of changing approaches and policies with regard to the poor, see Tanner, 1990.

21 A good example here are the views of the early Fabians – notably Sidney and Beatrice Webb and George Bernard Shaw – who tended always to portray the British worker, and more spontaneous outbreaks of workerist/collectivist political sentiment, as 'primitive' (see Barrow and Bullock, 1996).

22 The link between Baden-Powell's scouts and empire was, of course, an intimate one (cf. Warren, 1987).

23 Here there is an interesting contrast between Hargrave's 'Red Indianism' and that of the American Ernest Thompson Seton, whose work on scoutcraft inspired Hargrave's own. Hargrave seems in no way to have been particularly concerned either with real Native Americans or their fate. Seton, perhaps, could less easily ignore their plight, and indeed wrote at the beginning of his *Book of Woodcraft and Indian Lore*:

> As a model for outdoor life in this country I took the Indian, and have thus been obliged to defend him against the calumnies of those who coveted his possessions. (1912: v)

> I am not without hope that this may lead to a measure of long-delayed justice being accorded him. He asks only the same rights as are allowed without question to all other men in America – the protection of the courts, the right to select his own religion, dress, amusements, and the equal right to the pursuit of happiness so long as his methods do not conflict with the greater law of the land. (1912: vi–vii)

3

AMERICAN MODERN: ALIENS, DESPOTS AND THE REPUBLIC

American Transformations: 1880–1924

In a speech given in 1924 to mark the founding of Clark University some 45 years earlier, the American historian Frederick Jackson Turner, well known for the thesis that America was best characterised as a frontier society rather than merely an offshoot of northwestern European civilisation, spoke of the momentous changes that had taken place in the country within the lifetimes of the university's first graduates. America, he pointed out to his audience, was no longer a land of unsettled open spaces – 'practically all of the West unoccupied in 1890' was now occupied, the population of the country had almost doubled, urban population now exceeded the rural, and industry now dominated agriculture. Of the approximately 110 million inhabitants of the territorial United States, a large and growing proportion were foreign born, or of foreign born parents. And these people now came overwhelmingly from southern and eastern Europe 'instead of from northern and western, the source of the old immigration'.

These changes in the distribution, size and composition of the population were accompanied by equally momentous changes arising from technological innovation – the invention and widespread use of the telephone, automobile, overhead trolley and airplane. Human communications were also being revolutionised by the invention of the Kodak, now a common 'household instrument'; the moving picture which has 'deeply influenced the psychology of youth, for evil as well as for good'; and, most importantly, the radio. 'Truly,' observed Turner, 'the planet is shrinking.' Other inventions were also transforming everyday life, human health, industry and our understanding of the universe – electricity, industrial chemicals, the telescope, the advanced microscope, the spectroscope, and astrophotography; significant advances in medicine and engineering.

Among the results of all these changes was a huge increase in the global economic importance of the United States, making it by a long shot the world's biggest producer of iron and steel; a leading producer of petroleum and gold; and the biggest producer of agricultural commodities like corn, wheat, swine, cattle and cotton. As a consequence America was now the wealthiest country in the world, although that wealth was highly concentrated, and had probably become its leading military power. America was pioneering new forms of economic organization, not always to its advantage – huge trusts and corporations in what had become an 'era of high finance', and labour unions (Turner, [1924] 1959: 207–225).

While triumphaiist about American progress in the years since the Census department officially pronounced the closing of his beloved frontier, Turner worried about the consequences of at least some of these momentous changes. Turner shared with his 'progressive' colleagues, and indeed a significant proportion of middle class America, a vision of an American civilisation that was unique not, in his terms, merely a 'teutonism from the woods'. At the same time again, like many especially 'old stock' Americans, he felt profoundly ambivalent about the decline of rural life and values, the dominance of trusts and corporations, the militancy of some trade union organisers, the lack of progress of southern African Americans in the decades after emancipation, the state of America's cities, the corruption of urban politics and the capacity of America to successfully absorb so many migrants from southern and eastern Europe (see Gordon, 1964).

Turner, like most American intellectuals in this period, was engaged in a quest for a new American imaginary, one that would be able to accommodate the challenges to older visions of what it was to be American posed by the changes he outlined in his speech at Clark University. As it transpired, his own visions, first of a frontier civilisation and then of a country characterised by sectionalism, were not to have as great an impact as Turner had hoped. Given the commitment to the idea of progress, the end of the frontier meant that Turner's notion of a frontier civilisation was stillborn, while the growing preponderance of the urban population eroded ideas about America being defined by the values of the village and small town. Gradually American intellectuals abandoned, or substantially revised, their commitment to agrarianism and small townism, first ambivalent to the agrarian populism of the 1870s, then increasingly antagonistic to the political domination of especially northeastern cities by the small town vote of conservative upstate republicans. Even before the period covered by Turner's Clark address, the resolution of the Civil War in favour of the Union had laid to rest any idea of separate Americas and separable Americans – North and South, freemen and slaves – although some abandoned such visions reluctantly. The completion of the railway brought together East and West both physically and in the public imagination. And while many like Turner had great difficulties in coming to terms with the new migrants from southern and eastern Europe, those who tried were ultimately forced to rethink the vision, shared by probably a majority of nineteenth century 'native stock' citizens, of America as essentially an Anglo-Saxon, even a Protestant, civilisation. What could/should a modern America be like?

It is this story that I want to tell briefly here – the story of the transformations in American thought and culture that took place in the context of the processes of economic, political and cultural modernisation outlined in Turner's Clark address. The story has, of course, been told on numerous occasions before, being the subject of a good deal of soul searching even in recent years. But in telling it I have a particular aim – neither to defend conceptions of a culturally neutral American way, nor to reject them out of hand as merely another expression of particularistic nationalism masquerading as cosmopolitanism. My aim is more limited, and that is to show that, against both many of its advocates as well as its critics, American universalism is not and should not be seen as an abstract set of philosophical principles given for all time that provide America – and more recently the world – with permanent answers to questions of liberty, order and social justice. Instead it is a discourse that is very much contextualised, or, in other words it owes to its particular context most of its basic goals and understandings. Americanism, as I shall try to show, has changed almost beyond recognition in the crucible of American 'modernisation', that is in the period from roughly 1870 through the 1920s. From its most purely Enlightenment form in the thinking of someone like Thomas Jefferson, to their Protestant versions in the nineteenth century, modern American goals for the good life and for the best way of achieving it, basic assumptions about what it is that is universal in the human condition, the location of the boundary between public and private life, the vision of the nature of good government and the role that government should play in the lives of citizens – in these and other fundamental ways modern Americanism has shifted ground. And, particularly interestingly from the perspective of our theme, the shift in the period most commonly associated with cultural modernism in the West was produced at least in part by an encounter, or 'dialogue', between one, significantly more powerful, cultural group (mainly, as the saying goes, 'white, Anglo-Saxon, protestants') and others (most significantly, and in different ways, African Americans, Irish Americans, and 'new' immigrants from southern and eastern Europe and Asia). Finally, this 'dialogue' took place in and through particular social and political processes. In other words, the shift I am describing can best be understood as the product, not of a simple contest of ideas, not the consequence of a series of pure disembodied 'speech acts' or conversations, but as the outcome of some fairly intense political conflicts over the right to govern American cities, the extent to which governance should be impersonal and rational or personal and democratic, who has the power to 'speak for' the urban poor, and who should hold the balance of political and economic power among cities, states and the federal government in Washington. In other words, American political modernism, like other discourses with universalising pretensions, needs to be judged in its rather particular historical context. Whether, as its critics argue, it is exclusionary in effect, or whether instead, as its defenders maintain, it provides an important counter to the actions of despots and cultural essentialists bent on violating basic human rights, cannot be settled at the level of theory alone.

But this is, of course, to beg the question of the precise meaning of Americanism in the modern age. The privilege of speaking an exemplary modernism is, as we have already had occasion to note, most often granted to the aesthetic, literary and intellectual *avant garde* formed towards the end of the nineteenth century. But with notable exceptions, American 'high' art and literature in the late nineteenth century were oriented towards Europe. It is often argued as a consequence that late nineteenth century American intellectual culture was similar to that of Britain, a similarity at least implied by the frequent use of terms like Victorian, social Darwinist, progressive and liberal to describe both turn of the century Americanism in general, and the nature of its exclusions in particular. The ideas of prominent intellectuals like the 'social Darwinists' Charles Loring Brace and William Graham Sumner or the modernist theologian Henry Beecher, the 'social evolutionist' William Henry Morgan or the 'scientific racists' Agassiz, Morton and Brinton, are often taken to be typical of a late nineteenth century Americanism that differed but little from that of contemporary Britain.

But to see American modernism, whether aesthetic, philosophical or political, as the offshoot of British or European trends is misleading. Even the term 'liberal' as a description of American political thought towards the end of the nineteenth century is problematic. As one student of American liberalism comments:

> The word 'liberal' has taken on any number of meanings. This variability of hues reflects the ideological looseness of American politics . . . [in its] very broadest [sense it] suggests that virtually every American is a liberal. (Broesamle, 1990: xv)

Broesamle's resolution, to use liberal in a narrower sense to refer to 'the mainstream of American reform in this century, which has directed itself most fundamentally toward the welfare state . . .' (p. xv) is, perhaps, the most common if only because it reflects clearly contemporary American understandings of the term. But this is far from liberalism in its classical sense, and equally far from being an adequate description of mainstream currents in American political culture at the end of the nineteenth century.

Another term commonly used to describe American political and intellectual sensibilities from the late nineteenth century is 'progressive'. But John Buenker expressed what has become a fairly cormmon frustration with attempts to delineate the boundaries of progressivism in the American context:

> The Progressive Era was a period of time beginning in the 'ate nineteenth century and running roughly up until U.S. entry into World War 1. It was characterized by so many efforts to cope with the nation's political, social, and economic problems, and to promote 'progress,' that contemporaries and scholars alike have generally dubbed it 'progressive.' Fifty years of intensive investigation have failed to establish any consensus on the precise meaning of that elusive word. Even the participants disagreed vociferously about the 'progressiveness' of specific pieces of legislation, such as Prohibition, immigration restriction, or the disenfranchisement and segregation of southern blacks; nor has anyone agreed on what set of attitudes or positions made a particular individual a 'progressive,' since the term has been applied to many men [sic] holding opposite views on important issues. Even the cumulative effect of the period's reformist efforts have been called into question, with several scholars suggesting that the term 'progressive' is really a misnomer. (Buenker, 1973: vii)

As this suggests, the third key term applied to modernising political ideas from the late nineteenth century is 'reform' – a term which conveys quite well the developing view that the American system was neither perfect nor was it likely if left to its own devices to ensure the greatest good for the greatest number, contrary to the assumptions of social Darwinist liberalism. At the same time it was assumed capable of further progress by the intervention of principled individuals with special expertise. But doubtless this term, at least on its own, is as problematic as the other two, too vague and capable of multiple interpretation.

Yet even if we were to identify an American modernist intelligentsia or aesthetic *avant garde* equivalent to those of contemporary Europe, we would also miss what is a key feature of modern American culture more broadly, and that is precisely its tendency to reject the idea of a unitary high culture altogether. It is for this reason that the whole notion of an exemplary modernism is perhaps less appropriate in the American context than in any other, and the imperative to examine what I have been calling popular modernisms most compelling. A key feature of American modernism is, in other words, precisely an implied critique, if not an outright rejection, of European notions of modernity, including or even especially the way they rest on a distinction between 'high' and 'low' culture and hence of a single standard against which all cultural expression can be measured and thus a critique of a privileged position for the intellectual and aesthetic *avant garde*. We have had occasion to note the ways in which European modernism has interpreted this aspect of American culture, as evidence of a lack of high philosophical and moral principles. Yet it can also be argued that this American sensibility is itself modernist, since it derives as I shall try to show from a particular interrogation of 'civilization' that America shares with some other 'late modernisers'. An American version of modernism is therefore nowhere more manifest than in American popular culture as it developed from the last part of the nineteenth century.

To explore American popular modernism from the last years of the nineteenth century, I will begin with an example drawn from popular music. I do not do this because I claim any particular musical knowledge or expertise, but because musical influences and ideas about musical taste seem especially salient markers of identity in America both in the nineteenth century and throughout much of the twentieth, and because music provides an excellent arena for exploring the relationship between popular and exemplary modernisms.

The Phenomenon of John Philip Sousa

That said, nothing seems better to capture the mood of what were thought to be American values at least for a substantial segment of the middle classes in the late nineteenth century than the music, or better the whole phenomenon, of John Philip Sousa. A 'reading' of the Sousa phenomenon provides a valuable entrée into what it meant to be an American – and its corollary, what made certain people 'un-American' – at the turn of the century, perhaps more valuable than do readings of the 'scientific' works of Sousa's contemporaries such as the 'social Darwinists' Charles Loring Brace and William Graham Sumner, or racial theorists like Morton, Agassiz and Brinton or even of the music of notionally 'better', if far less popular modern composers such as Charles Ives.[1]

What has been called the Sousa phenomenon was identified, by Sousa himself and by his large audience, with the best of 'American values'. His band played to sell-out audiences all over the United States, and on extended overseas tours. There are not many Americans who do not know his most famous composition, 'The Stars and Stripes Forever', sometimes dubbed America's unofficial national anthem. This march reached the height of its popularity during – and itself doubtless contributed greatly to – the public jingoism that surrounded the outbreak of the Spanish-American War. It still finds its way into the repertoires of countless high school and college bands, being played in parades, Fourth of July celebrations, and sporting events in which America is being celebrated.

Sousa was a central figure in the emergence of an America popular music industry before the age of broadcast and recorded music. With the help of his manager he became a canny manipulator of new technology and the latest techniques of business management to generate hitherto undreamed of levels of income from musical composition and performance. Recognising early on the advantages to be gained from composing and playing music that appealed to the broadest range of musical tastes, and of the marketing importance of personality, Sousa was probably America's first musical superstar. His biographer Paul Bierley cites the following contemporary account that conveys something of the popularity of John Philip Sousa at the end of the century:

> In the military camp, in the crowded streets of the city when the troops march to the front, in the ballroom, in the concert hall, at the seaside and in the mountains, go where you may, you hear Sousa, always Sousa . . . It is Sousa in the band, Sousa in the orchestra, Sousa in the phonograph, Sousa in the hand organ, Sousa in the music box, Sousa everywhere . . . As a conductor, Sousa is of the people and for the people . . . The influence of his concert work among the masses is incalculable and the Sousa band is ever the pioneer in the cause of good music.
> ('The Era of Sousa', *Musical Courier*, 4 July 1898, cited in Bierley, 1973: 7)

Sousa remains best known for the marches he composed – including 'The Stars and Stripes Forever', 'Semper Fidelis', 'El Capitan', 'The High School Cadets' and 'The Washington Post'. Less well known now are his numerous other musical compositions, including fifteen operettas, some of which, like *El Capitan*, from which the song cited below has been extracted, competed successfully with the Gilbert and Sullivan productions so popular in the period. In addition, he wrote numerous suites, songs, waltzes, fantasies and other musical pieces.[2]

The march itself had developed towards the end of the nineteenth century in the direction of formalism, that is, according to the idea of a prescribed rule in march composition. Sousa's time was characterised by the use of 'marches of European composers [Schubert, Mendelssohn, Wagner] as models for the composition of concert marches' (Norton, 1983: 46). The main influence on Sousa's musical composition was probably Wagner, while his most important performative influences were Gilbert and Sullivan, composers of the most popular formal musical performances at the time when Sousa's career began.

At the same time, from mid-century, partly under the influence of Germanic musical culture, and partly because of the growing unionisation of musicians, the band was increasingly characterised by musical professionalism which led to the decline of street bands and the rise of the concert band. Now the 'emphasis [was] on original composition, the celebration of the individual composer, and the importance granted harmony as opposed to melody' (Norton, 1983: 44). The avowed purpose of the new musicians' unions, which Sousa himself supported, was 'to improve the quality of band musicians [which] resulted in a policy of screening and examining members before granting them union membership'. At the same time, unionisation led to an increase in the wages paid to professional instrumentalists (1983: 45). These changes contributed to the decline of amateur and professional street bands. While we may now associate Sousa's music largely with marching bands, in fact his marches were particularly adapted to concert performance rather than the march past.

In the absence of recording and broadcasting industries, most Americans experienced Sousa as a performer, and as the composer of sheet music, his popularity increased by his growing fame as a composer just as today any self-respecting pop musician has to be seen to make a contribution as both composer and performer. A violinist with classical training, Sousa earned a living with theatre orchestras until his first significant appointment as conductor of the United States Marine Band in 1880. Gaining fame as a composer of marches, in 1892 he teamed up with the Chicago impresario David Blakely to form the Sousa Band which very quickly gained a national and then international reputation, playing to growing and enthusiastic audiences around the United States and, from its first European tour in 1900, throughout the world. During the 1890s Sousa also found time to compose and produce operettas as well, the most successful being the popular *El Capitan*, first performed in 1896.

A committed self-publicist, Sousa communicated not just through his compositions and the performances of his band, but through endless newspaper interviews, and his own writings which included three novels – *The Fifth String* (1902), *Pipetown Sandy* (1905) and *The Transit of Venus* (1919), as well as an autobiography (Sousa, 1928).

What is the relation between the Sousa phenomenon and late nineteenth century Americanism? Enough has been said already to indicate that his music was judged, by both composer and audience, to be strongly patriotic.

It is interesting in this regard that a march with a highly patriotic title, 'The Stars and Stripes Forever', was inserted at the end of Act II in performances of the operetta *El Capitan* from the outbreak of the Spanish-American War, and that this unofficial national anthem has been trotted out ever since on public occasions demanding expressions of patriotic fervour. Most Sousa concerts were occasions for the playing of 'The Star Spangled Banner', patriotic audiences generally called for encores of 'The Stars and Stripes', the band wore military-type uniforms, and Sousa himself was a great one for mouthing patriotic platitudes, often to the dismay even of cultural conservatives (cf. Harris, 1983). A contemporary critic went so far as to describe Sousa as the 'Rudyard Kipling' of music (cited in Norton, 1983: 49). Noting the influence of Wagner's music on Sousa's, Pauline Norton writes:

> The appeal and popularity of both Wagner's and Sousa's music are understandable within the context of the general excitement, energy, and intense nationalism which so characterized the last decade of the nineteenth century. The belief in evolutionary progress that developed in that century was thought to have culminated in the 1890s . . . the 1890s witnessed a period when 'women became more manly,' and 'men became more martial.' By then the Civil War had become an event of the past, and a cultivation of militarism had begun which would culminate in the Spanish-American War. (Norton, 1983: 48)

But to argue that Sousa's music was patriotic is not to suggest that it was nationalist. Certainly as far as music itself is concerned, Sousa was a universalist. Arguing that music is somehow culturally neutral, Sousa wrote in his autobiography:

> An attempt to locate a melody within geographical limits is bound to fail. Rhythmic qualities are imitated in all popular forms, but music, although it has many dialects, is, after all, a universal language . . . Nor can one nationalize a melody by the placing of its harmonic structure. Because you meet a blonde in Spain, is she a Swede . . .? From a melody one cannot deduce its birthplace. 'Yankee Doodle' is old English and not American at all . . . No, I do not believe there is any such thing as nationalism in music. (Sousa, 1928: 354–355)

Sousa is elsewhere not above attributing meaning to the free-floating supposedly universal signifier of a melody. Of his favourite musical form, the march, he wrote: 'I think Americans (and many other nationals for that matter) brighten to the tempo of a stirring march because it appeals to their fighting instincts . . . A march stimulates every center of vitality, weakens the imagination and spurs patriotic impulses which may have been dormant for years' (1928: 358). Of his technique for composing marches, he wrote:

> Often I fix my mind upon some objective – such as the broad spaces of the West, the languorous beauty of the South, the universal qualities of America as a whole. And then comes its musical expression – be it thunder or sunshine. (1928: 359)

An English critic was in no doubt about the American qualities of Sousa's music, objecting to the un-European practice of the Sousa Band of playing encores automatically – without waiting for audience request – a practice he described as evidence of American 'hustle'. Describing the marches, the same critic argued that he had already heard them in music halls, pantomimes, cafés and on street organs, but hearing them live led him to recognise their 'ear-splitting blatancy,' saying: 'The Americans are, they themselves state, a great people, and apparently they like great noises' (cited in Sousa, 1928: 336). But Sousa quotes this critic only because it confirms his own image of Europeans as overly concerned with musical refinement.

Another key respect in which the Sousa musical phenomenon broke with the elitism of European art music lies in the general accommodation with even celebration of free enterprise capitalism and a kind of market-based populism that was unusual for example in European music of the time (especially as it was experienced by the audiences for very successful tours of the United States by popular European artists). As Neil Harris observes:

> The Sousa career was a managed one, created to stimulate and satisfy consumer interest and oriented to market-place approval. Skilful publicists fashioned the Sousa image, appealing to the mass market created by modern journalism. Musical history contains many instances of masters writing on demand for fame or income. The impresario-performer, brought to prosperity by clever promotional techniques, was well established long before Sousa's birth. But rarely before had a composer–conductor so clearly identified himself with the cultural needs and public taste of his day. Seldom had an artist more easily made his peace with the commercial ethos surrounding him, or become so unambiguous a symbol of community ambition. And in America at least, never had anyone achieved this for so long a period of time, basically unshaken in prestige by otherwise comprehensive changes. (Harris, 1983: 11)

As others have also remarked, Sousa's break with the Marine Corps Band, which under his direction reached considerable heights of popular success, including, as Sousa often reminds us, the enthusiasm of American Presidents, is of great symbolic importance. The decision to go into the music *business*, free of government support, is certainly strongly indicative of an American attitude towards the world of commerce, and it is no surprise that Sousa himself frequently railed against government support of the arts (see Harris, 1983). In spite of the contemporary development of what was called an American nationalist movement, by which was understood a push to nationalise public utilities and other assets in the public interest, Sousa's general suspicion of state involvement in the world of both business and the arts was much more typical of late nineteenth century American cultural sensibilities. Sousa, and many of his contemporaries, saw no contradiction between universal musical values and those of the market – insulating the former from the latter would merely serve the narrow nationalistic agendas of cultural elites.

John Philip Sousa did not share all of the views articulated by influential progressive intellectuals of the time. Perhaps most significantly Sousa was an enthusiastic patriot during the Spanish-American war, while most liberals, and indeed even the arch conservative William Graham Sumner, opposed it, seeing in America's adoption of an imperialistic mentality in fact a throwback to an earlier barbaric ideology that America had already superseded.[3] Here Sousa's views were closer to those of Theodore

Roosevelt, himself an important figure for most turn of the century progressives, and probably the most vocal backer of the invasions of Cuba and
the Philippines. And many other contemporary assumptions about the
importance of economic freedom, and the moral imperatives of hard work,
were clearly also part of Sousa's own less intellectualised philosophy. This
locates Sousa firmly in a developing tradition that sees American ideas and
institutions as exemplars not just for America, but for the world.

Certainly in the titles he gave to many of his compositions, in the militaristic overtones of the marches, in the conscious attempt to reach out to
audiences who found contemporary art music too challenging, Sousa's
compositions contained an American element. But unlike later American
composers in the 1920s and 1930s – Gershwin, Aaron Copeland, Randall
Thompson, Roy Harris – who in different ways sought to inject an
American content into their compositions by incorporating African
American, ethnic, or folk rhythms and melodies directly into their works
(Harris, 1983: 35; cf. Kahn, 1985) – Sousa self-consciously resisted such
musical particularism, remaining committed to a vision of music as a
universal language.

Listening to Sousa, audiences were in an important sense buying a
package of music, performance and the personality and visions of Sousa
himself, at least as that was constructed for public consumption, in much the
same way as late twentieth century audiences for popular music are
consuming, in addition to a purely musical experience, a total image generated by music videos, countless interviews with and gossip about musical
personalities and their lifestyles, and so on. People, in short, knew what
Sousa 'stood for', and large numbers of them liked it. It is here, more than in
the pure music, that Sousa-ism was an American phenomenon. Sousa's
audiences, then, would have been familiar with his views, and imbibed them
along with the stirring and relatively accessible musical content of each
performance.

Sousa was very concerned to establish the American credentials of his
own band. American audiences in the nineteenth century were quite used to
listening to European compositions played by Europeans, a large proportion of professional musicians were at least of European – primarily
German and Italian – origin. This was also true of Sousa's own band at the
outset, while Sousa himself was the son of a Spanish migrant of Portuguese
descent, also a bandsman in Washington, DC. Yet in his autobiography
Sousa proudly tells his readers:

> There are now eighty-four in my band. It has become almost entirely American in
> personnel. Last year – 1927 – there was only one player who was born abroad
> and he is a naturalized American citizen. That is quite in contrast to the early
> days when nearly all of them were foreigners, and the dramatis personae
> reminded you of a concert in Berlin and Rome. (1928: 334f.)

But this commitment to Americanisation was not nationalist in the
common understanding of that term, as Sousa's views on the differences

between European and American musical taste clearly show. In many of his interviews he was determined to demonstrate the evolution of American musical taste, and its superiority to that of European audiences:

> Many an immortal tune has been born in the stable or the cotton-field. 'Turkey in the Straw' is a magic melody; anyone should be proud of having written it, but, for musical high-brows, I suppose the thing is déclassé. It came not from a European composer but from an unknown negro minstrel. (1928: 341)

American audiences, Sousa informed his public, were superior to European ones because of their instinctive cosmopolitanism. While the Germans only like German music, the French French:

> Our population is more cosmopolitan in character, our tastes less limited and we are more open to the delights of eclecticism in music. Europeans claim to be international in their tastes, but to my interested eye they were pathetically provincial, perhaps deliberately so, for they always magnified their own music. (1928: 361)

And American composers too are the equal of any in the world, or soon would be:

> The rest of the world has had a long start, but the American composer with his heritage of creative genius from a race which has produced thirteen out of twenty great inventions of the past three centuries . . . [will soon catch up]. (1928: 361)

Sousa's well-publicised views on American music are significant for the way they testify to a somewhat contradictory attitude towards 'civilisation'. On the one hand many American intellectuals at the turn of the century accepted notions about a universal civilising process, and also that in important respects at least some European countries were more civilised than the United States. The task, then, was to strive towards these universal values that were European only because Europe had achieved them first. Here appreciation of culture in the Tylorian sense is taken to be a sign of civilisational maturity. To the extent that Americans were able to appreciate European music and art they could, then, be judged cultivated. To the extent that America could equal or, in the future, even surpass Europe in the field of high culture, it could be adjudged civilised.

Evidence of a certain consistency in his adherence to this civilising narrative is also found in Sousa's attitude towards music at what he took to be the 'lower' end of the civilisational hierarchy. Consider, for example, Sousa's comments on what was the predominantly African American musical form that began to replace Sousa-type music in popularity in the early part of the twentieth century. Of jazz Sousa wrote in his autobiography: 'The greater part of it is very bad.' Strongly rhythmical, its harmonic structure is not new but very old (1928: 358). It will disappear since 'it does not truly represent America to the world; it does reflect a certain phase of the world's life (not America's alone) since it employs primitive rhythms which excite the basic human impulses. It will endure just as long as people hear it through their feet instead of their brains!' (1928: 358).

Sousa as we have already seen was not averse to incorporating black musical elements in his own compositions – his remarks on 'Turkey in the Straw' are borne out by his occasional, and very popular, use of ragtime elements in his own music. But for Sousa black music could not stand on its own, it needed to be refined through the higher processes of advanced musical composition, that is through the skills of Sousa himself. The primitivist exclusions of blacks would also have been encouraged by the developing notions of musical professionalism. Professional concert bands, like Sousa's, would not have recruited from the ranks of street and ragtime musicians, but from those who received classical and/or professional training. Although I am unable to find a breakdown by race of the membership of Sousa's band, in all the pictures I have seen there are no black faces. One might want to account for this by the operation of a colour bar which doubtless prevented Sousa from using black musicians even had he wanted to do so given the amazing proficiency of black ragtime and jazz performers. But liberal primitivism I would suggest does not require a formal colour bar to exclude those who have been characterised as racial others. Speaking from experience, as a classically trained brass player who longed to emulate the improvisational skills of African American jazz musicians, I can assert that these are very different skills, and that even great jazz musicians would in all likelihood have been considered insufficiently professional by late nineteenth century unions and band leaders.[4]

Further evidence of these attitudes can be found in contemporary African American musical performance and in the ways in which Sousa-ist musical and performative themes were incorporated into contemporary black musical theatre. A frequent part of black vaudeville shows was a Sousa-type band. But these bands performed a parody of the Sousa band – at the same time mocking the military precision of bearing and performance of the Sousa band as they tended to confirm the image of black performers as undisciplined and sloppy.

That Sousa saw African Americans through the lens of a Tylorian-primitivism is confirmed in his fictional writing. That blacks were in some sense primitive Americans was clearly implied in the novel *Pipetown Sandy* where Sousa describes the racial attitudes of the boy Gilbert, an intelligent child who is admired and befriended by the eponymous hero of the story. When asked by Delia, the family's black cook, if there were black angels, and if not why she should give money at collection time at the church if blacks couldn't go to heaven, Gilbert tells her that blacks have white souls like everyone else. The only difference, Gilbert tells her, is the black pigment in her skin.

> 'Is dat de trouble wid me?' she queried, her face shining with perspiration.
> 'I can't recall any other reason. But, Delia,' he continued ingenuously, 'just think what it would mean to us. If you hadn't any pigment in your skin, the chances are you wouldn't cook for us, and then what would we do?' (Sousa, n.d.: 44)

This combination of an underlying universalism (in Tylor's words, the 'psychic unity of mankind'), a commitment to progress, betterment, self-improvement with a tendency to naturalise human difference are all typical of classical primitivist thought as we have seen.

There is, however, another side to all this that casts doubt on the equation of American 'progressivism' and Victorian liberalism. Underlying Sousa's musical Americanism is also a cosmopolitan critique of Europe and hence an attempt to reject at least certain understandings of the civilisational process as being overly closed and particularistic. At the same time as Europe is seen as the site of the highest civilisational achievements, it is also seen in crucial respects as inferior to the United States – as narrowly nationalistic, effete, class ridden, parochial, decadent, pretentious, even corrupt. A light hearted version of such a critique of Europe is found in the song from *El Capitan* which portrays a society rife with drink, gambling and corruption:

> The proudest ancestry on earth,
> Our golden goblets here we drain
> Of rarest wine of royal Spain;
> And so we sit the live-long day,
> While joyous minutes pass away,
> With cards and wine,
> Our life's divine,
> And pleasure has full sway.
> Each deceiving, thieving, sleeving,
> Each deceiving,
> With Castilian grace
> There's not a game that gamblers use
> The innocents to rifle,
> With which we do not trifle,
> We're down to ev'ry dodge and ruse,
> Our consciences to stifle.
>   (John Philip Sousa, [1896] 1994: 115–129)

In musical terms, Sousa intended his work therefore to be heard not as identical with European music, but as both different from and (ambiguously) better than it. If Europe is the site of musical civilisation, its music is also seen as being overly sophisticated and intellectualised, feminised, remote from the taste of the masses, narrowly nationalistic, and reflecting widespread social and political corruption or decay. Sousa's music is more in touch with the popular, more democratic, cosmopolitan and robust. Sousa and others, for example, accused European conductors of being too concerned to educate their audiences, Sousa by contrast was more interested in entertaining them.

Hence a particular example of popular Americanism towards the end of the nineteenth century injects something rather different into existing debates over civilisation, evolution and primitivity. I do not want to give the impression that this difference was unique to America. Given the 'globalisation' of ideas at least in the Anglophone world of the time, it would be surprising to find an Americanism that was untouched by contemporary developments in Europe, and vice versa. None the less, if only because there is a tendency in the literature, particularly in the literature on the origins and contours of American racism, to see in the late nineteenth century evidence only of social Darwinism and/or so-called 'scientific' racism, it is important to draw attention to this rather different popular understanding of America's civilisational destiny. The Sousa phenomenon evokes a critique of European notions of civilisation precisely for not being universal enough, for in fact being an expression of the rather specific cultural values of a narrow segment of society.

Baseball and the Republic

As I have suggested, many see in late nineteenth century America the dominance of a particular national imaginary that can be understood as in some sense 'Victorian', by which is usually meant some combination of social Darwinism/primitivism, or classical liberalism more broadly. If, on the other hand, Sousa-ism represents an important current of American culture of the time, and if we compare it to contemporary British modernism, then this way of characterising late nineteenth century Americanism becomes problematic. In spite of the clear presence of some basic liberal/primitivist assumptions, late nineteenth century 'progressive' American cultural assumptions differ in significant ways. What I am suggesting is that these assumptions that I have drawn out in the case of Sousa-ism are best understood for the way they manifest a rather different set of ideas about the pattern of American modernity, ideas that are frequently termed republican. The argument that there was a strong republican current in the American popular consciousness in this period finds further support if we examine other areas of popular culture in the late nineteenth century. One such area is sport.

Sport itself was, and obviously continues to be, thought of as a significant part of what it is to be American. Sousa-ism already testifies to the centrality of masculinist imagery in the developing American sensibility towards the end of the nineteenth century, a sensibility which was shaped in important ways by the concept of 'muscular Christianity'. This is even more clearly manifest in American attitudes towards sport.

While a variety of sporting activities have obviously been pursued by Americans since colonial times, it was particularly from the last decades of the nineteenth century that the new middle class native stock Americans began to promote physical exercise and sport as significant aspects of American character-building. The YMCA, combining exercise and Christianity in American cities, played a key role in all this.

Of the huge variety of sports that Americans have participated in, and viewed, two in particular, baseball and grid-iron football, have come to be seen as encapsulating specifically American values more than any others.

And it is interesting that these two sports achieved a good deal of their modern form in the last two decades of the nineteenth century. It is in this period that American football took on many of the rules, strategies, organisational features and patterns of spectatorship that we recognise as integral parts of the game today. In spite of the immense growth of the professional game, what are thought of as football's truly American aspects were developed first in the college game. The origins of modern football were very closely tied to America's most prestigious universities – Harvard, Yale and the University of Chicago. The most successful team was Yale's, and modern football coaching, the dominance of the forward pass and blocking as key strategies, and the most important rule changes associated with these strategies were pioneered by well-paid coaches at Yale and other prestigious colleges. The association between football and college education was a strong one, since the supposed merits of football were those of the college-educated elites. The sports sociologist Steven Reiss has written of the late nineteenth century debate on the merits of football in the following terms:

> America appeared ripe for a virile game that would verify courage and strength of character and foster such qualities as cooperation and obedience. Social Darwinists applauded football as a rough game, a test of the fittest, extolled by President Charles K. Adams of the University of Wisconsin for developing 'those characteristics that have made the Anglo-Saxon race pre-eminent'. (Reiss, 1995: 128)

But if football was a college game, played by future leaders drawn from the upper middle class, white, Protestant, Anglo-Saxon establishment, professional baseball truly has come to be viewed as the 'national pastime', its values frequently identified with that which is quintessentially American. On baseball, again in the late nineteenth century, Reiss writes:

> The baseball creed coincided with the prevailing broad-based progressive ethos that promoted order, traditional values, efficiency, and Americanization by looking back to an idealized past. The game's history and folklore expressed some of society's main values and goals. Baseball fostered social integration by promoting acculturation and hometown pride, by teaching respect for authority, and by giving factory workers much-needed exercise and diversion.
>
> The game was said to exemplify democracy because peoples from different social backgrounds sat together at the ballpark, which would reduce class tensions, promote democratic feelings, and provide plebians a model of proper behavior to emulate. Baseball was also believed to epitomize democracy since player recruitment and retention was based solely on merit . . . Identified as a rural game, baseball supposedly built character and developed such traditional qualities as fair play, discipline, and rugged individualism. It extended small-town life into cities, where playing and watching the game helped indoctrinate newcomers. Yet at the same time baseball was also perceived as a means to teach boys modern values such as teamwork and self-sacrifice . . . considered essential for future bureaucrats and factory workers. (Reiss, 1995: 165)

Boys were expected to emulate nineteenth century baseball heroes like Christy Mathewson, a college-educated player famous for his espousal of muscular Christianity.

In an important sense football and baseball construct very different American imaginaries. With its social Darwinist ideas about the superiority of the privileged classes, and the brutal on-field conflicts designed to promote the 'survival of the fittest', football strikes at least this spectator as having a very close affinity with the historicised discourse of primitivism described in the previous chapter. Some have pointed to the affinities between football and industrial culture, pointing particularly to the themes of adherence to a time clock, precise measurement and so on shared by both the sport and the factory regime. This contrasts with baseball, an apparently rural and open-ended game. In its myths of timeless, rural, small town origins, the idealised absence of on-field conflict and struggle, the supposed all-American virtues of its star players baseball most clearly articulates classical republican ideals.

In a very real sense baseball can have no history. When several years ago baseball players went on strike for higher wages and better conditions, and the season was drastically curtailed because management refused to yield, apocalyptic announcements about the end of the sport abounded. When an expansion team, the Florida Marlins, were seen to have 'bought' the World Series title by lashing out huge sums on expensive stars, only to sell them all in the following season, this vision of the final complete corruption of the republican virtues of baseball was re-enforced. All this is reminiscent of the blow to the cultural values of Americanism caused by the infamous black sox scandals. It is difficult to imagine seeing in the corporatisation of professional football a similar vision of collective doom.

One also needs to consider the relationship between 'respectable' American sports like baseball and other American sports and pastimes. If baseball in particular came to be closely associated with an emergent Americanism in the late nineteenth century, other sports and pastimes were at the same time considered undesirable by progressive reformers. Sports like horse racing and, especially, boxing, and games like pool were viewed with a great deal of suspicion by progressive intellectuals, journalists and politicians as likely to lead to corruption. One is reminded of the moralising of the bandmaster in the popular musical *The Music Man* first staged on Broadway and later made into a film starring Robert Preston. The huckster band leader who ultimately becomes converted to the cause of the wholesomeness and clean-living virtues of membership in the marching band, sings:

> I'm talking about trouble, right here in River City, and that starts with 'T' and that rhymes with 'P' and that stands for pool!

He could just as well have been denouncing other 'un-American' sports like horse racing or boxing. It should come as no surprise to learn that the lyrics and libretto of this popular 'republican' musical were written by one Meredith Wilson, one time flautist and leading personality in the Sousa Band, providing a personal link between the two main popular expressions of American turn-of-the- century republicanism, music and 'respectable' sport.

Of course baseball, the national pastime, was not as national as its boosters liked to imagine. A good deal of the vision of baseball as a democratic game of rural origins was a myth of late nineteenth century origins:

> The arcadian, integrative, and democratic attributes of professional baseball were largely myths. In reality, baseball was not a democratic game of rural American origins, a promoter of social integration, or a builder of character. Baseball was actually an urban sport that had evolved over time from the English game of rounders, and its finest players were raised in the city. (Reiss, 1995: 165)

In fact, the cost of tickets and transportation to ball parks located on the outskirts of the growing cities, and starting times that were inconvenient to blue collar labourers, prevented many unskilled workers from attending until the 1920s. Those that did come were segregated from the better off by different-priced sections. And unlike college football, and like the music industry that Sousa so enthusiastically embraced, baseball in these early years was most definitely not a simple rural pastime but an urban business. Team owners were businessmen trying to make money, or professional politicians working with business allies (nearly half of nineteenth century owners were politicians). Many were also streetcar executives who contributed to the development of baseball in order to create customers for the new street car lines that were pushing out into the urban fringes.

Apart from supposedly representing good, wholesome American values, baseball has for some time now been seen as an avenue for minority groups into mainstream American life. Reiss points out that social workers at the turn of the century saw it was a way of acculturating immigrant children into the American way of life, while others have seen in baseball an important vehicle of black advancement. And yet again, particularly in this early period, baseball was more exclusive than is often assumed. Contrary to the myth of a democratic audience, most spectators were mainly 'lower-middle to upper-lower class, and of WASP or old-immigrant stock' (Reiss, 1995: 170). And immigrant and black players were few and far between: '[V]irtually all [players] were white and the overwhelming majority were from native-born American, Irish, or German stock' (p. 166). The story of racial segregation in baseball is well known: until Jackie Robinson in the 1940s, some time after professional football was integrated, talented black baseball players were essentially restricted to the separate Negro Leagues.[5] And even new immigrants did not really get into baseball, nor see in baseball a respectable career for their children.

A Republican Vision?

This brief foray into the realm of American popular culture at the turn of the last century reveals some rather distinctive modernist currents if viewed from the perspective of contemporary British ideas about civilisation and primitivism. What I want to suggest is that American popular culture in this period is distinctly modernist, in that it seeks an interrogation of modernity and the processes of modernisation, but that it does so in culturally specific ways. The specific features of American popular modernism in this period, I would suggest, derive from the way they draw on a particular American intellectual and cultural tradition that is most frequently termed republican. Of course because they are now articulated in an identifiably modernist interrogation of America, these republican cultural and intellectual assumptions are here reconstituted. Because they are mobilised in new ways and under changed circumstances, they are far from being the same as they were in earlier periods. But the fact that at least American popular modernism emerges in this distinctive cultural context means that it too had its own rather distinctive characteristics, including the fact that it constituted itself self-consciously as a popular rather than a high version of modernism, and that it was self-consciously cosmopolitan, seeing in America an alternative to a class ridden Europe divided by an obsession with narrow national allegiances. I want to suggest that these themes in a developing American popular culture can be seen to draw on two longer-standing currents in American culture: first, Jeffersonian Republicanism, and second, a modernising Protestantism that itself has roots in the early nineteenth century Protestant revival.

Jefferson was, of course, more a product of the French republican than the British liberal Enlightenment, and his two central concerns were with the principles of 'good government' and the means for producing a 'virtuous' citizenry. The former would be achieved mainly through designing a system of government based on checks and balances that would prevent the natural inclination to maximise material gain from leading to the corruption of office holders. The latter would be achieved primarily through state education.[6] American civic or secular republicanism was transformed or even superseded in the early nineteenth century as a consequence of the Edwardsian revival of pietistic protestantism. By the latter part of the century, the combination of republican ideals and modernising Protestantism resulted in the kind of progressive, reform-minded republicanism into which one can place Sousa-ism, as well as many of the ideas behind the contemporary reform movement. Although some have seen in reformism a transitional phase in the incorporation of more historically based ideas about change and progress, the progressive era continued also to articulate the republican vision.

Republicanism, in the account by one of the best-known advocates of the view that there were very significant republican influences in American political culture (see Pocock, 1975; see also Ross, 1979), is characterised by a number of features that mark it off from the liberal/social evolutionist vision. It is concerned above all with the means of ensuring a virtuous life seen as best achieved through participation in political life. Above all, according to Pocock, early American republicanism was concerned with the threat to virtue posed by history, understood particularly by early republicanism as the development of commerce, to the religio-cultural integrity of the nation.[7] From the time of the Declaration of Independence, if not earlier, a key problem addressed by American republicans was how to establish a form of government that would guarantee the greatest happiness for the greatest number. And this was, contra the utilitarians and Spencer, most definitely a problem at least with a strong institutional dimension. Starting off with an anthropology rather similar to that of the utilitarians, seeing man as an animal concerned with maximising his own gain, the framers of the Constitution were concerned not just with how to counter these tendencies in civil society, but how to prevent their potentially damaging effects on those holding power. The solution was seen to lie in structuring government in such a way as to prevent the natural instinct for maximising personal gain of those in and outside government, by instituting a judicious balancing of powers among different branches and levels of government and between government and the people. Contrary to popular opinion, therefore, American versions of republicanism have not always taken democracy, in the sense of popular participation in government, as their central problematic. Instead, democratic participation is seen as one among several different ways of ensuring that those in government pursue the public, and not their own private, interest. Many indeed have seen in the history particularly of constitutional debate in America a history of a debate between those for whom the virtues of republicanism are of foremost importance, and those pressing for greater democracy – between what have been called Jeffersonian and Jacksonian versions of American political process.

But as this suggests there has also inevitably been a second string to the republican bow. As Jefferson argued, it was necessary not just to guard against the natural inclination of rulers to tyranny and corruption, but against the threat of the masses as well:

> In Jefferson's view, the threat posed by tyranny and corruption is addressed by the creation of multiple modes of representation, which simultaneously is viewed as multiple ways of exercising and, thus, providing a check on power. The threat posed by an amorphous mass is addressed by Jefferson in terms of a model of the cultivation of virtues and manners. In a modern, functionally and culturally diverse society, custom and tradition are not enough to guard against the formation of mass society. In Jefferson's view – and here he returns to French Enlightenment currents – education in the republican ideals and arts of ruling and being ruled can only guard against corruption. (Rundell and Mennell, 1998: 11)

Jefferson maintained the necessity of at least a period of universal public education, during which time:

> Instead . . . of putting the Bible and Testament into the hands of the children, at an age when judgements are not sufficiently matured for religious enquiries, their memories may here be stored with the most useful facts from Grecian, Roman, European and American history. The first elements of morality too may be instilled into their minds; such as, when further developed as their judgements advance in strength, may teach them how to work out their own greatest happiness, by shewing them that it does not depend on the condition of life in which

chance has placed them, but is always the result of good conscience, good health, occupation, and freedom in all just pursuits . . . (Jefferson, [1787] 1954: 147)

All students would be required to study the comparative history of government because in doing so they will see that in 'every government on earth is some trace of human weakness, some germ of corruption and degeneracy'. By learning to recognise these things, all will be in a position to become 'guardians of their own liberty', making it possible for the 'influence over government [to] be shared among all the people' (1954: 148). Jefferson also saw government playing a broader pedagogical role, advocating a state system of higher education in the sciences and humanities for a select few of outstanding ability from the poorest classes, government sponsorship of science, and the like.

We now know that the role that Jefferson envisaged the federal government might play in the production of an educated and virtuous electorate was greatly reduced in subsequent years. But it is important to note here that classical Americanism envisaged not, as some would have it, a purely *laissez-faire* system if by that is understood that no role whatsoever is envisaged for government in the lives of its citizens apart from protecting them against an infringement on their natural rights.

There is another significant difference between American republicanism and classical British liberalism that needs to be borne in mind. While as we have suggested British liberalism was strongly inflected by the progress of science from the late 1860s, Americans at least up to the end of the nineteenth century were more likely to find a grounding for their beliefs in religion. The significance of religion in American life, and in American intellectual life, of course has a long history, attributable in part to the significant role played in colonial settlement by those fleeing religious persecution in Britain. But of particular relevance to late nineteenth century Americanism were two things. First, as the historian Henry May among others has so clearly demonstrated, one key element of the Jeffersonian vision – its advocacy of a sort of civic humanism – was undercut in America shortly after the revolutionary period by the ascendancy of the religious re-awakening associated most closely with the preachings of the New England theologian Jonathan Edwards (May 1976, 1991). Manifest strongly in the views of prominent figures in nineteenth century republicanism, the influence of Edwards for example being particularly strong in abolitionist circles, ascetic, pietistic and/or Calvinist Protestantism probably played the intellectual role in America played by science among their British liberal contemporaries.

And while undoubtedly the scientific revolution associated with the name of Charles Darwin did make an impact on American liberals after the 1860s, equally if not more important was the emergence of a modernist Protestant theology out of the older Edwardsian tradition. While, therefore, British liberals may have looked to evolutionism in its various guises as an explanation for progress, in America development was taken to be evidence that progress was manifest, and hence that God's will was immanent, in the world (cf. Lears, 1981; Marsden, 1980; Massa, 1990).

This has been put in a somewhat different way by historians of American republicanism when they call attention to the lack of a historicist vision in American thought, hence a tendency towards millenarianism or utopianism rather than progressivism (in the historical sense) (see Pocock, 1975; Ross, 1979). And while utilitarianism and evolutionism might be used to explain the British liberal stress on the sovereignty of the individual, in America notions of individual sovereignty, responsibility and duty were derived to a much greater extent from a religious inflection that came increasingly to dominate republican thinking in the nineteenth century. Against what many believe, America at least in the nineteenth century was not the home of individualism in the liberal sense – opposition to the Federal State having more to do with republican assumptions about the need for guarantees for states rights, freedom of religion, the traditional republican opposition to standing armies and the like. In spite of the myth, emancipation through self-autonomisation seems less a feature of the American than the British cultural landscape. And this combination of cultural forces helps explain the particular form taken by American progressivism towards the end of the nineteenth century and, particularly, the way those within this republican tradition reacted to the major transformations that took place in America in the latter decades of the nineteenth, and early part of the twentieth centuries. Although it can, for example, be argued that the so-called progressive historians like Frederick Jackson Turner did to some extent show signs of developing a (European) historical consciousness, hence breaking with the ahistorical visions of classical American republicanism (see Ross, 1979), they none the less still showed manifestations of a commitment to classical republican goals.

Echoing certain of Jefferson's own arguments about the need to place history at the centre of public education, but adding to it a less ambiguous faith in progress already achieved, the progressives argued that history was not to be viewed as a discipline dedicated to the discovery of good things in the past. Instead, as particularly Robinson was fond of pointing out, the past was to be used for present purposes. This was linked to the centrality of reform, based on the fact that in the work of progressive historians:

[D]ominant thoughts and institutions fell easily under the suspicion of being the results of outmoded orthodoxies, kept in place by self-interests of groups and individuals . . . they were not content to let time's slow erosion of the past do its work. Too many of the past's elements had survived and, since they did not 'fit' into the present, exerted a drag on the progress of history towards its goal. Let historians, then, find the obstacles to progress . . . and destroy them in the interest of efficient progress . . . This simplification was helped by the suspicion – quite prevalent in the Progressive Era – that many ill-fitting elements of the past survived into the present not only through inertia but through the efforts of people who profited from the status quo and therefore wished to delay progress. (Ross, 1979: 62f.)[8]

This nexus of ideas – of republicanism, progressivism and reform – was, however, certainly shared with people outside the circle of academic historians. Given the religious underpinnings of American progressivism, it is perhaps not surprising to find that the reforming Social Gospel Movement also has its roots in the 1890s. Indeed, the strength of progressive reforming tendencies in American Protestantism carried through particularly strongly into African-American politics in the interwar and postwar periods as manifest in the central role played by black Protestant churches in the civil rights movement, itself strongly influenced by the kinds of progressivism we have discussed above (see Luker, 1991).

The basic elements of the new discourse articulated in the writings of the progressive historians, and the teachings of modernist Protestant theologians were shared by a larger number of middle class Americans involved in one way or another in the movement for social reform – a term that has been applied to a loosely structured but growing movement comprising mainly middle class, native or old immigrant stock intellectuals, artists, professionals, ministers of the church, journalists and teachers, most of whom exercised their reformist zeal directly or indirectly through charitable bodies and settlement houses, citizens' action committees, good government pressure groups, schools and colleges and religious organisations (cf. Crunden, 1982).

Progressivism, republicanism, reform – together these terms indicate the parameters of a developing cultural sensibility towards the end of the last century. This vision was clearly universalistic in intent. Its advocates envisaged at least an America, and many also a world, fully governed by a particular set of moral and political principles. This new progressivism also shared with the longstanding republican tradition a commitment to good government, understood as a form of government that would minimise the possibility of those in government using their office for maximising their own personal powers and/or material rewards. And they also placed the Jeffersonian stress on public education and Protestant evangelical aims back on the progressive agenda, stressing the need for high-minded people to intervene actively in society to ensure the full realisation of the American dream. Labour and agrarian unrest, the predatory activities of big businesses, unscrupulous operators of urban sweatshops and tenements, machine politicians – all the consequence of industrialisation, urbanisation, immigration and the rural crisis brought on by the development of American economy and society in the late nineteenth century – would, if left unchecked, undermine the ideals of republican government. Only active intervention on the part of reformers could prevent this from happening.

There is an important sense in which questions of religion underpinned American republicanism from the outset, since a good deal of the appeal of constitutional republicanism lay in the protection it offered to the diversity of Protestant believers in the colonies. A shared history of religious dissidence perhaps explains the desire to enshrine religious freedoms in the constitution. Here republican guarantees are seen as an outgrowth of this early religious diversity of American society.

Yet clearly also to the extent that the model of the diverse nation was based on religious differences among Protestants, it would also have difficulty accommodating both differences between ascetic Protestantism and other more ritualised religions (first Catholicism, then orthodox Judaism and others), as well as forms of cultural diversity unrelated to religion.

How representative of mainstream American opinion were these ideas? This is of course a difficult question if only because there were at the turn of the century multiple American imaginaries just as there are now. Doubtless then as now the content of Americanism was contested by blacks and whites, men and women, immigrants and 'natives', government and people. But perhaps something at least of a new middle class vision of America becomes manifest not so much in their own intellectualised and idealised pronouncements, but in the sphere of popular culture. Because middle class tastes in music and sport, to name two fields in which national imaginaries were being forged and transformed in the popular consciousness at the end of the last century, were less likely to be chosen consciously, examining them is more likely to provide insight into what at least certain groups really felt about what it meant to be American in the late nineteenth century.

And as we have seen in the music of Sousa and the ideals of baseball, popular Americanism in the late nineteenth century differed in certain key respects from contemporary forms of popular modernism in Britain, most notably in the continued importance of religious themes and undercurrents, in the prevalence of utopian and millenarian elements, in their concern with virtue rather than simply efficiency and rationality, and in their cosmopolitan/multireligious understanding of America's own path to civilisation. Finally, the absence of strong historical themes in popular republicanism, particularly evident in the rules and ethos of the game of baseball, affected the ways in which republicans conceived of the problem of what we would now call cultural diversity. Primitivism, of course, sees diversity largely as a consequence of temporal variation, thus primitivists can place different cultures and societies firmly on a temporal axis leading to a single universal future. The absence of this temporal dimension suggests that in American popular culture otherness will not so clearly be seen in terms of before and after.

Instead, diversity in America is understood in two rather different senses. First it might be said that the cosmopolitan dimension of Americanism shows an indifference towards diversity, a sense that cultural, and most importantly religious diversity is in itself no bad thing so long as different religious and cultural groups accept the legitimacy of the rules that govern the (culturally neutral) public sphere. On the other hand, this leaves open the possibility that there may also be individuals, or more likely groups, who refuse to play their part in society, by failing to play by these rules of the public sphere, preferring instead to look inward to their own distinctive values for guidance. In this case, the other-to-the civilised is as likely to be constituted as different or alien, as it is to be seen as an earlier version of the civilised self. We have seen this for example in the way Sousa positions his music in relation to that of Europe. But this theme in American modern republicanism is perhaps most clearly manifest in the attitudes towards immigrants in American cities towards the end of the nineteenth century.

Republican Exclusions: Primitives and Aliens

At least at the level of cultural practice, republicanism in the so-called progressive era seems to have erected barriers to the full participation of both blacks and new immigrants. Was this a contradiction between theory and practice, or did republicanism itself generate the propensity to exclude these groups as in some sense un-American or incompletely American? The possibility that late nineteenth century American republican discourse had the potential to generate exclusionary impulses is suggested if we examine the way in which many white, 'Native stock' intellectuals represented African Americans and immigrants in their own discourse.

When one looks at the views expressed about African Americans and immigrants by late nineteenth century American writers and social commentators, one is faced with an enigma in the way in which they represented non-white, non-Anglo-Saxon Americans. The differences in the ways in which *fin-de-siècle* Americans thought about the Americanising capacities of African Americans on the one hand and new immigrants on the other provide important clues both about the subsequent transformation of the progressive paradigm in general and the different fates of blacks and 'white ethnics' in the years after the First World War. I say enigmatic because, contrary to what most commentators on race and ethnicity in America might lead us to expect, it was white immigrants from southern and eastern Europe (and to an extent also Asians) who were at least initially looked on as considerably more problematic than were ex-slaves and their descendants, leading those unfamiliar with the differing historical experiences of blacks and the white immigrants since that time to suspect that it would have been the latter and not the former who would have had greater difficulty in realising the American dream. But of course as everyone now knows, at least in terms of their levels of economic and social mobility since the turn of the century, 'white ethnics' have had significantly greater chances of success. After all, if an important part of the American intellectual establishment was more inclined to view blacks in a favourable light, as both being more likely to cast off their poverty and oppression, and more deserving of support in their attempt to do so, then surely they, and not the children of white immigrants, should have ultimately 'Americanised' more successfully, if that is understood not just as a cultural transformation, but as the achievement of economic, political and social levels comparable to those of the rest of the population. Does this, perhaps, tell us something about the exclusionary dimensions at least of Americanist discourse at the outset of the period under consideration? Trying to discover why this might have been the case provides us with important insights into the process known as Americanisation.

> We congratulate ourselves all the time on the increased means of producing wealth, and then we take the opposite fit and commit some great folly in order to prove that there is something grander than the pursuit of wealth. Three years ago we were on the verge of a law to keep immigrants out who were not good enough to be with us. Now we are going to take in eight million barbarians and semi-barbarians, and we are paying twenty million dollars to get them. (William Graham Sumner [1892], in Bannister (ed.), 1992: 293)

Using the familiar device of contrasting a universal (American) self with a primitive (not yet American) other, the prominent American sociologist William Graham Sumner expressed the view that the new immigrants flowing into American cities from southern and eastern Europe were incompletely civilised – not primitives in a state of nature, but occupants of a middle level of barbarism between civilised and uncivilised. But while the evolutionist Sumner had no qualms about using such primitivist language to describe these new immigrants, and while others classed new immigrants with other members of the 'lower races', many late nineteenth century 'native stock' Americans were more ambivalent in their attitudes towards immigrants and immigration. *Contra* the primitivists and racists, they were instead inclined to interpret what they undoubtedly saw as their undesirable qualities as arising as much from their diverse religious and cultural backgrounds and the environmental circumstances they faced in America as from their prior civilisational states. What was most problematic about them as far as many observers were concerned was that they were inclined to be manipulated by a particular breed of urban politicians, the unscrupulous owners of sweatshops, saloon keepers, gamblers and the like, generally assumed to be people of their own nationality already living in the United States. Cultural and religious solidarity rather than a lack of culture was seen as the immigrant's main failing. In other words, many late nineteenth century observers tended to cast the 'problem' of immigrants more often in a culturalising than in a primitivising mould.

That these attitudes towards the new immigrants from southern and eastern Europe differed from those commonly associated with nineteenth century liberalism becomes evident when we compare them with a set of representations that were more typical of classical liberalism, that is of African Americans. Compare, for example, the differing impressions of Jacob Riis of the living conditions of immigrants and blacks in New York tenements. Riis, author of the acclaimed *How the Other Half Lives*, who through his articles in popular New York dailies probably did more than anyone to draw the attention of Americans to the appalling situation of the urban poor at the turn of the century, was born in Ribe, in Denmark, in 1849. He travelled to New York in 1870 and spent the next seven years bumming around the eastern states before becoming police reporter for the *New York Tribune*, and then the *Evening Sun*. He later developed a friendship with Theodore Roosevelt when the latter was Chairman of New York

City's Police Board. At one point Riis worked as a colleague of Lincoln Steffens, doyen of the muckraking journalists. Riis knew most of the leading reformers, especially in New York, including Dr Charles Pankhurst the crusading Protestant minister and Felix Adler, educational reformer and founder of the Ethical Culture movement. He focused his concern on a single area of New York, 'The Bend', in Mulberry Street on the Lower East Side, and as journalist, author and pioneering photojournalist he launched a wave of attacks on conditions in tenements, the use of child labour, the so-called sweating system, the treatment of truants, and conditions in the city's schools.[9]

Riis is best known for his campaign to tear down tenements, although he had less to say about where their residents might go when their housing had been destroyed. The recurring images of tenements in his writing and photographs were of darkness and filth. The greatest need in his opinion was to open them up to the light. It is interesting in this regard that the discovery of flash photography was so important for him. He used photographs and lantern slides to illustrate his lectures and books to 'open the eyes of the public', and the flash allowed him literally to shed light on the appalling darkness of tenement life. He also continuously stressed the need for fresh air. Its absence, he said, caused disease and high mortality rates. Opening the tenements up to fresh air was as important as letting in light, and the developing Fresh Air Program, whereby city children were sent for a period to board with people in the country, and the creation of public parks and school playgrounds where children could enjoy light and fresh air in the city were very important to him. Significantly, the ultimate aims of tenement reform in Riis's eyes were to create better citizens through promoting the virtues of political participation:

> With tongue or pen, the argument shaped itself finally into the fundamental one for the rescue of the home imperilled by the slum. There all roads met. Good citizenship hung upon that issue. Say what you will, a man cannot live like a pig and vote like a man . . . The tenement had given to New York the name of the 'homeless city.' But with that gone which made life worth living, what were [sic] liberty worth? With no home to cherish, how long before love of country would be an empty sound? Life, liberty, pursuit of happiness? Wind! Says the slum, and the slum is right if we let it be . . . (1901: 320f.)

A forerunner of twentieth century reform in New York, and unlike those who followed him, Riis remained hostile to welfarism *per se*. This attitude is most evident in his attacks on tramps and soup kitchens, which he felt perpetuated idleness and a lack of individual responsibility. None the less he shared broadly, if not always consciously, in prevailing progressive attitudes – specifically in the ambivalence towards culturally alien immigrants and an admiration for blacks as more or less similar to American 'natives', if still in a more primitive state than most whites.

In *How the Other Half Lives*, published originally in 1890, Riis gives his impressions of the different groups living in New York's tenement districts.

One of his earliest remarks on these districts concerns the absence of the English language: 'The one thing you shall vainly ask for in the chief city of America is a distinctively American community' (1962: 15).

Italians are characterised largely by their participation in the so-called '*padrone* system', in other words by the fact that they were enmeshed in a patron–client system alien to the organisation of American work places. One place this operated was in the business of recovering items in the city's garbage dumps: 'The discovery was made by early explorers that there is money in New York's ash-barrel, but it was left to the genius of the *padrone* to develop the full resources of the mine that has become the exclusive preserve of the Italian immigrant.'

Like most other observers, however, Riis found the Chinese to be the most clannish and inward-looking of America's new immigrant communities, in spite of their great success in business: 'Whatever may be said about the Chinaman being a thousand years behind the age on his own shores, here he is distinctly abreast of it in his successful scheming to "make it pay" . . . all attempts to make an effective Christian of John Chinaman will remain abortive in this generation; of the next I have, if anything, less hope' (1962: 68).

Another group that, according to Riis, was both commercially oriented, but culturally closed, were the Jews: 'Thrift is the watchword of Jewtown, as of its people the world over. It is at once its strength and its fatal weakness . . . Money is their God. Life itself is of little value compared with even the leanest bank account . . .' (1962: 78f.).

Of course, here Riis is dealing in stereotypes, even demeaning ones, although given the prevalence of such attitudes it would have been more surprising had he not done so. My aim, however, is not to produce a presentist critique of Riis, but instead to draw attention to certain rather specific features of these stereotypes. While perhaps demeaning, it is notable that these representations – of Italians, Chinese and Jews in New York – are in no simple sense primitivist. In some ways Italian, and especially Jewish and Chinese immigrants in turn of the century New York, are here portrayed not as primitive but as hyper-modern. Jewish thrift, Chinese business acumen, Italian monopoly are in a real sense merely extremely efficient adaptations to a commercial economy. But in each case what prevents these groups from being seen merely as successful American entrepreneurs appears to be the fact that they are inward looking, exclusive groups – the Italians keep non-Italians out of the garbage business, Jews and Chinese shut outsiders out of their dealings.

The Chinese, for example, are said to 'consider themselves subject to the laws of the land only when submission is unavoidable, and . . . they are governed by a code of their own, the very essence of which is rejection of all other authority except under compulsion' (1962: 74f.). And commenting again on the Italians, Riis also bemoans their secretiveness, even to the extent that they will protect criminals of their own group if it would otherwise mean informing to the police:

By far the most cheering testimony that our Italian is becoming one of us came to me a year or two ago in the evidence that on two occasions Mulberry Street had refused to hide a murderer even in his own village. This was conclusive. It was not so in those days. (1901: 275)

These inward-looking or 'clannish' qualities were what, for Riis, appeared to distinguish these groups from other Americans. Can one say that for Riis the otherness of these new immigrants was a consequence of their 'cultural essentialism'? It was certainly their tendency to associate with each other, to shut out the outsider's gaze or at least to ensure that interaction with the outside world was strictly controlled and not permitted to break group ties that Riis found most problematic about the new immigrants.

This culturalisation of the American discourse on new immigrants was manifest more widely at the time. This becomes evident when we look at the way new immigrants were characterised in articles in some of the better known periodicals published in the 1880s and 1890s, their contributors sharing most of the goals of more prominent intellectuals of the time. The main problems associated by most of these observers with the new immigrants were urban – problems of labour unrest, destitution, crime, violence, public unrest, drunkenness etc.

Many drew attention to the higher propensity of new immigrants to engage in criminal acts, pointing to statistics showing the relative high proportion of foreign-born among convicted criminals. The following, taken from an article that appeared in *Popular Science Monthly*, is typical:

The criminal influence of the alien with its steady increase can be traced back in our history . . . [A]nd yet so gradually has it grown upon us that we have now become thoroughly accustomed to a condition of things which should have been extremely shocking to our rugged ancestors as they are sometimes called. (Fisher, 1896: 625)

When our system of foreign immigration first began to reach [high levels], about the year 1820, its effect on our manners and morals soon attracted attention. The Native American party, which arose soon after 1840, based its strongest argument on the enormous increase of crime which followed the advent of the foreigners. The belief and confidence in the cheap labor of the immigrant were very strong in those days, or the people would never have been willing to go on with the system in the face of the shocking revelations of pauperism, crime, and corruption which became more and more apparent from 1830 . . . (p. 625)

The census of 1880 attempted to summarize the relative proportions of the foreign population which were paupers and criminals as far back as 1850 . . . [and this shows that] [t]he foreigner in proportion to his numbers furnishes by far the greater part of pauperism and crime. (p. 625)

The Massachusetts census of 1885, which was taken with great care and completeness, shows the same condition of affairs. The foreign born of that State were 27.1 per cent of the whole population, and yet they furnished 44.03 per cent of the paupers, 40 per cent of the prisoners, and 36.87 per cent of the convicts . . . The statistics of the national census of 1890 reveal the same condition. The native white element of the population is 54 per cent, but it produces only 43.19 per cent of the whole prisoners. The foreign white element, counting foreign born and the

children of foreign born, is only 32.93 per cent of the population, and yet it
produces 56.81 per cent of the whole prisoners. (p. 626)

Foreigners – Irish labour organisers including the Molly Maguires, and
'anarchists' and 'socialists' from eastern Europe – were also held account-
able for most of the labour unrest of this period. One observer even takes
care to distinguish between 'Celtish' and 'Saxon Ulsterite' Irishmen, arguing that

> The largest proportion of the delinquent classes is derived from the Celtic
> element. The Irishman is practically a man without a country; he owes an ill-
> rendered fealty to the British crown until he leaves his native island and swears
> allegiance to the American Government, but the oath rests lightly upon him; all
> the patriotism which he possesses is centered in that ill-starred rebellious depen-
> dency of Great Britain on her west. While on the surface more easily assimilable
> than the Teuton because he speaks the language of his adopted country, he is first
> an Irishman, then an American, and such only so far as it is an America of the
> green flag. A distinction must, however, as already observed, be drawn between
> the natives of the north and those of the south of Ireland – the Saxon Ulsterites
> and the Celts. From the latter is derived the large proportion of our delinquent
> classes; the Molly Maguires were Irishmen, and it is the Irish who have had the
> largest share in the corruption of our governmental institutions. The Ulsterites,
> on the contrary, being principally of Scotch and English stock, partake of the
> characteristics which mark the British alien in America. (Hyde, 1898: 396–397)

And in the same article, the author links the rise of socialism to new
immigrants, especially in New York City:

> The anarchist and ultra-socialist parties do not, as is commonly supposed, derive
> their chief support from the Teutonic element; their ranks are rather recruited
> from among these members of the Semitic and Slavonic races. . . . It is here [in
> immigrant areas of New York] that the socialists expect to elect . . . an
> assemblyman to represent them at Albany. . . . It is in this section of the city that
> the socialists are centralizing, that the most active party leaders are colonizing.
> Such imperfect statistics as are available reveal the fact that the Hungarian,
> Polish, and Russian population stands in the ratio of 5:1 to that of all other
> nationalities. Many of the first three named peoples are not yet voters, but each
> year the naturalization mill turns them out by thousands as free electors, after
> they have solemnly sworn to uphold the Constitution of the United States. Yet
> the socialist ideals are entirely at variance with the true theory of the American
> government as conceived by the early makers of the American state. The ques-
> tion, then, confronting us is whether the process of assimilation or the growth of
> socialism will be the most rapid. (pp. 397–398)

Paradoxically, while immigrants were held responsible for organised
resistance to capitalist exploitation, they were also blamed for their propensity to be manipulated by unscrupulous employers and political bosses.
George Ethelbert Walsh, for example, wrote in the pages of *The Chautauquan* that of 'all the evils which are born and fostered by unrestricted
immigration the so-called "sweating system" of labour is one of the most
conspicuous', since among other things it deprives native Americans of
work by undercutting their wages (Walsh, 1890: 174). These immigrants
caught up in sweatshops he described as 'slaves to endless toil until relieved

by death' (p. 175). And they do so because they are lacking the republican virtues of American workers. If the latter were 'intelligent and thrifty', and hence unlikely to be trapped into the appalling conditions prevailing in sweatshops, the former, because of an ethnic attachment to the bosses or *padrone*, and their own ignorance as 'low, downtrodden material from Europe' were ripe for such exploitation. These immigrant workers were exploited, Walsh suggested, because they spoke no English, failed to assimilate, did not communicate with their fellow workers, and were unaware of the opportunities offered by American business. To succeed they needed to shake off their inward-looking, clannish/tribal dispositions and loyalties and their dependence on sweatshop despots and stifling patron client ties (p. 179).

While certainly condescending, the sorts of stereotypes perpetuated by mainstream commentators on the problem of immigration in late nineteenth century America were by no means simple products of primitivist assumptions. Unlike primitives, immigrants were cast in the role of aliens, lacking in American (republican) virtues and bound up in economic and political institutions that were seen as betrayals of republican values. The inability of immigrants to speak English was frequently singled out for attention, as was their tendency to look inward, within their national communities, rather than outward, to the America in which they found themselves. The failure was therefore as much a failure of communication and attitude as it was a primitive ignorance. Immigrant communities were characterised by ties of patronage and dependence, clear evidence that immigrants differed culturally from mainstream Americans who were far more independent (outside the bonds of the elementary family), who indeed refused to bow to anyone, and who would have been too proud to rely on handouts from their supposed superiors. These institutions lacked that central principle on which republican institutions were based, that is the strict separation of the personal/the private/the economic from the public/ the political/the state.

Immigrants also manifested religious beliefs and practices that appeared distinctly alien from the standpoint of ascetic Protestantism. To mainstream Protestant Americans, the dominant religions among new immigrants – Catholicism and Orthodox Judaism – with their heavy reliance on ritual observances and practices, with the stress they placed on social bonds among the members of the religious congregation, also appeared distinctly alien.

And as aliens, these new immigrants appeared to constitute a significant threat to the American way of life. Given their assumptions about immigrants we should perhaps not be surprised that many saw in the high rates of poverty and poor living conditions endured by urban immigrant groups, in higher rates of criminal behaviour among the foreign born, in the participation by immigrants in the labour movement, in the role played by immigrant elites in the business of sweatshops and urban political machines and the like yet further evidence of the large cultural gap between themselves and immigrants from China, and southern and eastern Europe. After all, could one not walk around the neighbourhoods of New York, Chicago and other large American cities and find evidence that one was in another country altogether?

If we now turn to prevailing impressions of African Americans we find important differences. In the lifestyles of African American tenement dwellers, for example, Jacob Riis found a marked contrast with those of immigrants. Perhaps the contrast was most strikingly articulated by Riis in his use of his central metaphor of light and darkness. What seemed for Riis most to mark off the living places of African Americans was that they were light and clean, while those of Chinese, Italians, Jews, were, as we have seen, described always as dark and secretive:

> Cleanliness is the characteristic of the negro in his new surroundings, as it was his virtue in the old. In this respect he is immensely the superior of the lowest of the whites, the Italians and the Polish Jews, below whom he has been classed in the past in the tenant scale. ([1890] 1962: 112)

That this view was shared by white landlords was demonstrated, according to Riis, by the testimony of a large real estate firm to the effect that they:

> would rather have negro tenants in our poorest class of tenements than the lower grades of foreign white people. We find the former cleaner than the latter, and they do not destroy the property so much. We also get higher prices . . . (cited in Riis, 1962: 113)

In his description of life in black areas of New York, Riis evinced a great deal of empathy, an empathy clearly absent in his accounts of life in European immigrant quarters of the city. In spite of their 'imperturbable cheerfulness', blacks according to Riis were the victims generally of 'poverty, abuse, and injustice' (1962: 115). Despite their superior qualities as tenants, blacks paid higher rents, a consequence of the 'despotism' of the city's landlords. In fact, generally African Americans, who had come to New York from the American South, found themselves forced to accept employment at far lower levels than their intelligence and qualifications entitled them to:

> Ever since the war New York has been receiving the overflow of colored population from the Southern cities. In the last decade the migration has grown to such proportions that it is estimated that our Blacks have quite doubled in number since the Tenth Census. Whether the exchange has been of advantage to the negro may well be questioned. Trades of which he had practical control in his southern home are not open to him here. I know that it may be answered that there is no industrial proscription of color; that it is a matter of choice. Perhaps so. At all events he does not choose them. How many colored carpenters or masons has anyone seen at work in New York? In the South there are enough of them and, if the testimony of the most intelligent of their people is worth anything, plenty of them have come here . . . (1962: 111)

If African Americans had any faults in Riis's eyes, they had to do with an apparent childish simplicity – a willingness to accept their lot cheerfully, and a certain extravagance in money matters, since they appeared to 'love

fine clothes and good living a good deal more than . . . a bank account'
(1962: 115). This view of the African American as merely a white man at an
earlier stage of civilisation, a person, moreover, fully capable of becoming
white as it were, was confirmed for the readers of an article in *The Monist*
by an author described as a prominent Italian man of science:

> If, instead of comparing the intellectuality of the colored race with that which the
> white race has acquired, it were possible to take the intellectual development of
> the white race many years ago,when the social-economic system was at the same
> level with that of the real colored races, I am convinced that many of the illusions
> in regard to the superiority of the white race would be destroyed. Now, it is a fact
> that while we frequently speak of race and define what we mean by it, yet in
> practice it is almost absolutely impossible to make any distinction that will hold
> . . . [C]olor . . . varies widely among the same people. The same may be said of
> stature. If language is taken as the basis of classification, the results obtained are
> even less trustworthy. (Fiamingo, 1898: 385)

> The spirit of exclusivism finds its natural basis in ignorance, in blind indi-
> vidualism. The cautious human egoist sees that the only source of welfare and
> wealth is labor, and for two individuals who find it profitable to work together in
> order to increase their mutual welfare, diversity of race, of color, of form of the
> head, of nationality or social class, constitutes no impediment. If all men are once
> convinced of this truth then the spirit of exclusiveness will disappear. (p. 414)

If, then, immigrants, especially those from southern and eastern Europe,
were characterised as the bearers of a more or less profound cultural
otherness and hence irretrievably lacking in republican virtues, African
Americans by contrast were seen as essentially similar to 'native stock'
Americans. To the extent that their circumstances were different from those
of (white) American natives, this was accounted for by their relative inno-
cence, a simplicity that was seen as almost child-like in character. African
Americans were therefore constituted in accounts such as those by Jacob
Riis as primitive in the sense that they were portrayed as existing in a state
prior to, rather than radically different from that of white Americans.

Solutions proposed to the problems posed by urban poverty were,
therefore, very different depending on whether American reformers were
addressing themselves to the 'Negro question' or the 'problem of immigrants'. For African Americans the issue was fairly clear cut. They merely
needed 'improvement' – education and assistance of various sorts under the
guiding hand of more experienced and knowledgeable whites, much as
children need the guidance of adults. Blacks might have been considered to
be in some sense *incompletely American* but they were most certainly not
seen as *un-American*.

Contrary to those who assume that systems of cultural differentiation are
somehow 'softer', that is more mutable than racial hierarchies, for turn of
the century Americans it was the culturally distinctive migrants who, it
was assumed, posed the greater problem for America. Unlike African
Americans, the new immigrants were not seen as innocents whose ignorance
merely had to be overcome through education. As distinctly and culturally
non-American, turning them into Americans required instead promoting a

profound cultural transformation, a transformation that usually went under the heading of 'Americanisation', before republican virtues could be instilled.

This contrast between culturally distinctive European immigrants and primitive African Americans, was quite generally shared by turn of the century white native-born Americans. It accounts, for example, for what with hindsight appears to be a curiously sanguine view of the future of race relations in the United States articulated by prominent American progressive theorists at the turn of the century. In his study of the progressive historians, for example, Breisach points out that the race problem was largely absent in their work. Turner de-emphasised slavery as a defining feature of American civilisation in favour of the importance of the western frontier, and even here made only occasional reference to 'The Indian problem'. On the other hand, it is known that he had considerable misgivings about the wave of new migrants (Breisach, 1993: 80). Turner's more influential contemporary, James Harvey Robinson

> expected race problems to disappear once human relations assumed a sufficiently rational character, and [Charles] Beard did not see race as a source of problems in the cooperative society of the future . . . because racial differences were manifestations of evolutionary differences between less and more fully developed peoples; the race problem, like many others, resulted from a time lag, not from biological differences. (Breisach, 1993: 63; see also Robinson, 1912)

This was a fairly predictable result of the prevailing understandings of progress and evolution of turn of the century American intellectuals in general. Writing again of American historians, Breisach maintains that with the exception of Becker they avoided the epistemological agonies especially of German historicism. Evolution they adopted loosely as confirmation:

> [T]hey fell back on that concept when they wished to recast the meaning of progress in modern terms . . . Making history the story of evolution gave history a scientific quality .. [They] followed common usage and expectation when they treated evolution as a synonym for a development 'upward' or progress . . . In contrast to other post-Darwinists, Progressive historians also ignored such Darwinistic concepts as the struggle for existence, the survival of the fittest, and a pure environmentalism, which could not be accommodated into their view of progress based on the collective increase of rationality and on rational efforts at reform. (1993: 57)

And of course it was not just white liberals who accepted both the notion of the 'perfectability' of the black American and the need for 'improvement'. Prominent African Americans of the time, most famously Booker T. Washington, were themselves great supporters of an idea of 'self-improvement' that stemmed from the dominant assumptions of white progressivism with its corresponding views of the improveability of the primitive. Contrary to popular impression, moreover, this discourse on primitiveness and civilisation, of improvement and self-improvement did not die once the 'Uncle Tomism' of people like Booker T. Washington had been cast aside. In one form or another it has continued to inflect ideas about black oppression and emancipation through the writings of influential intellectuals of the so-called Harlem Renaissance, to many involved in the American civil rights movement in the 1960s. An assessment of its origins and implications is, therefore, probably as pressing now as it ever has been.

The distinction between the ways in which turn of the century America constituted two distinctive others – African Americans on the one hand and migrants from southern and eastern Europe on the other – allows us to look at the relationships between universalising discourses and exclusionary practices in ways that differ significantly from general abstract discussions of the strengths, and weakness, of Americanism on the one hand, and the history of American nation building on the other. To examine these issues, it is important to ask about the relationship between these quite separate exclusions – the one racialised, the other culturalist – and prevailing understandings of Americanism. Were these exclusions in some clear sense outgrowths of American 'progressivism' in the late nineteenth century? Why should the grounds for excluding blacks and immigrants have been so different? Has liberal thinking about the 'Negro question', based as it has been on particular understandings of the evolution of American civilisation, been more inclusive as a result of its greater attachment to universal principles? How universal are these principles in any case – are they inflected, like previous universalisms, by particular cultural values and assumptions? Why given what we now know about the very different histories of the two groups should Americans have viewed relations with immigrants as somehow more problematic than those with blacks? And why, given that immigrant 'aliens' have been viewed with such tremendous suspicion, have successive waves of ('culturally different') immigrants appeared in fact ultimately to have been more 'successful' in their pursuit of the American dream than have African Americans? What changed to produce these contrasting effects?

The answers to at least some of these questions can be found in the way in which American 'progressive' theory was put into practice by progressive reformers from the late nineteenth century, and the particular outcome of the subsequent struggles between advocates of reform and the defenders of what most of them took to be their principal enemy, the dreaded 'political machines' which held local government in most of the major American cities. Here we shall see that context is important in assessing high theory. Here a version of republicanism that is logically exclusive can shift its ground and become relatively more inclusive, and, on the other hand, a theory that appears more inclusive (in this case of black Americans) can be mobilised in practice precisely to exclude the groups it aspires to include.

Notes

1 For an attempt to locate Ives within the progressive movement, see Crunden, 1982.
2 For a complete list of Sousa's compositions, see Bierley, 1973: 233–240.

3 See Sumner's 1899 address 'The Conquest of the United States by Spain', reprinted in Bannister (ed.), 1992.

4 This recalls the story from Sousa's autobiography about a production of *El Capitan* when a theatre manager said they could not have a black actress playing a leading role. Sousa was urgently contacted by the conductor saying they should refuse to go on. Sousa says that the conductor's attitude did not surprise him since he was from New England. But Sousa himself, a native of south of the Mason Dixon line, understood the objections of the manager and agreed to replace the black actress with a white actress in black face.

5 One of the best accounts of the history of African Americans in baseball is the study by Jules Tygiel (Tygiel, 1957).

6 For a useful overview of republican traditions of civilisational analysis, see Rundell and Mennell (eds), 1998.

7 The classic arguments of American republicanism are those of Thomas Jefferson (see Jefferson [1787], 1954). See also Rundell and Mennell (eds), 1998.

8 James Harvey Robinson, for example, cites Beccaria approvingly to the effect that 'the past was after all only an immense sea of errors from which there emerged here and there an obscure truth' (1912: 249).

9 The best source for Riis's life and developing attitudes towards urban squalor is his autobiography (Riis, 1901).

4
CIVILISATIONAL VIRTUES IN THE MALAY *KAMPONG*

The Malay language film *Semerah Padi* (Red Paddy), produced by Shaw Brothers, the Singapore-based giants of the Malayan film industry, was released in 1956, just one year before Malaysian independence. It was directed by, and also starred, a young Malay actor named P. Ramlee. Ramlee had made his directorial debut in the previous year with *Penarik Becha*, a major box office success with the Malay movie-going public in Singapore and in cities and towns throughout the peninsula. P. Ramlee's rapid rise first to stardom and then to directorial success was promoted by Shaw Brothers in response both to the demands of a movie-mad Malay public, and to the calls by Malay nationalists in Singapore for greater Malay involvement in the creative side of the film business, as well as for increased Malay content.

P. Ramlee was the name taken by a Malay of Sumatran descent born in a village in Penang State in 1929. A musician, he played in local dance clubs and composed his own music which was heavily influenced by the samba, rhumba, Latin and swing music then popular in British Malaya.[1] In 1948 he won a talent contest and as a result was recruited by the Singapore-based film company where he continued his musical career, and rose to become the best-known figure in Malay film, first as actor, then as screenwriter, director and romantic lead in a string of at least 64 feature-length films. Having established himself as the foremost Malay entertainer of his time from his base in Singapore, he returned to Kuala Lumpur in 1964, and continued to compose, perform and direct films until his death in 1973. He was awarded the title of Tan Sri posthumously by the government, and continues to be revered, not just by ordinary fans of his films and music, but by a government always on the look-out for iconic figures from the Malay community. A museum has been established in his former home in Kuala Lumpur, and recently much of his music and many of his films have been re-released in popular video cd format by the satellite broadcasting company Astral.[2]

Ramlee's arrival on the Singapore film scene coincided with a period of intense pressure on the local film industry by Malay nationalists based in Singapore who wanted to 'Malay-ise' local film. The film industry in Singapore had been pioneered by Indian capital and personnel – and the earliest Malay language films presented mainly Indian themes and plots remade in Malay with local actors. The first of these, *Laila Majnun*, was a platonic Middle Eastern love story, with Islamic overtones, and it proved popular with the Malay movie-going public. *Laila Majnun* was produced by Bombay Chemical Company which felt it could tap the huge market developing among Malays of the peninsula for American, Indian and Chinese films by supplying them with original Malay language films. They screened *Laila Majnun* in independent theatres, supplying projection equipment themselves. But their success prompted Shaw Brothers, the Chinese company that controlled most established cinemas in Malaya, to go into the production of Malay language films themselves. Between 1938 and the outbreak of the Second World War, Shaw Brothers produced eight Malay films, *Mutiara, Bermadu, Hanchor Hatt, Topeng Shaitan, Ibu Tiri, Terang Bulan di Malaya, Tiga Kekasih* and *Mata Hantu*.

During the Japanese occupation the import of western films as well as local production was suspended, but in the postwar period a local Indian businessman produced his only Malay film *Seruan Merdeka* (Freedom Call), a dramatic story of an underground movement to fight fascism. *Seruan Merdeka* was unusual because its two heroes were Chinese and Malay and they led the underground movement together. In subsequent years only a very few such multiracial films were made, including *Selamat Tinggal Kekasihku* (1955), directed by L. Krishnan, and *Gerimis* (1968), directed by P. Ramlee himself.

Seruan Merdeka did not get a very wide screening, since Shaw Brothers prevented the productions of other companies from showing in peninsular cinemas which they effectively monopolised. Instead, in the 1950s the typical pattern was for films to be produced by Chinese capital (Shaw Brothers), directed by Indians,[3] with 'Malay-ised' versions of Indian and Chinese plots, and acted by Malays speaking in Malay. This formula proved successful for the predominantly Malay audiences, and it was into this structure that Ramlee himself was slotted. His first 25 films were produced between 1948 and 1955 by MFB (the Malay film-making arm of Shaw Brothers), and directed by B.S. Rajhans, L. Krishnan, S. Ramanathan, K.M. Basker, and B.N. Rao.

But Malay nationalist calls for greater Malay involvement in the film industry – calls spearheaded by the Singapore Malay Journalist Association, which railed against the encroachment of foreign, and the misrepresentation of Malay, culture – forced Shaw Brothers to look for Malay directors. Their first effort, *Permata Diperlimbahan* (1952), directed by former Assistant Director Haji Mahdi, was badly made and a commercial failure, leading some to argue Malays were incapable of mastering western technology. But the demand for Malays to direct Malay films did not go away, indeed it became stronger as more cultural organisations joined in the call. As a result, they turned to the singer and actor P. Ramlee who was asked to direct *Penarik Becha*. He went on to direct over 30 more films, about half for Shaw Brothers and half for Merdeka (the Malaysian company) after his return to Kuala Lumpur.

What versions of Malayness did Ramlee's films construct for their audience? How did Ramlee himself, first as actor and then as screenwriter and director, interpret or 'consume'[4] the ideas of Malay nationalist intellectuals and political leaders for his Malay audience? In attempting to answer this question it is important to recognise not just the similarities, but also the important differences between Ramlee's version of Malaya, and that of the high priests of Malay cultural nationalism – novelists like Shahnon Ahmad or nationalist political leaders like the young Mahathir Mohamed, both of whom wrote influential accounts of the Malays and their 'dilemma'.[5] It should also be reiterated that the cultural products that now all bear Ramlee's name would not have been a product only of one man's free imagination, or unmediated responses to the cultural demands of nationalists. Shaw Brothers would have certainly attempted to ensure that the films were commercially viable, and others (directors, writers, actors, etc.) would also have had an input. And as this suggests, in so far as Shaw Brothers strove to tap into the desires of a Malay audience, these films could be said to have been constructed by directors, actors, producers and audience in interaction with each other. Ramlee himself admitted that he had been influenced by such noted Asian flim makers as Ray and Kurosawa. I use Ramlee here, then, in much the same way as I used Sousa in a previous chapter – not to discuss the artistic vision of a single person, but to examine a cultural phenomenon constructed explicitly by and for the developing public of a modern culture industry.

There was a prodigious output of films and music associated with this Ramlee phenomenon. If we focus mainly on the films of the Singapore-era of his career, still there is an immense range of thematic material ranging from Middle Eastern-type fantasies, to historical drama, to contemporary melodrama and romance. None the less, a rather limited range of themes to do with class and 'blood', Islam, Malay tradition (*adat*), the qualities of leaders and, above all, romantic love are dealt with over and over again.

What strikes the viewer of these films is that these themes are played out almost entirely against the backdrop of the Malay rural village or *kampong*, and the characters are, with very few exceptions in some of the later films, identifiably Malay to a man and woman, even though Malays at the time constituted only one of the three main 'races' or 'ethnic' groups that together made up the population of British Malaya. Even the locales of films like *Ahmad Albab* and *Abu Hassan Pencuri* (a Malay version of *The Thief of Baghdad*), ostensibly a Middle Eastern village and a king's palace (*Istana Raja*) in Baghdad respectively, are effectively 'Malay-ised' and recognisably Malay in many respects. The other films, both historical and contemporary, are unambiguously located in Malay villages. Cities may be referred to, or even, as in the case of *Antara Dua Darjat*, actually portrayed (Singapore not Kuala Lumpur is the identified site of contemporary Malayan urbanism, while Malacca is the offstage centre in the historical dramas). But villages are where almost all the action takes place, the stage on which even people from the city must be judged. Urban influences, and urban people are almost uniformly corrupting if they are acknowledged at all. Moreover, the characters in these films are all ethnic Malays. Chinese and Indian Malayans are not stereotyped or racialised, they are quite simply absent. In Ramlee's film world cities exist offstage as it were, and non-Malays do not exist at all.

The stereotype of the Malay village in many Ramlee films is one that would have been recognisable to his Malay audience as an example of that imagined space within which all Malays live. Each of these films is interspersed with such scenes of idealised village life – men and women working together happily in large groups in the irrigated rice fields, honest craftsmen working with their hands, young men gathered in housing compounds playing *sepak raga* (a Malay cross between soccer and volleyball), spinners of tops, groups of women washing and bathing on the riverbank, and lovers meeting in isolated garden land (*dusun*) on the village fringe.[6]

In Ramlee's films, the *kampong* is the Malay universe complete unto itself, and normal *kampong* life is the very definition of Malay virtue. Indeed, it is precisely that which threatens the *kampong* and village life that constitutes the essence of the melodrama in most Ramlee films. People or events that threaten the normalcy of the village condition set off events, conflicts and resolutions that constitute the plot line of almost all his films. It is by examining what constitutes that threat, and how that threat is overcome, that we can best approach the underlying notions of Malayness that pervade Ramlee's early films. And the film about a fictionalised village called *Semerah Padi* is an excellent place to begin.

Civilising Nature and the Beast Within: Islam and Malay Modernism

Semerah Padi is a story of threat and village response that in turn exposes important underlying assumptions about the virtues of Malay civilisation. It is a historical drama, set in an unspecified golden age of Malay culture.[7] The background threat to the villagers of *Semerah Padi* throughout much of the film is posed by a band of apparently non-Muslim wild men from the nearby jungle (*hutan*). They first appear in the figure of one of their number who, the villagers learn, has been carrying out a wild affair with the wife of one of the villagers. When villagers burst in on the couple writhing in animal-like passion, they are dragged off and sentenced to death by the village Chief acting 'according to the laws of the Koran'. But the adulterer's brother vows to seek revenge on the village of *Semerah Padi*, and until they are finally defeated by the villagers under the leadership of the village warrior (*panglima*), played by Ramlee, they mount terrifying attacks during which they rape, burn and pillage from their secret hideouts in the jungle surrounding the village.

The film tells of a romance between the young village warrior named Aduka and the beautiful Dara, daughter of the village Chief (*penghulu*). Following her father's wishes, however, Dara becomes betrothed instead to a second warrior and deputy to the Chief, one Taruna, who is Aduka's closest friend and whose parents approach the Chief to arrange the marriage of their son. It soon becomes clear that while Taruna, being already enamoured of Dara, is delighted with the arrangement, Dara is succumbing unwillingly but obediently to her father's wishes. Aduka takes it on the chin, but not without a good deal of melodramatic moping. A kind of ceremony according to Malay custom (*adat*) duly takes place, although the actual wedding, which is due to follow the rituals associated with an Islamic wedding (*nikah*) does not follow, since in the mean time Taruna is called to lead a group of men appointed by the Chief to fight in the Sultan's army against pirates who are plaguing the coast.

While Taruna is away fulfilling his duty to both Sultan and Chief, Aduka and Dara are dramatically thrown together when he rescues her from the clutches of the bad guy who is leading the terrifying raids on the citizens of *Semerah Padi* by the forest-dwelling friends of the adulterer put to death in an early scene. After questioning by Dara about why he has been avoiding her, they both confess their love and, the film suggests discreetly, they consummate their forbidden love in an isolated hut.

Taruna returns triumphant, but soon realises something is wrong, and seeks out Aduka. Aduka eventually confesses by telling him that Dara is no longer a virgin (*gadis*), and urges Taruna to punish him by putting him to the sword. Taruna declines, saying that Aduka has forgotten God, and it is God who will punish him, and urges Aduka to run away. But Aduka is determined to accept his just punishment and confesses to the Chief, Dara's father, who as the political and religious leader of the community administers the punishment dictated by Islam, namely a public whipping for both Dara and Aduka. Although Taruna and other villagers beg him to stop the beating, the Chief remains firm.

Finally, Taruna visits a hurting and depressed Aduka at his mother's home, and tells Aduka that as he has now been punished according to the laws of the Koran, that Taruna also forgives him, and that Aduka can now marry Dara. The film ends with a version of the Muslim wedding ritual (*nikah*) and, presumably, Aduka and Dara live happily ever after.

The theme that unites these diverse plot lines is laid out quite early in the film in a number of scenes. For example, early on Taruna comes to report to the Chief, having been away in the 'interior' clearing the jungle so that irrigated rice fields (*sawah*) can be opened up by the villagers. The term actually used is *ulu*, literally 'upstream'. Among Malays the contrast between *ulu* and *ilir* ('upstream' and 'downstream') denotes a whole series of oppositions between jungle or bush and village, hence also between nature and culture, or, when applied to people, between country bumpkin and cultured villager or, more generally, primitivity or barbarism and civilisation. When the Chief praises Taruna for his efforts clearing the jungle, he speaks explicitly of the process as a civilising effort, of taming nature and turning it into habitable and cultivable land. This, he clearly indicates, is the civilising work of Malays.

In the scene in which the village Chief pronounces the death sentence on the adulterers, he begins by asking the man, Jejaka, what village he comes from. This is a common opening conversational gambit among Malays and Indonesians, even among those who live in cities, and indicates clearly the importance of village 'citizenship' even for urban Malays who may have long since abandoned their village residence. Instead of giving the name of a village, Jejaka replies: 'Wherever there is a pretty woman!' This clearly inappropriate and disrepectful response enrages the Chief, who proceeds to tell the couple: 'You are sinners against God, traitors to your country, your nation and religion.' Adultery is, he tells them, the worst crime against the laws of Islam, 'a law that separates men from beasts.' Having no *kampong*, coming from the *ulu* or the jungle, and committing adultery are all signs that Jejaka is uncivilised.

Underlying much of this is a distinction between what Malay and Indonesian Muslims call *Nafsu* and *Hawa*,[8] between desire and feeling. A good Muslim, it is believed, is someone who can overcome his physical/ natural desires (*nafsu*), and control them by means of an elevated or civilised subjective will (*hawa*). It is perhaps not surprising that someone who has no *kampong* should also be someone who gives in to base desires. It is at least implied here that Jejaka is neither a Malay (he has no *kampong*) nor is he a Muslim (since he does not even appear to recognise that he has committed a sin).

But, of course, the underlying theme of adultery is far more central, since it completely colours the lives and relationships of the main characters. Aduka and Dara throughout much of the film, members of the virtuous *kampong* republic, wrestle continuously with *nafsu*, their base sexual desires. Indeed this supplies perhaps the main dramatic tension, at least for those watching the film mainly for its romantic plot line (which has a tremendous appeal to a Malay village audience) rather than, say, for the action scenes (which appeal more especially to young Malay men watching such a film). What makes them models of Malay virtue is that they recognise this battle within them, and, when Aduka fails to control his *nafsu*, he not only accepts punishment but begs for an even more extreme punishment. Having been punished 'according to the laws of the Koran', he is then redeemed, and allowed to marry Dara. It may be significant here that Dara's marriage to Taruna was clearly never consummated, nor even was it formally completed in the eyes of God.[9]

Semarah Padi is a remarkable film for the way it combines a dramatic plot line and strong romantic themes with a rather thorough representation of the parameters of the virtuous Malay village republic. It portrays very clearly ideas central to a particular vision of a Malay–Muslim civilising project, but combines it with all the elements of a good romantic melo-drama expected by Malay audiences of the time. With its love themes, the suggestion of sex, adultery, battles, fighting and suspense, *Semarah Padi* remains an extremely engaging film to watch.

Many of these themes are taken up in other Ramlee films as we shall see. Adultery between characters who are romantically involved yet somehow separated by unjust circumstances, for example, seems to be a continuous obsession of Ramlee the film maker. And the clear messages about the virtues of *kampong* life echo throughout his filmic production. But before turning to these themes, it is worth asking about the nature of Ramlee's *kampong* idyll, since for all that it appears to evoke a golden – precolonial or premodern – age of Malay civilisation, it also contains themes and elements that can only be termed modernist, and it is these that are of most concern here.

We are of course used to assessing nostalgic narratives of the kind found in *Semerah Padi* in a rather different way – as testimony to the eruption of the premodern into modern consciousness, or to the rejection of modernity and celebration of the premodern. We might as a consequence be inclined to see in the Ramlee phenomenon evidence of the hold of a particularistic nationalism on the imagination at least of the Malay masses in the period immediately before Malaysian Independence in 1957, perhaps itself a consequence of an appeal to cultural essentialism encouraged by leaders' pursuing their own political agendas. In either case, Malaysia appears to fail the test of political modernity given the apparent absence, at least until quite recently, of any unifying national vision, and the central saliency of racial differentiation among the political masses, compared to the racial and cultural homogeneity that appears to characterise the iconic French experience.[10] In Eugene Weber's influential account of the emergence of national consciousness in France, for example, the key category 'Frenchmen' would appear to be both a universal and inclusive one (Weber, 1976), while the central category in the history of Malaysian nation-building – 'the Malays' – explicitly excludes what was at any one time up to one half of those residing in the territory governed by the British colonial state and then the government of the independent Federation. Viewed from this perspective, the Malaysian nation state would appear to be very fragile indeed, while French unity seems completely unproblematic.

But such an assessment derives from the problematic vision of modernity and modernism as abstract phenomena, disembedded from particularistic historical and cultural contexts, one difficult to maintain even for the French case.[11] In this regard, it is important to see the extent to which Malay ideas about the nation developed precisely out of a critical engagement with a colonial particularism masquerading as universalism. Witness, for example, a typical British view of their colonial subjects. Richard Wheeler was an Englishman who spent seven years in British Malaya, mostly in the state of Perak. Upon his return to England he felt compelled to write a book, published in 1928, which he somewhat paradoxically entitled *The Modern Malay*. Wheeler's first encounter with Malays was in Singapore where travellers:

> will see some boys diving for coins from primitive dugouts or playing ball with their passles with great dexterity as the ship comes in; these are of primitive Malay stock. Malay women are not allowed out in the street, as Muslim women are in Egypt and Java and other places where the struggle for a living in thickly populated areas has led to a breakdown of Muslim theory, at least as far as the

poor are concerned. But the few Malay men who are visible, mostly lounging in corners, look like women to the visitor, because they all wear the national skirt or 'sarong' practically down to their feet, with a feminine blouse or 'baju' loosely hanging over that. (Wheeler, 1928: 20)

But, Wheeler observed, cities are not the natural habitat of Malays:

The Malay does not flourish in cities, and has done nothing to develop them . . . The Malay must be sought for in the country; and even there his presence is not conspicuous at first glance, though the national custom of keeping women confined to the house . . . must be allowed for . . . save for a certain number seen on the roads and railway stations, mostly engaged in doing nothing in particular. (p. 21f.)

Wheeler pursues this narrative of a rural people in harmony with their environment describing Malays as 'aristocrats with their own philosophy',

that of the countryman who is content to live and let live amid restful and natural surroundings, while strangers from the continents of Europe and Asia live feverish lives in the quest for wealth and material things. . . . Few races offer a better opportunity for the study of this problem than the Malays. Their old traditions and beliefs have suffered no violent break; their docility and friendliness create a favourable atmosphere for that progress which is certainly necessary and which has already made great strides. But on the other hand a certain lassitude and passivity, partly natural, partly climatic, partly born of Islam, are favourable to a state of stagnation which, if not vitalized by new currents, can only end in decay. (p. 23)

Peasant villagers are the 'real Malays' of the peninsula:

conservative, prejudiced, loyal, affectionate, disinclined to take up new or extra work, improvident, loyal but not fanatical Muslims, with little education in the technical sense, knowing as a rule little or nothing of any language but their own, and that often chiefly in one of the many dialects . . . They are essentially village or 'kampong' dwellers, rarely moving far from their hamlet, whether it be set on poles over the sluggish waters of some crocodile-haunted estuary or mangrove swamp, or buried by some stream-side amid the thick foliage of the forest, broken only by the rice-fields which provide the chief subsistence and chief industry for the inland dwellers. These, near the sea, merge insensibly into the 'Orang Laut', or primitive Malays, who gain their living by fishing; the piracy of former times is replaced by rubber smuggling . . . In this and other ways the Malays are by no means averse to hard work when they can see a chance of both profit and sport. To them the lure of the city makes no appeal; they are dazed and even frightened by rapid streams of traffic and the noise of restless multitudes . . . (p. 193f.)

Turning to Malay history, Wheeler echoes a theme of much orientalist literature when he argues that at the dawn of British colonialism, the Malays had experienced centuries of 'decadence':

Here and there able and fortunate rulers . . . brought temporary prosperity to their districts. For the rest, the States were feeble and disunited. For hundreds of years the Peninsula had been raided by Portuguese, Achinese, Bugis and Siamese, torn by inter-State wars, and by feuds between rival chieftains . . . (p. 109)

Rulers imposed executions and mutilations; there was no medicine 'worthy of the name'; there was 'decay in religion and art', drunkenness and gambling; debt-slavery was universal and schools were unknown; the old skills in metalwork and weaving were fast disappearing; piracy was rampant; and the small population of Malays was swamped by a 'Chinese invasion' (pp. 109–114).

The Malay, observed Wheeler,

> has a keen appreciation of the use of a little money, if it can be got without undue exertion; but he does not see the force of sweating all day long for wages for someone else, and the higher classes are quite content to gain honour and position in the Government service rather than worship filthy lucre. (1928: 128f.)

All this appeared clearly to justify the British presence:

> For though much credit is due to the courage and labour of the Chinese, and not a little to Indian immigrants too, it cannot be too clearly grasped that nothing permanent would have been effected in Malaya except under Pax Britannica. (1928: 131)

Wheeler was a traveller who none the less managed to articulate rather clearly the relationship between British impressions of their Malayan subjects and the colonial mission. More definitive accounts of both, of course, were provided by colonial officials themselves, none more articulate, or with more first hand experience of life in peninsular Malaya around the turn of the century, than Hugh Clifford. Clifford was clear about the nature of the colonial project:

> What we are really attempting . . . is nothing less than to crush into twenty years the revolutions in facts and ideas which, even in energetic Europe, six long centuries have needed to accomplish. No one will, of course, be found to dispute the strides made in our knowledge of the art of government, since the Thirteenth Century, are prodigious and vast . . . (1993: 11)

Hugh Clifford was by no means a typical representative of colonial officialdom in British Malaya. Instead his thoughts are important precisely because he was distinctly atypical in the depth of his knowledge of and sympathies for the colonial subjects of the Malay peninsula, particularly the Malays. He first came to Malaya in 1883, and ended up staying for twenty years in various posts in the colonial administration, mainly in Perak and Pahang, and returned in the late 1920s as Governor. He acquired a good working knowledge of the Malay language, experiencing the 'frightening fascination' of living with 'a culture alien to his own, and coming to accept in some measure an alien system of values' (Roff in Clifford, 1993: xiii). Clifford, it is said, developed a strong sympathy for the Malay peoples, even entertaining doubts about the colonial project for its negative impact on the them:

> Clifford found in himself a strong natural sympathy with all classes of the Malay people, and the beginnings of a nagging doubt about the wisdom of wrenching a medieval society (as he liked to think of it), into the modern world . . . (p. xii)

In the passage cited above on the colonial mission, Clifford went on to confess a sympathy with the Malays who were 'suddenly and violently' transferred from their path of 'natural development', and 'required to live up to the standards of a people who are six centuries in advance of their national progress' (Clifford, 1993: 11).

Yet for all his experience of and empathy for his Malay subjects, and in circumstances which led European colonial ideologues elsewhere to proclaim the wisdom if not of independence, then at least of promoting forms of development more in keeping with indigenous cultural values,[12] Clifford clung firmly to the universalising narrative of 'civilisation' that characterised the ideology of the vast majority of British officialdom in colonial Malaya. Indeed, so close does Clifford's framing of the Malay question fit the classical 'apology for imperialism' that he could almost have been reading from the script of Edward Said's *Orientalism*. This particular group of colonial subjects are constituted as a racial other, a group of people who, although occupying the same historical time as Europeans, manifest in their social, economic and, particularly, political organisation all the characteristics of British society at an earlier time period.

The comparison with medieval Europe is particularly significant here. Malayan society in the nineteenth century is most commonly characterised as feudal, seen by nineteenth century British liberals as a society subject to the whims of petty princes and lords engaged in meaningless acts of symbolic status enhancement and conspicuous consumption, and captive to magical beliefs and superstition. Malays were therefore also most at home in the countryside, happier with the practice of agriculture for subsistence than industry, unwilling to work for wages, in short lazy[13] by the standards of modern bourgeois society. The Malays were backward, therefore, precisely because their political system discouraged hard work, thrift, providence and the achievement of 'real' goals. Progress inevitably meant overthrowing the arbitrary rule of the rajas and sultans and then educating the common Malays in the arts of modern economics and politics – things that the British were uniquely qualified to do, not for their own selfish reasons (like the Chinese), but because they of all the races in Malaya could do so disinterestedly.

Another feature of much orientalist discourse is also manifest in British images of the Malays, namely the way in which racialised and gendered discourses are closely intertwined. Wheeler portrays the Malays as both weak and feminine at the same time. Malay men, for example, are explicitly portrayed as feminine in both manner and dress, further strengthening the impression that they need protection against the more 'masculine' Chinese.

Finally an element of orientalist discourse crucial to Said's argument, but frequently overlooked, is also present here, namely the idea of decadence. In his discussion of French and British orientalists, Said pointed out that they saw the contemporary Middle East (and India) as debased in civilisational terms. It is this, importantly, that according to Said enabled orientalists to maintain that they could know the Arab, or the Indian, better than he could know himself, since true knowledge required knowledge of ancient languages, texts and archaeological remains. British observers like Wheeler also depicted Malay society as decadent – one which only the British could therefore know and improve.

From the point of view of late nineteenth century British liberal observers, at least the Malay peoples of British Malaya constituted a backward race, in this sense not all that different from the backward working classes at home, although with respect to the Malays British observers were more inclined to adopt a primitive-mania than the phobia they displayed towards the working classes at home. But similarly this race of not yet modern Malays could only become civilised through the benevolent intervention of the British themselves. Wheeler's 'modern Malay' was a British invention, or at least a British project.

As one might expect from a colonial officialdom wedded to primitivist ideas about racial advance, the anticipated end point of colonial nation builders in British Malaya was the emergence of a modern state, by which was understood a state ruling over a 'Malayan nation' of patriotic citizens regardless of religion, race and culture. Once the more 'backward' groups had been pushed along the path of civilization, a certain universal homogeneity of all citizens would be achieved. When, for various reasons, the British began to anticipate independence for their Southeast Asian colony, it is no surprise that they proposed a constitution based on supposedly European principles, including a 'multiracial "Malayan" patriotism to which they could devolve power' (Harper, 1996: 239).

And not surprisingly this proposal for what was called the 'Malayan Union' failed, not least because it was widely opposed by most sections of political opinion within the colony who recognised quite clearly that these supposedly universal principles were in fact derived from the cultural assumptions of an extremely narrow group of colonial subjects. As such it could not provide a culturally neutral public sphere within which the diverse interests of Malays, Chinese and Indians might be arbitrated:

> Colonial nation-building was an illusion. It attempted to cultivate a hybrid which had no real social roots beyond an English-educated, urban middle class based on the bureaucracy. It was contested at all levels of Malaysian society and was defeated by an Alliance made up of ethnic parties dominated by the United Malays National Organization (UMNO), later known as the National Front. (Harper, 1996: 239)

Nationalism in Malaya, then, was constituted in opposition to patriotism, not because one was culturally inflected and the other not, but because the 'culture' in the latter was explicitly recognised for its association with a very small group of middle class, anglicised colonial subjects who could in no sense 'speak' the culture of a homogeneous nation. Therefore sentiments more commonly equated with European nationalism in Malaya were quite explicitly sectional or communal. They did not embrace, and in most cases did not seek to embrace, all colonial subjects. There was therefore a Malay nationalist movement, but never a pan-Malayan one, while the other races were forced into a position from the start of merely seeking guarantees that in the new Federation, their rights to citizenship, if not membership in the nation, would be guaranteed. To quote Timothy Harper once again:

> The constitutional framework for the nation that emerged out of these debates – the Federation of Malaya – was very ambiguous. It gave limited citizenship rights to non-Malays; yet this citizenship did not amount to a nationality, and the citizenship rights for non-Malays in no way impinged on the special rights of the Malays. Malayness was enshrined in the Constitution; the new political entity was translated as *Persatuan Tanah Melayu* [literally Association of Malay Territories]. The 'Malayan' had no status, no legal definition at all. It was a state, but not a template for a nation. Thus, there remained fundamental contradictions between the formation of a new nation-state and the cultural basis on which it was to evolve. (Harper, 1996: 240)

While the nationalist imperative gave rise to a variety of understandings of what did constitute the culture of the nation, it came as no surprise that all were in one way or another self-consciously particularistic, not necessarily out of a rejection of modernity *per se*, but because modern universalism was itself exposed as self-evidently particularistic. The popular discourse on the virtuous *kampong* so clearly articulated in the films of P. Ramlee was one such attempt to define the contours of a modern Malay nation. Not surprisingly, a close look at other themes in the Ramlee *œuvre* reveals similar attempts to address pressing issues of concern to a modernising Malaysia.

Good Blood: Bad Blood – We Are All Human Beings

It might seem odd at first to argue that a discourse on the virtues of village life should be labelled modern, even if it is embedded as we shall see in a modern call for Malay sovereignty. And yet I would defend this characterisation for two reasons. First, like other counter-imperial discourses in the modern world, Malay cultural nationalism was self-consciously culturally particularist precisely because it rested on a critique of the pretence to universalism contained within colonial liberalism. The kind of colonial emancipation envisaged by Malaya's British rulers, while clothed in universalist language, was, as we have seen, based very much on the cultural presuppositions of a particular group of English-educated, middle class Malayans. In exposing the particularism of these claims, Malay nationalism self-consciously paraded its cultural roots, and these were to be found in the idea of the virtuous Malay *kampong*.

But this emerging popular vision of a Malay civilisation rooted in the *kampong* could be labelled modernising in another sense, since it also involved a full-blooded critique of Malay tradition from the standpoint of a universalising vision of human emancipation. But this emancipatory vision rested to a far greater extent than did contemporary liberal visions on notions of loyalty to a just patriarch (cf. Woodiwiss, 1998). A good example is found in its explicit critique of 'traditional' principles of Malay rule based on the privilege of aristocratic lineage. While present in a submerged form in

Semarah Padi, the critique of a system of social relationships structured by the presumed superiority of aristocratic blood comes much more to the fore in many other Ramlee films. One of the best known of such 'anti-aristocratic' films was *Antara Dua Darjat* (Between Two Levels/Classes), directed by Ramlee and released by Shaw Brothers in 1960. Once again a film with a strongly romantic theme, *Antara Dua Darjat* is set in the present, in a village somewhere in the State of Johore, the southernmost state on the Malay Peninsula. It begins with a scene in a large house in the village where an apparently wealthy man (Ungku Makri) is honeymooning at the request of his new wife, Zaleha. Present also is the wealthy man's best friend and their maid. During a dramatic thunderstorm first the maid and then Zaleha think they see a ghost peering through a window calling Zaleha's name. The audience soon learns that the apparition is not after all a ghost, but an ordinary villager and musician called Ghazali (the Ramlee character) who lives with his mother and cousin in a modest house in the main part of the village. Ghazali is berated by his cousin for continually returning to the big house, like a 'crazy man'. 'Zaleha is dead,' he tells him.

Much of the rest of the story unfolds through flashbacks, the main one being Ghazali's. Through the telling of his story we learn of Ghazali's first meeting with Zaleha, the daughter of a wealthy and aristocratic villager. Her car becomes stuck during a rainstorm, and the chauffeur goes in search of help, coming upon a group of musicians practising on the verandah of a village house. When the musicians, among them Ghazali, help push the car out of the mud, Ghazali sees Zaleha in the back seat and eventually persuades her to help push. She does so willingly, without regard for her obviously superior status.

They meet again at a birthday party thrown for Zaleha, with fancy guests in formal attire dancing to the music of Ghazali's band, hired for the occasion. The party ends with a group gathered round Ghazali's piano crooning a birthday song, a scene that could have come straight from a Bing Crosby movie. By this time it is evident that Zaleha and Ghazali have fallen in love. But we also know already that the love affair will be difficult. Zaleha has already been berated by her father for helping to push the car; he reminds her in no uncertain terms that being of aristocratic blood, she must avoid both physical labour and mixing with ordinary village folk.

Ignoring her father's warning, Zaleha uses the occasion of one of his many trips to Singapore to go to a remote garden accompanied by her maid to pick flowers. There she meets Ghazali, who comes here to seek inspiration for new songs, and their romance begins to flower. When the father returns, he once again berates Zaleha for going out in the *kampong*, and mixing with people of a different class (*darjat*).

But he also decides to hire her a piano tutor, who turns out, fortuitously for Zaleha, to be Ghazali. Zaleha learns western musical notation, and makes such rapid progress that in a short space of time she is able to play both a Tchaikovsky piano concerto, and a romantic ballad composed especially for her by Ghazali. At the same time romance blooms, and the two are pictured again in the *dusun*, paddling in the village stream, and holding hands strolling over a covered bridge. Finally they arrange to meet on the fringe of the village at night, with the maid sleeping in Zaleha's room to disguise her absence. At this meeting they declare their mutual love and embrace, although we the audience sense that something terrible is about to happen.

Inevitably the father and Zaleha's equally arrogant and 'blood' obsessed half-brother discover the ruse, track the lovers down and, with the help of some thug-like retainers, beat Ghazali unconscious and drag Zaleha back to the house. The full details of the night's events are not fully explained until the end of the film, when all the main characters have had their chance to 'flash back'. But we do learn that Ghazali's cousin saw Zaleha's apparent corpse being carted off in an ambulance immediately after Ghazali's beating, and we assume that she is, as the cousin keeps telling Ghazali, now definitely dead.

The occasion for more of the story to be revealed is provided when Ghazali and Zaleha finally do meet again, when he is called in by her husband to tune a piano. In Zaleha's flashback we learn that she did not die but was drugged and transported to Singapore by her family, that she had been defended against her father's wrath by her mother (a former bar girl, whom the father married hypocritically in spite of his obsession with blood and status), that in the ensuing argument her step-brother had killed her mother, that the step-brother had been arrested and her father had ultimately gone mad and been confined to a lunatic asylum, and that she became engaged to be married to Mukri, another Malay of noble blood and an international businessman who hoped to marry Zaleha to get hold of her father's property. Curious, she had begged Mukri to take her back to the village and the big house for their honeymoon.

After much agonising, both Zaleha and Ghazali recognise in each other the youthful lovers and, this time on the occasion of a trip by Mukri to Singapore, they resume their romance, committing adultery in the process. Mukri had asked his friend to keep an eye on Zaleha in his absence, but having learned the true story of Zaleha's and Ghazali's romantic history, he first covers up for them, and then pleads on their behalf for Mukri to divorce Zaleha and allow her to marry her true love. Mukri becomes enraged, seemingly kills his friend, and returns to the village with a shotgun to kill Ghazali. As he is about to fire he himself is shot, the friend (who has dragged himself up from the previous murder attempt) agrees to take the blame thus clearing the way for Ghazali and Zaleha to marry and live happily ever after.

Once again the theme of adultery is at the centre of a Ramlee film. This time the adulterous couple are not punished according to Islamic law. They are instead excused, largely it seems because Mukri turns out to be such a bad sort whose marriage to Zaleha had yet to be consummated. Mukri in turn, as it transpires, had a mistress in Singapore whom he promised to marry just as soon as he got hold of Zaleha's property, another thing stacked against him. This time, for whatever reason, the 'laws of the Koran', never referred to, appeared considerably less harsh.

Although the film, then, is very much concerned with the issue of adultery, equally important is the theme of blood, for through the characters of Zaleha's father, her half-brother and of her husband Mukri, we are invited to view the evils of appeals to status based on blood. Here the principle of high status deriving from aristocratic descent is portrayed as a violation of the spirit of *kampong* life, to say nothing of the threat it poses to the fulfilment of real love. But the standpoint is not the *kampong* only, since the virutes of the kampong are also presented as universal human virtues. Not only are the characters who claim aristocratic lineage corrupt and money-grabbing to a man, they also prove to be hypocrites. Zaleha's dutiful mother, who defends Zaleha against her father's lecturing and outbursts of temper, turns out to have been a bar girl with no aristocratic blood, who married the father for love. Zaleha's elder half-brother, unlike Zaleha a pure-blooded aristocrat, is so prone to violence he actually kills his step-mother. Mukri, the successful businessman, pictured returning from overseas on a BOAC jet, is interested only in Zaleha's property, and apparently forges a letter from her insane father to persuade her to marry him. All along he was keeping a mistress somewhere in Singapore. To make matters worse, Mukri makes a cowardly attempt on the life of a friend whose only crime was a compassionate plea to allow true love to run its course. The supposed superiority of those of noble blood is continually proven to be a sham – a pretence for both sexual and financial chicanery. The contrast with the virtuous and unpretentious *kampong* folk could not possibly be lost on the film's Malay audience.

The critique of the pretension to superiority of men of aristocratic blood, and the contrast with the virtues of the 'poor but honest' common folk, runs through many Ramlee films. Nowhere is it more clearly articulated than in *Abu Hassan Pencuri*, a version of *The Thief of Baghdad*, released in 1955 and directed by B.N. Rao. Here the Ramlee character, the petty thief Abu Hassan, falls in love with Tengku Faridah, daughter of the King (Raja) of Baghdad, and wins her love in return. But her father the King is appalled at Faridah's desire to marry the good-hearted Abu, seeking a more suitable spouse for his daughter among the princes of all the neighbouring kingdoms. Only after Faridah is kidnapped by one of their number, and the King offers his daughter's hand in marriage to whomsoever can rescue her, is the way cleared for true love to triumph at the expense of blood. Abu Hassan and his friend, with some magical intervention, duly rescue Faridah, and the King finally agrees to allow the two to marry.

Here the critique of the pretensions of blood is explicit in a number of scenes involving Faridah and her father. What is especially interesting is that in this film, as in most of those in which the question of aristocratic lineage is dealt with, it is the female lead who is given opportunity to carry the argument. In each of these scenes Faridah gently criticises her father's assumption that only a man of aristocratic blood should be allowed to marry a princess and, hence, live in the palace and ultimately rule. In the scene cited at the beginning of this book, Faridah first chides him and then strenuously resists the idea, scorning the assumption that blood makes any difference at all. We may be differently endowed with aristocratic lineage, she says, but after all we are all human beings (*manusia*), we all share the same fate (*kami semua sama nasib*) – a bit of dialogue that is repeated continuously throughout the film. Abu Hassan's miraculous rescue ultimately proves his worth, even in the eyes of the Raja.

This popular critique of aristocratic privilege is linked to a central part of the Malay nationalist project, one that is often lost sight of by those who see in popular conceptions of Malay-ness a traditionalist rejection of modernity. James Scott, whose influential work on popular conceptions of morality and justice among Malay peasants, for example, rightly sees them as articulating a critique of the moral economy of capitalism in particular and instrumental rationality and the discourse of rational mastery more generally. He reports on the widespread use by Malay villagers of an unfavourable contrast between local elites motivated by instrumentalism, and apparently more traditional patrons and landowners who were willing to meet minimum peasant demands for subsistence and justice (Scott, 1985).

But it is equally important to note that this is not a simple backward-looking ideology about the behaviour of Malay elites in some golden age of Malay history. To do so would be to miss the centrality both in popular discourse and the ideas of nationalist intellectuals and political leaders of a parallel critique of aristocracy, and all traditional forms of authority, a critique based on a commitment to the equality of all human beings. From the time of the early Islamic modernist Munshi Abdullah, Malay nationalism has been linked explicitly to an attack on the traditional Malay rulers (rajas) for their despotism and arbitrary exercise of power, for their wasteful consumption and for their later collaboration with the colonial regime (cf. Milner, 1995). It is not surprising that many Malay nationalists use the term 'feudal' to characterise traditional Malay society,[14] echoing the critiques of colonial liberals of traditional forms of Malay rule. The popular version of this nationalist critique is to be found in the attack on the idea that aristocratic lineage should bring with it the right to rule that is so central to many of Ramlee's films.

It was precisely this popular hostility to the Malay aristocracy that led Malay nationalists to lose patience with their leaders in the first decade of Independence, posing an early threat to the government of Malaysia that some have blamed for the violence and instability of the late 1960s.[15] And it explains the unwavering hostility of the current regime to the 'special privileges' enjoyed by the sultans. This has been interpreted by some observers as further evidence of the prime minister's desire to erode the principle of the separation of powers. But while he is undoubtedly hostile to any challenge to his own executive supremacy, this fails to explain the popularity among Malays of attempts to curb the powers of the so-called traditional rulers.

The popular critique of blood privilege found throughout the Ramlee *œuvre*, therefore, is at the same time a modernising discourse on good leadership in general. A good leader here is not someone born to the role, not someone who literally lords it over the good folk of the *kampong*. Instead, he is personified in the ordinary man who has earned his position by showing himself to be stern, wise in the ways of Islam and Malay custom and just, an otherwise ordinary villager admired for his personal qualities, a leader in short personified by the traditional village chief (the *penghulu*), not the person with aristocratic blood running through his veins and an inherited title.

It is thus possible for a discourse to be at once opposed to the further instrumentalisation of everyday life and at the same time modernising – the former, to use the distinction made by Castoriadis (1991), concerns the modernist principle of rational mastery, the latter instead focuses on autonomy. But if this Malay nationalist notion of emancipation is quite clearly modernising, it also differs from classical liberal notions of individual autonomisation in the emphasis given to the virtues of good leadership rather than individual liberty. The popular critique of aristocratic privilege articulated in Ramlee's films is not an attack on hierarchy so much as a critique of arbitrary rule. The tendency to emphasise the rights and duties of rulers and ruled over the rights of individuals is frequently seen, by advocates and critics alike, as evidence of the survival of traditional Asian values into the modern age. Yet as the discussion above suggests, it is more accurately described as a modern alternative to more individualised notions of emancipation of the kind found particularly in British liberalism.

The sociologist Andrew Woodiwiss, following Weber, characterises this discourse as 'patriarchalism', arguing that it is 'a mode of governance where, whilst social relations remain distinctly hierarchical, the content of benevolence is democratically decided and its delivery is legally enforced' (1998: 3), hence making it at least arguably a viable alternative to liberal versions of modern political autonomisation. Moreover one could go further to suggest that similarly modern forms of patriarchalism are not unknown in the West, as the example of at least some political machines in early twentieth century American cities discussed below will show.

And while in popular versions of Malay nationalism, such as that constructed in the Ramlee films, there is evidence that the principle of autonomy is manifest in popular discourse on the good leader, the place where autonomisation (the idea of the emancipated, self-created subject) is most evident is in the representation of romantic love.

Love Conquers All

In his study of intimacy in modern societies, Anthony Giddens engages in an argument with Foucault, not in order simply to dismiss Foucault's arguments about modern sexuality as a mode of discipline, but to draw out the ambivalence of modern intimate relationships. Romantic love, which according to Giddens is peculiar to modern society, and the intimate relationships which it infuses are not just about the oppression of women, though doubtless they can and have functioned in this way. Instead, modern intimacy based on romantic love, argues Giddens, is also 'the harbinger of the pure relationship'. In this sense modern intimacy 'implies a wholesale democratising of the interpersonal domain, in a manner fairly compatible with democracy in the public sphere' (Giddens, 1992: 3).

Giddens argues that romantic love is a distinctively modern practice, emerging during the nineteenth century in Europe when marriage ties began to be formed based on 'considerations other than judgements of economic value' (1992: 26). While the idea of passionate love may be universal, romantic love associated particularly with courtship and marriage is, for Giddens, a distinctively modern discourse. This notion of romantic love as the basis of marriage relations began, argues Giddens, among the bourgeoisie and from them spread to the rest of society. Romantic love introduced the idea of narrative into the lives of individuals, and so not surprisingly its emergence is linked to the rise of the novel. Romantic love entails the idea of freedom; it tends to be associated with ideas of sublime love rather than sexual ardour alone; it generally entails the idea of love as instant attraction (love at first sight); and is linked with the ascendancy of reason (1992: 40–41). The emergence of romantic love, according to Giddens, was linked to a number of other changes associated with the modernisation of society: the creation of the home as a 'distinctive environment set off from work . . . and hence . . . a place where individuals could expect emotional support, as contrasted with the instrumental character of the work setting' (1992: 26); the development of the idea of the possibility and desirability of limiting family size which in turn contributed to the development of the idea of sexuality, part of a 'progressive differentiation of sex from the exigencies of reproduction'; changing relationships with parents; and the invention of both childhood and, particularly, the cult of motherhood. It can therefore be associated with patriarchy. But romantic love, Giddens suggests, is essentially feminised love and as such can both oppress and empower women. Unlike passionate love,

> romantic love detaches individuals from wider social circumstances in a different way. It provides for long-term life trajectory, oriented to an anticipated yet malleable future; and it creates a 'shared history' that helps separate out the marital relationship from other aspects of family organisation and give it a special primacy. (Giddens, 1992: 44–45)

Many of these themes are played out in the Ramlee films. Indeed, just as the romance and the novel are co-terminous, reflexively providing a language through which people can construct their own lives and search for intimacy through the concept of romantic love, so Ramlee's films both reflect a modernisation of intimate relations in Malay society, and, as the first form of mass entertainment, also served to constitute such modern relations.

While Ramlee's films give us an insight into a variety of themes in popular discourse on the 'Malay dilemma', there is little doubt that their main appeal is generated by their romantic storylines. The films are all basically about romantic love in the Giddens sense, the obstacles posed to it, and the ways its male and female characters overcome the odds to establish intimate relations. In *Antara Dua Darjat* the love between Ghazali and Zaleha is ultimately fulfilled after years of their being separated by the vagaries of *darjat* (rank/status). Dara is kept apart from her beloved Aduka throughout most of *Semarah Padi* until they have overcome her father's desire that she should marry Taruna. Abu Hassan has to wait until Faridah breaks down her father's opposition to her marrying a commoner, and has ultimately to prove himself a better man than her aristocratic suitors, in *Abu Hassan Pencuri*.

In the 1968 film *Ahmad Albab*, a Middle Eastern fantasy directed by Ramlee for Merdeka during his Kuala Lumpur years, a Sjech (sheik) is determined to marry off his three daughters. The two foolish daughters agree to his wishes, and marry the two scheming young men whom he persuades. The third, Mastura, a thoughtful and thoroughly virtuous modern young woman, refuses, saying she will find her own husband and chooses Sjawal, a simple village boy whom she loves. The father's choices turn out badly – both promise their fathers that they will rob their father-in-law of all his wealth, but end up pawning their wives' jewellery, flirting in cabarets and, eventually, thieving to keep afloat. Sjawal, however, becomes successful, and uses his wealth to help his fellow villagers and, ultimately, his hapless brothers-in-law, whom he bails out when they are imprisoned for theft. Even the Sjech is brought on side when he realises that it is Sjawal who has made a success of his life. Wealth, happiness – everything comes from God, Sjawal informs his father-in-law at the end of the film and, he might have added, a marriage that is a personal project of husband and wife. Here as elsewhere in Ramlee's films, romantic love shifts what is constituted as the traditional relationship between father and daughter, son-in-law and father-in-law. No longer, it is implied, can relations with parents determine (*paksa*) a daughter's own romantic narrative.

Moreover, as Giddens implies, romantic love is feminised in the Ramlee stories. They almost always tell of intelligent and modern daughters reversing roles with fathers – it is now the former who are wise, the latter either tyrannical or foolish. Marriages may oppress wives, but in Ramlee's stories that happens only when marriage is based on economic considerations. Otherwise it empowers them, or so the ideology goes.

Not a particularly successful film, none the less *Ahmad Albab* reworks many of the central themes of most Ramlee films – a young woman's right to choose her own husband, rather than to have one forced on her by a father's wishes which are, in any case, motivated by greed rather than concern for his daughter's happiness. Marrying for love, here as elsewhere a commoner and ordinary villager, is always better, and almost inevitably also brings its own rewards: happiness and, more often than not, wealth as well. Marriage explicitly for wealth usually ends in disaster.

Derivative Modernism?

Before moving on to consider the exclusionary possibilities of this third example of popular modernism, we must anticipate an objection to the argument that it is possible to consider Malay modernism to be on a par with the liberalism and republicanism already considered. The objection goes like this: certainly we can find traces of a universalising modernist sensibility in a place like colonial Malaya. It would be surprising if this were not the case given the cultural and intellectual hegemony exerted for so long there by the British. But Malay modernism is surely no more than a 'derivative' phenomenon, to borrow the term used by Chatterjee similarly to criticise Indian nationalism as a colonial imposition, given wider credence because it was articulated by English-educated Indian elites during the colonial period (Chatterjee, 1986). A softer version of the same objection would have it that Malaysian modernism is to be understood as the 'indigenisation' of notions of modernity flowing into the country from outside, here through the distinctly western medium of modern cinema. This would still have the effect of denying that in this case we are dealing with a phenomenon of the same order as, for example, English liberalism or American republicanism.

In terms of the images they construct, P. Ramlee's films manifest some at first sight rather striking parallels with British representations of Malay culture and society, which might lead one to the view that all Ramlee did was to reverse the negative assessment of the Malay village life inherent in the writings of British apologists for empire like Wheeler. Certainly both Wheeler and Ramlee were engaged in what some of have been tempted to call the project of the 'invention' of tradition. But on closer examination, it would be difficult to defend the notion that no significant differences exist between Ramlee's and colonial representations of the Malay village republic. In the latter, for example, Malay villagers are clearly viewed through the lens of liberal evolutionism, which explains among other things the frequent use of natural imagery to describe both the Malays and their surroundings. Consider again Wheeler's images of the Malay village, 'whether it be set on poles over the sluggish waters of some crocodile-haunted estuary or mangrove swamp, or buried by some stream-side amid the thick foliage of the forest' (1928: 20). Contrast this with the image of the village of *Semarah Padi* in the Ramlee film of the same name. Far from being viewed as standing in harmony with nature, the Malay village is seen as a prime example of a nature tamed, even mastered, by a Malay–Muslim civilising impulse. Here as elsewhere, the parallels between the Malay discourse on the virtuous village republic, and the primitivising discourse articulated by colonial writers like Clifford and Wheeler, prove to be rather superficial.

This objection that Malay popular modernism is a derivative discourse can be seen ultimately to be specious. This is not to deny that 'ideas' exert 'influences', both within and across national boundaries, although why the former should be considered unproblematic, while the latter attract labels like derivative remains a mystery. But the important point here is that modernism in a place like Malaysia was in no simple sense derived from the West. Forms of modernist discourse can be shown to have been contemporaneous with, rather than subsequent to, the two other national imaginaries considered here. Consider, for example, the case of Abdullah Abdul Kadir or Munshi Abdullah (1797–1854). While he has been considered by Malay historiographers to have been a mere mouthpiece for western, especially British, liberalism, and hence an early apologist for colonial intervention, an important recent study has shown that Munshi Abdullah's 'liberal' critique of Malay society, and particularly of a political regime within which the raja (king) was the focal point, drew as much on Muslim and Malay sources as it did on European ones (see Milner, 1995). The quite original notion of emancipation through attachment to the just patriarch testifies to this fact.

Much the same can be said of the central themes articulated in the films of P. Ramlee. The developing discourse on romantic love with its positive valuation of freedom and its criticism of compulsion (*paksa*) in the formation of intimate relationships is, as we have seen, a central theme in the films of Ramlee, indeed it could be said to be the dominant theme in Malay popular culture as a whole. Given the focal position of romance in western popular culture, one might again be tempted to see in this parallel evidence of cultural borrowing, even cultural imperialism.

And yet it would be greatly to oversimplify this complex of romantic ideals in Malaysian film and music if we were to see it as a mere copy of western ideas about intimacy. Certainly 'western' and 'eastern' ideas about romance have influenced each other, although just as certainly the influences have not all been one way. But equally certainly the romantic complex in Malay popular culture emerged in the context of a particular set of historical changes in Malay social and religious life that began at least as far back as the mid-nineteenth century, and, as recent studies have suggested, it has for some time been heavily inflected by internal developments within Malay culture itself. In short it may well be that the ideas about romantic love more recently articulated by P. Ramlee have their origins in far older Malay cultural traditions (see, for example, Hooker, 2000; Wazir, 1990).

Doubtless, then, the reasons for the more or less simultaneous appearance of modernising cultural impulses in such apparently widely dispersed social universes need further exploration. But it makes sense to consider the three to be part of an interrelated discursive field of contestation within Anglophone modernity – rather than assuming from the start, for example, that while white former colonial subjects in North America were capable of an original modernist synthesis, their brown counterparts in Southeast Asia were not. Just as early twentieth century primitivists in Britain contested the liberal utopia of an urbanised, technologically advanced Britain, just as North American republicans were forced to orient themselves, if highly critically, to ideas of European civilisational maturity, so Malay 'cultural nationalists' were drawn into a conflict with the British for the right to define the contours of a Malay(si)an nation state. In all three cases these modernist sensibilities were inflected by or drew upon more localised cultural meanings, all interrogating modernity from somewhat different terrains. But it is as misleading to speak of any one as derivative of another, as it would be to see in any one a simple case of the indigenisation of a set cultural meaning first created elsewhere.[16]

Malay Exclusions

We have traced an emerging discourse in Malay popular culture in the years before 1957 when Malaysia achieved independence from its British colonial masters, at the same time looking at the ways in which its central themes served to interrogate those very same processes of economic, political and social modernisation that made popular culture possible in the first place – urbanisation, economic transformation, bureaucratisation, the constitution of a public, technological changes in the entertainment industry, the rise of modern culture industries in the region and the like. The Ramlee phenomenon can be seen as a response to these developments at the level of popularly constructed meanings, calling into question as it did modern processes of commodification, bureaucratisation, and the instrumentalisation of everyday life. It did so from the terrain of a Malay–Islamic village republic where a virtuous modern life be could be lived by ordinary Malays.

But modernisation is not a homogenising process. As everywhere where modernity has transformed the life ways of a people, modernisation in Malaya did not give rise only to homogeneous communities of village-dwelling Malays. On the contrary, the very processes that gave rise to Malay popular culture, and that enabled the formation of this particular form of popular consciousness, also generated increasing rather than decreasing levels of social and cultural diversity in the region.

Malayan economic modernisation, for example, took place only through a large-scale influx of 'foreigners' into the peninsula. British and other western entrepreneurs, along with Indian and Arab traders, and Chinese merchants and capitalists, were instrumental in the development of the capitalist economy, while migrants from the Indonesian archipelago, China and India supplied the labour without which the colonial economy would have been impossible. Between 1881 and 1900, for example, nearly two million immigrants from China came to the Federated Malay States, mainly to work in the burgeoning tin mining industry itself controlled by Chinese capital. The result was that by the turn of the century the total number of

Chinese in much of British Malaya was about equal to the size of the Malay population (Milner, 1995: 91). While many Chinese migrants were temporary, new migrants more than made up the numbers of those returning to the homeland. And through the first few decades of the twentieth century, the character of the Chinese migrant community gradually changed. At first mainly transients determined to return to China, Chinese Malayans, including a growing number who were locally born, increasingly came to view themselves as permanently resident.

Indians too have a long history of travel to the Malay peninsula. For centuries they had come as merchants, religious proselytisers, even rulers. With the development of a modern plantation economy, the pace and style of Indian immigration changed as poorer Indians from the South came to work as plantation labourers. By 1911 Indians constituted 10 per cent of the population of British Malaya, the proportion rising to 14.3 per cent in 1931 (Kratoska and Batson, 1992: 314). Neither Chinese nor Indian immigrants and their descendants constituted homogeneous groups. On the contrary, both groups were highly diversified on linguistic, cultural and religious grounds. The modern classification of the peoples of Malaysia and Singapore into four discrete groups – Malay, Chinese, Indian, Other – is very much a modern invention.[17]

Constituting a discrete population of Malays, therefore, similarly required imposing a homogeneity on a group of people that was both internally diverse and lacking in any clear sense of their own identity. Many who came to be classified as 'Malay', or whose descendants subsequently became Malay, were themselves relatively recent migrants. The development of modern Malay peasant communities of small-scale cash croppers and rice farmers was the outcome of substantial immigration and mixing of peoples, many of whom came from what was then the Netherlands East Indies (now Indonesia). The flow of people into British Malaya in the early colonial period points to just how recent and culturally diverse the population of 'Malays' really was:

> Many areas of the peninsula previously under forest or swamp and occupied, if at all, only by aborigines were settled by indigenous Malays and by Javanese, Banjarese, Sumatrans, and other immigrants from the archipelago during these years . . . Indigenous Malays migrated from Kedah and Perlis to the Krian, Kurau, and Selama areas of Perak; Patani Malays [from what is now Thailand] moved south to the upland districts of Ulu Krian and Ulu Perak in Perak; Kelantan Malays settled in Kuala Selangor . . . and in almost every district of Perak. A large increase in the non-Chinese population in western coastal Johore dated from the 1870s, when Malay and then Javanese pioneers in the alluvial lowlands cleared forest and planted . . . [crops] for their own use and for sale in Singapore . . . Javanese immigrants settled in coastal areas in Klang, Kuala Langat, and Kuala Selangor; they also settled inland in the Ulu Langat valley in Selangor. Banjarese from southern Kalimantan [Indonesian Borneo] migrated to the Krian district beginning in the 1870s, drained swampland and began intensive wet-rice cultivation there. Banjarese also settled in Kuala Selangor on the coast. In the 1880s and 1890s, both Javanese and Banjarese cleared the alluvial swamps of Lower Perak and the Dindings and planted coconuts and rice. Sumatrans

pioneered settlement in inland areas of Selangor . . ., Perak, and northern Johore as tin miners, petty traders, and wet-rice agriculturalists. The migratory flows initiated in these years between specific areas of the Indonesian archipelago and regions and districts in the peninsula continued over the next fifty years, reaching a peak during the two decades from 1911 to 1930. (Nonini, 1992: 53f.)

Given this immense diversity of peoples and cultures associated with the development of modern Malaya, it is appropriate to ask how popular Malay modernism handled the question of diversity.

We have already seen some of the ways in which popular culture in other parts of the Anglophone world engaged with the diversity in their midst, and the exclusions which resulted from them. In Britain, liberal evolutionism and then primitivism were in different ways at least in part a response to the apparent 'otherness' of the working class, constituting workers as primitives in opposition to a homogenous civilised/modern self. American popular republicanism constructed the category of America out of a contrast with a decadent Europe, at the same time constructing African Americans and new immigrants as either not yet American or deeply un-American.

Malay nationalism constituted its image of Malayness largely in opposition to the elitist cosmopolitanism of its British rulers and the small, anglicised Malayan elite who served them. In doing so they drew on certain longstanding themes in rural Malay culture, but also and significantly on assumptions spread through a Malayan version of Islamic modernism. Earlier, in the nineteenth century, such an identity could scarcely be said to have existed at all.[18] Popular notions of Malayness were therefore a precipitate of the changes wrought during the period of British colonial rule and Ramlee's narratives provide an excellent guide to the contours of this new Malay identity, particularly as it developed in the popular consciousness.

But what strikes the outside observer about Ramlee's images of Malayan society perhaps more than anything else is their almost total lack of reference to the non-Malay population of the peninsula. The viewer of the films discussed above could be forgiven for assuming that perhaps apart from forest-dwelling aboriginals, represented as primitive versions of the Malay self, not yet able to control their base desires, Malaya was populated entirely by culturally homogeneous village communities of Malay-speaking Muslims. Unlike the case for turn of the century Britain or the United States, early Malay popular culture was characterised by a complete and total silence about the lives of more than half of the population living within the boundaries of what was to become the modern state. These peoples do not appear as stereotypes, negative or positive. If we are to judge from a viewing of Ramlee's early films, they simply did not exist at all. While contemporary liberalism and primitivism seemed on the whole to view human diversity as a consequence of natural difference, and popular republicanism cast the other in the mould of the cultural alien, Malay–Islamic modernism, at least in its popular guise, constructed the other only by refusing to name it at all.

This hole or gap in popular Malay consciousness is difficult for an outsider to understand or even appreciate. But judging from my own experience living in a Malay village for an extended period of time, and numerous visits of differing lengths to Malaysia since the mid-1970s, there is little doubt that the silence about 'ethnic' Chinese that so strikes a viewer of Ramlee films is very real, especially among Malay villagers. A westerner, used to both the widespread practice of ethnic and racial stereotyping back home, as well as to broad concern or even interest in cultural otherness in academia, tourism, journalism, comedy, and advertising as well as daily conversation, is quite unprepared for the fact that Malays, most of whom are in daily contact with Chinese and members of other 'ethnic' groups, rarely show interest or even concern with them at all. Their presence in Malaysia may be acknowledged, occasionally hostility may be expressed, but it very rarely goes beyond that.

This is not to suggest that Malaysia is a society where the fact of diversity is unrecognised. On the contrary, it is a society that, at least until recently and among certain groups, is deeply racialised. In the everyday lives of citizens, it is no exaggeration to say that racial identity is a matter of absolute first principle for almost all Malaysians. It is literally the first thing Malaysians notice about a person, and the first thing they want to know about someone whose racial identity they have yet to establish. The system of racial identities/identifications is in some sense then the phenomenological foundation of all social life in Malaysia. It is, or at least was until very recently, probably the key determinant of everyday social interaction, the first principle in determining networks of friendship as well as residential arrangements, and the choice of marriage partners. While patterns of spatial segregation laid down in the colonial period – Malays in villages, Chinese in cities and towns, Indians on plantations or in urban areas depending on occupation – have broken down in the years since Independence as a consequence of new employment patterns and rapid urbanisation, residential and to a decreasing extent interactional segregation remains the norm.

The racialisation of Malaysian society is no less marked at the institutional level. The main political parties have always been race-based. There has never therefore been a single ruling party as in Singapore and Indonesia, but always a ruling coalition of race-based parties. Yet within all branches of government the domination of Malays is ensured, and the problems of the Malay 'community' are always the top priority of the state. Because the category Malay is also a legal category it is the subject of legal definition.[19]

Finally, as one might expect, conflict, whether in the national political arena or at the local level is almost inevitably constructed as racial conflict. Malaysia has not experienced racial violence on anything approaching the scale or intensity of places like Sri Lanka, Rwanda or Guatemala, or even parts of Europe. None the less, the bloody race riots of 1969 remain strong in the collective memory of most Malaysians, and the fear of re-occurrence is strong, particularly among the older generation.

But all this takes place in a context in which, for Malays at least, the category Chinese is a more or less empty one. Although the term 'racial' is most frequently used to describe this classificatory scheme, there is no developed thinking – scientific or otherwise – on the nature of race and racial difference, very little history of popular racial stereotyping in the popular media, almost no research by Malay academics on Chinese history, language, or culture. While Chinese in everyday conversation are quite happy to make jokes based on Malay stereotypes, it almost never happens the other way around. Apparently when the prime minister felt Malays should be encouraged to be more entrepreneurial by emulating Chinese Malaysians, he had to appeal by proxy as it were to the advantages of adopting a Japanese work ethic. This may partly have been a consequence of Malay hostility to Chinese Malaysians, but it doubtless was also a response to this silence about the Chinese in Malay popular culture.

Just as this 'exclusion by silence' is difficult to appreciate, so it is also hard to explain why it came about. It may have its origins in an earlier system through which one's status and identity were entirely determined by one's links to a political ruler or raja, rather than being the consequence of membership in a cultural community (cf. Milner, 1982). Groups like the indigenous *orang asli*, although they did not share affiliation to Islam, could none the less be recognised as primitive versions of the Malays, not so much because of cultural similarities (although these did exist), but because they did play an identifiable economic and political role within Malay kingdoms. Even as slaves, or potential slaves, they acquired a particular status in the traditional political systems on the peninsula.[20] Similarly most cultural groups in the region – in both Indonesia and Malaysia – have rules about incorporating what are generally referred to as 'latecomers' (*orang datang*) into village communities, through the granting of use rights to land for farming and house plots. In this way such newcomers are gradually incorporated into village communities, first through opening up new land for cultivation, then through intermarriage. Chinese labourers, merchants and entrepreneurs did make contracts with sultans and kings, but usually not to carry out traditional village agricultural activities, and these contracts gave them no social or political status whatsoever. Together with early Chinese patterns of circular migration, this may explain why early Malay nationalists always treated the Chinese among them as temporary, even when later on it became evident that many considered themselves resident with no intention of returning to China.

Certainly British attitudes towards the Chinese would have contributed towards this tendency to treat the Chinese as essentially irrelevant to the long term future of the nation – although so necessary to the economy of the colony, the Chinese were invariably seen by the British as interlopers, and not as potential beneficiaries of the British civilising mission. If anything, as the above quotations from Wheeler show, the British viewed the Chinese as a threat to the Malays, the latter always seen as the main object of British attempts to civilise its colonial subjects. The special position of the Malays was generally accepted by the British colonial rulers, and the fact that it carried over into the attitudes of postcolonial governments shows that one of the central planks of the Malay nationalist platform in no way contradicted colonial policy.

The ways in which separate social spaces were constructed for Malays and Chinese in the colonial period also goes some way towards explaining how it could appear that the two races occupied entirely independent social worlds. For many Malays in the colonial period towns were not seen either as centres of civilisation or as alien places but as completely separate social universes, an impression certainly confirmed in the Ramlee films. In *Antara Dua Darjat*, discussed above, some of the action takes place in Singapore. And yet we see very little of Singapore itself, nor do we even catch a glimpse of any Chinese characters in this overseas Chinese city at the heart of the colonial polity and economy.

Although this extreme social segregation of Chinese and Malays may have broken down, particularly since the early 1970s, pressures to maintain residential segregation remain strong in places like Kuala Lumpur and Penang, particularly for those Malays who can afford to live on all-Malay housing estates, and in predominantly Malay neighbourhoods. Once, when going around a small Malaysian town with a Chinese friend, a town I thought I knew from previous visits, I was struck by the extent to which Chinese and Malay town dwellers carry radically different maps of urban space around in their heads, the main routes of their daily lives very rarely intersecting. This segregation is further hardened by the food taboos of most Malays, who will not even go to the same coffee shops as Chinese friends for fear of being served food that is not *halal* or being in the presence of those drinking alcohol. Those who do go to such places to avoid the strictures on Malay eating and drinking know that they are leaving their own social universe, even if temporarily.

It remains to be seen whether recent changes in Malaysia are serving to break down this particular Malay culture of silence about Chinese Malaysians. But what it does show is that popular Malay–Islamic modernism as it developed in the colonial period was just as exclusionary as were British primitivism and American republicanism, although this time othering took a very particular form. For many Malays in the late colonial period it was as if the Chinese really did not exist.

Notes

1 The secondary material on P. Ramlee cited here is taken from Lockard (1998), especially on his music, and from various web sites which provide information on his film career.

2 Astral is a subsidiary of Maxus which was owned mainly by Ananda Krishna, a prominent businessman known to be close to Prime Minister Mahathir Mohamed, although as a result of the 1997 financial crisis, Krishna sold a substantial holding of Maxus to British Telecom in what one commentator described as a 'firesale'.

3 Between 1947 and 1962, Shaw Brothers employed no less than ten Indian film directors: B.S. Rajhans, S. Ramanathan, L. Krishnan, K.M. Bashker, B.N. Rao, V. Grimaji, K.R.S. Shastry, Phani Majumdar, Diresh Gosh and Kidar Sharma.

4 I am using the term consumption here in the sense given to it by the Japanese sociologist Yoshino, whose work on the idea of Japanese uniqueness (*nihonjirnron*) is particularly insightful. Yoshino maintains that much of the literature on national identity, especially in Japan, rests on interpretations of the intentions of the state, or of political and intellectual elites, and thus ignores the problem that these images may well be 'read' or 'consumed' in divergent ways by their intended audience. It is therefore important, if one wants to understand how non-elite Japanese think about national identity, to examine these processes of consumption. For example, to understand the popularisation of *nihonjinron* ideas, he examines not the texts of novelists and intellectuals, which have a fairly limited readership, but the texts produced by popularisers of these ideas intended for company employees (see Yoshino, 1999).

5 Mahathir's *The Malay Dilemma*, first published in 1969, was banned by the leadership of the political party he now heads, UMNO. Shahnon Ahmad is probably the most widely respected Malay novelist in the post-Independence period, and in spite of significant differences, there are also some important parallels between Shahnon's early accounts of Malay village life, and the image of a backward Malay race in urgent need of uplift painted by the future prime minister (see Kahn, 1994; Mahathir, 1970; Shannon, 1977).

6 These are some of the main tropes of the village that have since appeared time and time again in novels and plays and, more recently, in a culture industry appealing to the nostalgic yearnings for the *kampong* experienced by urban middle class Malays (see Kahn, 1996).

7 The prototype of which in most such Malay historical dramas is the Sultanate of Malacca, which was taken over by the Portuguese in the early sixteenth century. So we assume films like *Semerah Padi* are set in the time before the coming of the Portuguese, a time generally considered to be a golden age of Malay civilisation.

11 A lucid discussion of the *hawa/nafsu* opposition is provided by James Siegel in an early analysis of Islam among the Acehnese of northern Sumatra (see Siegel, 1969). For a discussion of this opposition in a Malay context, see Wazir Jahan Karim (1990).

9 The ceremony carried out according to Malay custom (*adat*) is described in the film only as a ceremony of betrothal (*bertunangan*), implying that a proper marriage can only be recognised after the Muslim *nikah*.

10 The distinction between a 'normal' French model of modern nation building, and a 'pathological' German one, appears in the work of Louis Dumont, among others, who resurrects the contrast between supposed French universalism and German particularism to explain the success of national socialism in the latter but not the former. The possibility of making such a distinction also informs Habermas's critique of national identity, but corresponding support for the civic values of citizenship (Habermas, 1995), and Appadurai's critical observations on nationalism, and his defence of patriotism (Appadurai, 1993). See Llobera (1996) for a summary and critique of Dumont's contrast between French and German forms of nation building, and Chatterjee (1986) for a similar critique of the liberal distinction between good and bad, or normal and pathological, nationalisms.

11 For a specific critique of the French pretence to cultural neutrality, see Lebovics, 1992.

12 At much the same time, for example, colonial officials and scholars in the Netherlands East Indies were abandoning both the classical imperial project of civilising the natives, and the 'social Darwinist' schemas that underpinned it (see Kahn, 1993).

13 Syed Husin Alatas's influential book on colonial images of indigenous Southeast Asia investigates this myth of the lazy Malay (Syed Husin Alatas, 1977).

14 See, for example, Syed Husin Alatas (1977).

15 One manifestation of this unhappiness with the UMNO leadership is found in the success of the alternative Malay party, the Pan Malay Islamic Party, in this period, a success that at least one author puts down to a large swing to PAS of poorer rural Malays (see Kessler, 1978) who felt betrayed by an increasingly elitest UMNO.

16 The effective way in which he questions both the general view that early Islamic modernism was merely a derivative form of western 'social Darwinism', and the specific

judgement of Munshi Abdullah as mere mouthpiece for British colonialism is one of the great strength of Milner's study. For the countervailing view of Islamic modernism, see various contributions to a Symposium on Islam and modernity held in Kuala Lumpur in the 1990s (Symposium, 1994).

17 For a detailed discussion of the creation of these categories by colonial census takers, see PuruShotam, 1998.

18 'In religion, language, literature, manners, clothing, legal systems and style of their political life, Malays gave numerous foreign visitors the impression they constituted a single community or what was sometimes called . . . a "nation". These elements of unity, however, were apparently more obvious to outsiders than to Malays themselves . . . in the early nineteenth century, Malays were concerned primarily with their differences rather than their shared features. They did not consider themselves to belong to what we today would consider a single political unit and, as we shall observe, many Malays appear not to have been conscious of themselves as members of a common race. No supreme Malay sultanate existed. In the nineteenth century some Malay histories certainly told of a noble sultanate once based in Malacca on the west coast. Several of the nineteenth century rulers traced their genealogies back to that sultanate . . . On the other hand, states like Kelantan, Kedah . . . and Deli (on the coast of Sumatra) had no such connections but do not seem as a consequence to have been considered inferior in culture and tradition . . .' (Milner, 1995: 14).

19 The Federal Constitution defines a Malay as:

[A] person who professes the Muslim religion, habitually speaks Malay, conforms to Malay custom and: (a) was born before Merdeka (Independence) Day, in the Federation or Singapore or born of parents one of whom was born in the Federation or Singapore, or was on Merdeka Day domiciled in the Federation or Singapore; or (b) is the issue of such a person. (Article 160, cited in Syed Husin Ali, 1981: 2)

20 Harper has shown that the *orang asli* were not an isolated or marginal group in the precolonial Malay world, but that they played a very specific role within the precolonial division of labour (see Harper, 1997).

5
ENCOUNTERING THE OTHER: MODERNISM AND RACISM

I began this study of modernity and racism by observing the co-presence of countervailing currents in modern thought and culture, one current particularising, the other universalising in ambition. I also suggested that it may be possible to see a tendency for one or other current to become dominant in particular times and places. At least in Britain, America and Malaysia, the past decade seems to have witnessed a rather general shift away from an earlier preference for particularising thought towards new forms of universalism, forms still rooted in arguments about the links between science, ethics and human nature that have their origins at least as far back as the eighteenth century. What should we make of this apparent re-dedication – not just on the part of western intellectuals, but more broadly in popular culture in both East and West – to what some have called the 'project of modernity'? In particular is the development from the late twentieth century of a universalising modernist sensibility likely to provide an antidote to the racism and violence that have characterised much of the twentieth century. Or instead is 'new modernism' likely to heighten racism and racial conflict for reasons outlined by late twentieth century critics of modernity. Is the connection between the modernist project and racialised practice to be attributed to historical accident, or is there instead a deeper and more intimate relationship between modernism and the practices of racial exclusion, conflict, even genocide that are bracketed historically by the eruption of early and late twentieth century modernisms?

To pose the question is also to note the existence of directly opposing answers to it. Modernist intellectuals assert that modernism – understood as the reflexive dimension of modernity – stands in direct opposition to racialising ideologies and practices, while modernism's postcolonial, postmodern, feminist and multicultural critics have argued that the two are intrinsically connected.

An analysis of popular modernisms within a delimited field – America, Britain and Malaya in the period of modern nation building – suggests that neither of these answers is adequate, if only because the question they purport to answer is posed at far too abstract a level. This is itself a consequence of a tendency – on the part of modernity's critics and defenders alike – to see in modernisation at least the possibility for a modernity ultimately disembedded from its social, political and cultural contexts. What the focus on popular, as opposed to exemplary, modernism shows among other things is the extremely problematic nature of a conceptualisation of modernity uncontaminated by culture and history. Instead, especially in respect of the question of the origins of modern racism, it is possible to argue that just as modernity can never be a pure state of social and cultural being, neither is it separable from the modern imaginaries that make it possible.

If this much is granted, then the particular understandings of modernity given to us by social theory – as rationalisation, differentiation, autonomisation – emerge out of a specific and hence limited exemplary discourse on the modern constructed within German social philosophy after Kant (see Pippin, 1991). While sharing some of the elements of continental high social modernism, British, American and Malaysian popular modernists emphasise other markers of the modern constellation – the triumph of civilisation over nature, the threat of instrumentalisation to a virtuous state and citizenry, the creation of the virtuous village republics and just leaders etc. Each of these popular discourses on modernity is characterised by modern assumptions about human nature, and the possibility of deriving from these assumptions moral, ethical and political principles that are universal in their scope. Each is similarly characterised by that reflexive interrogation of modernisation that is said to be a defining feature of continental exemplary modernism. But each rests on a rather distinctive vision of the natural human condition, a vision that in each case is inflected by historically specific national, religious and cultural values.

The above interrogation of a diversity of modern imaginaries, and hence of a multiplicity of modernities, therefore reveals a more complex relationship between modernity and exclusionary practice than might have been assumed at the outset. We should not be surprised to find in them an analogous diversity of constructions of otherness ranging from notions of the other as a primitive version of the modern self to the other as irreducibly alien, from a visible and speaking other to one that is more or less completely invisible and silent. It remains to be seen whether these rather diverse modern imaginaries shaped concrete social encounters between self-conscious moderns and others in ways that could be deemed racist in the period after their emergence, and at the same time how the histories of such encounters did, or did not, provoke in turn a reassessment of modernity in popular culture.

To do so, however, is no easy task. None of the modernist sensibilities discussed in previous chapters can in any way be taken as representative of the vision of a single nation. Whatever the strengths of the ethnographic approach adopted here, providing a complete picture of American, British or Malaysian attitudes towards otherness is not one of them. Not all native stock Americans were republican, nor all Englishmen liberal. And certainly not all citizens of a newly independent Malaysia subscribed to the Malay–Islamic vision of the virtues of modern *kampong* life constructed in the films of P. Ramlee. There is no reason to believe that cultural contestation was not just as marked in America, Britain and Malaysia at the beginning of the twentieth century as it was at its close.

It would also be a mistake to assume that the basic assumptions of republicanism, liberalism and religious (if not specifically Malay–Islamic) 'fundamentalism' were not found throughout the anglophone world of the late nineteenth century. There is no reason to assume that each national tradition was culturally discrete and sealed off from cultural developments outside its borders. Finally, however one answers the question of the link between modernist discourse and racially exclusionary practice, it cannot be assumed that the causes of the latter lie completely in ethos or world-view. Indeed, as we shall see, the nature of racism and racial conflict is shaped as much by social, economic and political factors as cultural circumstance. As a consequence, to search for a one-to-one correspondence between each of these modernist sensibilities and particular national patterns of dealing with otherness would be fruitless. There is more to this than the traditional anthropological distinction between idea and practice, but this rather trite dichotomy at least serves the purpose of warning us against any naive attempt to derive a history of race relations from a few simple characteristics of a national culture. All this is to say that not only is the question of the link between modernism and racism inevitably posed at too abstract a level, but that a definitive answer to it may never be possible.

That said, even a cursory comparison of the more recent histories of race relations in America, Britain and Malaysia in the twentieth century suggests both that there have been significant differences as well as similarities, and that the differences are at least more comprehensible in the light of their different discursive starting points discussed in previous chapters. We are therefore forced to draw the conclusion that significant forms of popular modernism do have some sort of impact on racialised practice and, therefore, that a link does indeed exist between modernism and racism in all three cases. But given the contextualised understanding of modernity used here, it should also come as no surprise that popular modernism in all three cases also underwent significant transformations as a result of the confrontation between modernity and its others, leading once again to the conclusion that modernism is not and should never be understood as a pre-given set of abstract principles, but that it has its own particular and diversified history. To the accusations of racism levelled against it by its critics, modernism can only plead guilty. But it can also argue for mitigating circumstances – racism is no unitary phenomenon, and precisely because it is contingent and embedded in particular historical and cultural circumstances, modernism can become more inclusive.

To see that this is so, rather than attempting exhaustive racial histories of America, Britain and Malaysia in this concluding chapter, I want instead merely to gesture towards the significance of changing forms of popular modernism in shaping racialised practice in all three cases by means of a number of observations about the way such shifts have come about, and what implications they had for racial politics from the end of the twentieth century in each place.

Republicanism, Reform and Culture: The Changing Face of American Progressivism

A puzzle in modern America's encounter with its others concerns the contrasting fates of two groups uniformly characterised by 'native stock' Americans as somehow outside the American mainstream: blacks seen as not yet American on the one hand, and alien immigrants from southern and eastern Europe and Asia construed as deeply un-American on the other. While at the beginning of the twentieth century it was the latter who were seen as posing the greatest threat to the achievement of the republican utopia, most would agree with hindsight that it has been the former who benefited the least from the American century. At least as far as the liberal mainstream is concerned, descendants of eastern and southern European immigrants, and to a certain extent of Asian immigrants as well, no longer constitute a problem for America, indeed they are in many ways now considered as much a part of what it means to be American as any other group in American society. African Americans, however, continue to experience racism and economic and political marginalisation almost as a matter of routine.

In this respect one could say that what I have called American popular modernism has shifted ground. Against those who see in modernism an unchanging commitment to racial and cultural exclusion, in America groups formerly excluded have now been more or less included within the universal category American, while new exclusions have emerged. And this shift was provoked, I want to propose, not so much by an intercultural dialogue, but by a conflict that was at once cultural and political, a conflict that more than any other served to shape a distinctive American system of race relations by the last few decades of the twentieth century. In particular this system of race relations has been characterised by a politics of cultural identity, a clash among groups for both power and recognition that has been simultaneously political and cultural. It is this perception that to be modern is simultaneously to be represented in the political process and in the cultural arena (by which is generally understood the media), hence the engagement in the practice of what some call a politics of recognition, that as much as anything else shapes the emancipatory goals of American citizens. It is the dominance of these goals in turn that explains why America should be seen, particularly by outside observers, as obsessed with race, culture and identity to the exclusion of other modern political and economic aspirations.

This politics of recognition is manifest at all levels of American society, and in a variety of arenas. One such formative arena has been the sphere of urban politics. Here a politics of recognition can be seen to have been formed out of the longstanding conflict between urban political machines and reform movements from the early decades of the twentieth century, which has set the pattern for a cultural politics that has been pursued ever since. Because as institutions political machines were based as much on personalised political relations of patronage and clientalism, because they seemed to violate basic ideas about the need for a separation of powers, because they encouraged rather than discouraged interconnections between economic gain and politics as a pure vocation, and because they became closely associated with new immigrants, as far as republican reformers were concerned urban political machines represented all that was wrong with contemporary America. Political machines were invariably represented by reformers as having strong links with the criminal underworld. Although such urban machines had a very long history in American local and regional politics, many reformers saw their rise as directly linked to the presence of the new immigrants from southern and eastern Europe in the latter part of the nineteenth century. John Philip Sousa's caricature of the corrupt court of a Spanish despot as a reformer's nightmare was a commonly held view of machines, presumed often to be alien institutions imported into the United States by European immigrants.

Estes Kefauver in the foreword to a book fittingly titled *Barbarians in our Midst* on the history of Chicago politics and crime, wrote in 1952: 'The stranger coming into such a community rubs his eyes in amusement at the sights he sees . . . Can this be the Orient, he asks himself, where by centuries old usage, the giving and taking of bribes is the custom of the country?' (in Peterson, 1952: ix). An upstate New York Republican senator in the 1910s spoke of 'proletarians . . . crowding the seaboard cities. They elect legislators and are strong enough in number to enforce their demands for equality, according to their ideas, which are not American ideas' (cited in Buenker, 1973: 18). Shefter provides the following analysis of these campaigners for reform:

> Since the end of the nineteenth century, antimachine campaigns in New York have been initiated by what might be termed the city's reform vanguard. The funders, directors, and financial backers of the organizations through which this vanguard has operated were drawn from the city's upper classes, especially from among wealthy New Yorkers who financed organized charity. But the most numerous and active members of this vanguard were young practitioners of professions that produce, disseminate, and implement respectable opinion on political and social issues – among them, academic social scientists, social workers, clergymen, and journalists. The first two of these professions were born at the turn of the century, and the latter two were transformed by the rise of the Social Gospel and the muckraking tradition. As David Hammack says of the members of these newer professions, these highly trained men – and women – were seeking public outlets for their newly won expertise and . . . were ready to devote a good deal of effort to local politics. New York's reform vanguard was a would-be leadership class whose members sought to supplant machine politicians as the key actors in municipal government . . . Exposés and investigations were a central reform strategy. The exposure of incompetence, the discovery of graft, or, best of all, the discovery of ties between machine politicians and the underworld could destroy the legitimacy of the incumbent municipal administration. (Shefter, 1989: 142)

As this suggests, reform was not just a political but a cultural project. Primarily Protestant, and of native stock, reformers campaigned on a wide variety of fronts. As Buenker points out:

[t]heir ethnic and class assumptions led many genteel activists to expend an inordinate amount of time and energy on moral crusades to uplift the new stock lower class. Prohibition, Sunday blue laws, censorship, and attacks on gambling and vice were often held to be viable solutions to the problems that plagued the city, and the causes of these perversities were generally seen to lie in the immigrant presence. (Buenker, 1973: 26)

As important expressions of urban popular culture, music and sport were not immune from the attention of reformers. Particular sports like boxing and horse racing, characterised as both decadent and un-American partly because they were closely associated with the heavily foreign-born urban underclasses, drew the ire of reformers seeking to regulate or ban them. And jazz, the unique artistic contribution of African Americans to American popular culture, was also widely denounced as primitive and decadent, particularly because it had its origins in a nightclub scene usually associated in the minds of reformers with drink, drugs and the (ethnic) underworld (see Morris, 1980; Reiss, 1995; Wagner, 1997).

Excluded in the discourse of republicanism as alien, however, political machines, sweatshops, immigrants and popular pastimes like jazz, betting on the horses, boxing and so on were none of them truly external to the general processes of American modernisation described by Frederick Jackson Turner in his 1924 address at Clark University. Perverse modernities they may well have been in the eyes of the reformers, but they demand the attention of anyone seriously concerned with an inclusive understanding of what it has meant to be modern and American since the early twentieth century. There is, in other words, another history of American modernisation that has been silenced in standard republican accounts of American progress. This is not in any straightforward sense a subaltern history for it is not a history of peoples and institutions somehow external to the processes of economic, political and cultural modernisation or of a completely voiceless and oppressed underclass. It is instead a history of what were construed as perverse forms of modernisation by high, republican, modernism. And out of these perverse institutional and cultural forms emerges a challenge both to republican historiography and to the reform movements themselves. It has been in this conflict with republican reform, I want to suggest, that the contemporary system of race relations in America was formed, a system characterised by a politics of representation in both senses of the term: representation as political and as cultural process. At a discursive level the opposition to reformism takes the form of a claim to cultural authenticity by or on behalf of the non-Anglo, non-Protestant inhabitants of American cities. It is no accident that it was in America in the years after the First World War, when the conflict between reformers and machine politicians was at its height that intellectuals at least should have discovered the notion of cultural relativism as an alternative to the republican discourse on the alien and un-American nature of immigrant life.

Drawing the link between cultural conflict and the contest between reformers and machine politicians in American cities in the early part of the twentieth century has been facilitated by the appearance of revisionary histories of machine politics that have uncovered the ways in which urban machines were able to appeal to new immigrants. Against those who saw machines as wholly perverse political institutions, for example, Buenker has pointed out that

> [t]he machine performed various functions for the immigrant. Employment was his most pressing need and the most common political arrangement was the exchange of votes for jobs both in government and with private businesses holding city contracts. In addition, the machines' minions also became pioneers in social work at a time when public assistance was unheard-of and private charity wholly inadequate . . . A bucket of coal, a basket of food, a rent payment, funeral expenses, clothing, and other material benefits were made available to those in need, as were interventions with the law such as providing bail, cutting the red tape to receive a license or permit, or getting charges dismissed. (1973: 4)

The machine furnished a career ladder in politics for some immigrants, it helped with naturalisation and voter registration and provided a focus for political and social life for many others. Buenker points out that the political clubhouse, usually over or behind or next door to the saloon, became one of the social centres of immigrant life. Picnics and outings were the high points of the social year in most wards. The machine in other words was the pivot of a political system that 'provided ethnic minorities with vital benefits that the economic and social order often denied them' (1973: 5; see also McNickle, 1993).

A good example of a politician reviled by reformers for his underworld associations, and his involvement in prostitution and vote buying, was 'Big Tim' Sullivan, Boss of New York's 4th Ward (Bowery) and later a State Assemblyman. A recent study of Sullivan's career shows that contrary to the views of contemporary reformers, Sullivan's patronage of his largely immigrant constituency had very important positive benefits, that he was an advocate of women's suffrage, that he played an important role in the promotion of a popular entertainment industry – especially vaudeville – and that he was a benefactor of poor and of immigrant groups. Indeed it has been argued that Sullivan was to become a major force in the push for the institution of a system for the provision of welfare by local government (Czitrom, 1991).

There is some debate over the degree to which urban political machines on their own provided any lasting benefits for immigrant groups, Steven Erie among others expressing a degree of scepticism (1988). But there is little question that in their quest for the immigrant votes, in addition to providing members of marginalised immigrant groups with jobs, welfare and political clout, party machines certainly served to raise both the cultural consciousness of recent immigrant groups, and their expectations. Neither could subsequently be ignored by anyone running for political office in American cities, and a case can be made that a good deal of the early welfare reform on the part of local and state government was a response to immigrant demands (see Buenker, 1973: 31–33; Shefter, 1988).

A comparison of the activities of early reformers, hostile to any provision of welfare on the part of government, and the activities of city government under the mayoralty of Fiorello La Guardia shows clearly the transformations in urban politics brought about by the conflict between the republican reform movement and urban machines. From the 1930s onwards progressive American thinking on cities had changed drastically – becoming welfarist and closely associated with the practice of ethnic politics. The result in many places was the development of a marked split in the republican movement, between 'liberals' like La Guardia and his supporters, and rural, Protestant and conservative party members. La Guardia eventually lost the support of the Republican party, at the same time forging an alliance with a renewed Democratic Party under Roosevelt which provided him with Federal funds to support his welfare reforms.[1]

The link between this developing force in American urban politics and an emerging set of rules for racial and ethnic advancement is neatly captured by Buenker, who argues that:

> Ethnic politicians gave compatriots greater visibility, enhanced prestige, renewed self-respect, and an influential friend at court. The astute politician cultivated the immigrants' ethnic pride by defending him against nativist attack, observing his customs, and concerning himself with conditions in the homeland. Mostly, the machine played the politics of recognition, granting political office and party positions to representatives of any ethnic group large enough to merit consideration. (1973: 5)

In this sense the conflict between reform and machine can be said to have been the main formative influence on twentieth century race relations in the United States, characterised by a particular kind of cultural conflict, a politics of recognition marked by the competing claims for political representation and cultural authenticity on the part of immigrant groups. Against those who would see in identity politics, and claims about the relativity of cultural values, the main threat to the rights of immigrant groups, it was precisely their participation in such a politics of recognition that prised open a highly exclusive social regime, making it possible for these alien groups to overcome their economic, political and cultural marginality. It remains to be seen why it was that African Americans were apparently less able to exert this kind of influence.

This is a difficult question to answer definitively, but at least two factors seem to have reduced the ability of African Americans to pursue the same path as immigrant groups. On the one hand, for whatever reason, blacks were excluded from, or at least marginalised by the urban political machines at the time when these were experiencing their greatest successes. It was not until the 1960s that urban blacks became involved as a group in urban politics in a self-conscious attempt to follow in the footsteps of earlier generations of immigrants. By this time there had already been significant changes in urban machines as a consequence of their far tighter integration into the Democratic Party. Under the Roosevelt presidency, and then again under Kennedy and Johnson, the Federal government became the main source of material resources, allowing city governments to disperse the funds and favours that made machine politics successful in an earlier period. And with the election of Ronald Reagan even these Federal funds dried up considerably, leading to a further, even fatal decline of local networks of welfare and patronage. This was accompanied by the fragmentation of the older solidarities forged among diverse ethnic groups through first political machines and then local government around issues of welfare and workers' rights. According to one observer it was the withdrawal of the flow of resources from Washington into the cities that began with Reagan that is the main reason for the failure of what were called rainbow politics in the 1970s (see Erie, 1988).

On the other hand, while individual African Americans have certainly benefited from the policies of advancement arising out of the complex of liberal/primitivist assumptions and practices within which blacks, unlike immigrants, have been enmeshed since the latter part of the nineteenth century – integration, educational funding, equal opportunity, affirmative action, and the like – it also appears to be the case that such policies if anything serve continually to reaffirm the backwardness of those they judge to be not yet civilised. *Contra* Lee Baker, who has recently argued that African Americans would do well to abandon culturally relativist claims to the authenticity of African American culture in favour of liberal evolutionary ideas about deprivation and advance, the above analysis suggests that it has been their failure or inability to become involved in a successful politics of recognition that has preserved the economic and political marginality of African Americans as a group, while at the same time permitting a relatively small number of them to advance (cf. Baker, 1998). It remains to be seen whether a new system of relations between black and white Americans will emerge in the same way that new relations were forged between 'native' and 'ethnic' Americans in the decades since the 1920s.

It might be argued, then, that the American pattern of dealing with otherness has crystallised around a system that has been labelled 'multicultural', within which groups classified as culturally alien and hence incapable of subscribing to American values of democracy and freedom engage in a politics of recognition. Contesting a self-consciously universalist understanding of America has involved, perhaps paradoxically, an insistence on the relativity of cultural values, in turn broadening the cultural understandings which serve to define America. And those who have succeeded in this task are those who have been able successfully to advance the case for their inclusion by means of a politics of patronage. The rules of the game were laid down in part by the dominance of the republican discourse discussed in an earlier chapter.

Race in Britain: From Liberalism to the Critique of Essentialism

In an article first published in *The New Yorker* in 1997, the prominent African American intellectual Henry Louis Gates Jr reported on his impressions of black London, drawing attention to a contrast with American urban life that many others have remarked on:

> Yet if the barriers of class seem higher in England [than in America], those of race seem far more permeable. I'm always struck by the social ease between most blacks and whites on London streets . . . Through [Brixton], blacks and whites seem comfortable with one another in a way that most American urbanites simply aren't and never have been. 'The advantage we have here in England is that you are more likely to be accepted for who you are', one black Londoner tells me. 'People don't judge you by who your partner is or who your friends are.' (Gates, 2000: 176)

In spite of the fact that the apparent greater ease of interaction between black and white Britons is in part simply a consequence of racial dispersion, Gates has captured an important difference between an American and British system of black and white relations. His impression of the greater interactional permeability of racial boundaries finds confirmation in more substantive studies of social interaction in London (cf. Baumann, 1996).

What is at issue here is not whether the situation of black Americans or black Britons is somehow better. In both cases racially exclusionary practices operate at all levels of society, producing levels of economic and political marginalisation that leave blacks as a group relatively worse off than their white and ethnic counterparts. Unlike others who have reported on this contrast, Gates is not overly sanguine about the state of race relations in Britain. He recognises the presence of both significant white racist sentiment in Britain and of relatively high levels of deprivation and marginalisation among Britons of Caribbean descent. He even reports that at least some black Londoners perceive that the situation of black Americans is in many ways to be envied. So where does the difference lie?

There are clearly a large number of differences between the black experience in Britain and the United States. While there have been blacks in Britain for centuries, in contrast with the United States their numbers were relatively insignificant until after the Second World War, when the demand for cheap labour, together with changes in nationality laws led to a new wave of immigration. Among these new immigrants, although they never constituted the majority, were people from former colonial territories, particularly the West Indies. And regardless of the fact that blacks formed a minority of immigrants, British debates over immigration almost inevitably focused on those of black and later Asian origin. There is a growing body of opinion, against those who have maintained that race did not become an issue in British debates over immigration until racial unrest in the late 1950s, that in fact race and migration had become intimately interconnected by the time of the 1948 Nationality Act, and that both Conservative and Labour governments from 1945 were already constructing black immigration as a potential source of problems in British society. So in contrast to America where anti-immigrant sentiment consolidated against culturally alien 'new' immigrants from southern and eastern Europe, in Britain the race and the immigration debates have tended to be co-terminous at least since the War (cf. Carter et al., [1993] 2000; Solomos, 1989). This meant that in Britain nativist anti-immigration opinion and racism were connected, while in America this was not always the case.

Given that labour immigration has a long history in Britain, going back at least to far earlier waves of immigrants from Ireland, to say nothing of more recent immigration from Europe, on what basis were immigrants from the Caribbean singled out for this special attention? Why was it considered that this particular group of migrants would pose a threat to political stability, a constant theme of anti-immigrant discourse in Britain from 1945? In spite of the volumes of published work on immigration, racism and identity in modern British history, very little attention has focused on how political and intellectual elites actually represented blacks as different not just from natives but from other immigrant groups, or indeed on popular racial stereotypes prevalent in the mainstream of white society. Such a study is not proposed here, but it seems to me a good case can be made for the dominance of a liberal-primitivist discourse on blackness not just among overtly exclusionary, nativist Britains, but among their anti-racist critics as well.

As a recent arrival in London in the 1960s from America, I can still remember how shocked I was to find overtly primitivist representations of blacks in British popular culture, representations that were unthinkable in polite American society of that time. Advertisements for tropical fruit drinks shown in cinemas, for example, depicted happy African natives with prominent lips cavorting through the jungle; the appearances of blacks on the football pitch was inevitably accompanied by chants about jungles and bananas by baying crowds of spectators making ape-like sounds – either of which would have led to riots in contemporary American cities. Although perhaps more circumspect, anti-immigration politicians left little doubt that blacks constituted an uncivilised race, governed by their natural instincts, a propensity for violence and criminality, and hence distinctly out of place in a country like Britain governed by what were presumed to be universal civilised values. At least in overtly racist discourse, the differences between black and white were represented as differences in level of civilisation and, hence, of relative closeness to nature.

Of course such a discourse permitted individual blacks to escape the stereotype – in ways noted by Gates in his piece on black London – provided that they had achieved a level of civilisation through an Oxbridge education, and mastery of the requisite English accent and cultural trappings. But that even overt racists accepted the civilisability of immigrants from the Caribbean suggests a deeper connection between racism and mainstream liberal opinion. To focus on overtly racist ideas, like those of Enoch Powell and his supporters, or of far right racist groups like the National Front, the BNP and the like would of course give a misleading picture of British racial discourse even in the 1960s. A more complete picture emerges when we balance the overtly racist imagery of uncivilised blacks with the more measured discourse of liberal intellectuals on the causes of racism and on ways of improving British race relations. Much of the attention of recent critics has tended to focus on the racial assumptions present in the work of prominent race relations intellectuals, but if only because some of these ideas circulated more widely in popular culture, such analyses should be balanced by a closer look at popular culture. Consider for example the racial humour in the very popular television series *Rising Damp*, a 1970s vehicle for the comedian Leonard Rossiter.[2] Part of the show's comedic effect lay in the interaction between the three main characters – the landlord Rigsby (played by Rossiter), the female tenant (played by Frances de la Tour), and the male tenant (played by Richard Beckinsale) – with Beckinsale's roomate, Philip (played by Don Warrington). Philip is an Oxbridge graduate and son of an African chief who confounds the racist stereotype of the uncivilised and simple black by being more educated, more British and hence more civilised than anyone else. The racial humour derives from the confrontation between Philip and his likeable but foolish roomate, the hopelessly romantic Ruth and, above all, the vainglorious and money-grabbing Rigsby. But it needs to be pointed out that this challenge to the racist stereotype in no way undermines the primitivist narrative that also underpins anti-black racism. The difference is that liberalism is more open than overtly racist discourses to the possibility of black civilisability. Here the black character, Philip, is more civilised than the whites, confirming the liberal assumption that individual blacks are as capable as whites of achieving civility through the acquisition of traits and characteristics already achieved by middle class Englishmen (but not yet by the main white characters in *Rising Damp*).

Now we have seen how a very similar liberal discourse on the perfectability of blacks in the American situation leaves a large residual category of not-yet-civilised blacks, comprised of those who, in the British context, are simply not able to follow Philip's route to an, ambiguous, Englishness. In the American case this has been one of the factors behind the so-called rainbow strategy, through which African Americans have attempted to engage in a politics of recognition similar to that pursued by an earlier generation of immigrants. While there is evidence that this has also taken place in the British context, although more often in the name of immigrants from the subcontinent than among descendants of the Caribbean migrants, a rather different development can be detected among at least prominent black British intellectuals, and artists. That this rather specifically British response to racism has at least begun to penetrate the arena of popular culture is evident from the somewhat surprising success of a more recent British television show, *Goodness, Gracious Me!*[3]

The source of racial humour in *Goodness, Gracious Me!*, a program be it said much admired by the black and Asian intelligentsia as well as right thinking whites, is quite different from that in *Rising Damp*. Here the mainly Indian characters also frequently go against stereotype by taking on one aspect or another of the dress, attitudes and behaviour of the English middle classes. An example is an episode in which a middle aged Indian couple dress up in the outlandish golfing gear favoured by affluent white suburbanites. But this time the humour lies not in the challenge this poses to a picture of Anglo-Asians as uncivilised. Instead by behaving innocently as more English than the English, it is the trappings and pretensions of Englishness that are being ridiculed and that the audience is being invited to laugh at. This program explicitly challenges the equation of Englishness with higher levels of civility, showing at the same time the extent to which the British understanding of civility is heavily inflected by the culture of the English tribe. Unlike American popular multiculturalism, no attempt is made here to seek recognition for an authentic Indian culture to be placed alongside English culture. Indeed 'essentialised' visions of Indian culture are also continually ridiculed in the episodes of *Goodness, Gracious Me!*

Although a parallel politics of recognition has also been manifest in Britain, it does not appear to have played such a significant role in the history of British race relations. Here, partly due to the dominance of liberal-primitivist narratives, the struggle by groups adjudged non-modern/alien takes a rather different form. What is now at stake is the supposed racial-neutrality of existing notions of the modern. In the United States new immigrants were construed as so culturally alien that they could not be accommodated within a vision of America and hence also of human-ness inflected by both republican and ascetic Protestant values. The cultural biases of this particular form of universalism is precisely exposed by notions of cultural relativity and multiculturalism.

By contrast British notions of the civilising process rested on an understanding of the process as both a universal and natural one. British narratives of modernisation in other words have always presumed that the English were distinctive not because of the unique cultural characteristics of citizens of the United Kingdom, but only because the English, particularly white middle class Englishmen, were farther along the road to a universal human future than anyone else.

As a result, perhaps the most significant challenge posed at least to the classical liberal British modernising agenda is the argument that far from being universal, this agenda is shaped by particular racial assumptions which underpin it. If the conflict in America then became a *cultural* one, critique of British notions of civilisation took the form of a challenge to its naturalising/racialising dimensions. A dominant British liberalism was literally unable to recognise the fact that its understanding of freedom, progress and democracy was inflected by particular racial assumptions. The revolution in cultural studies pioneered by the Birmingham school, and by Stuart Hall in particular, which began to unpack the ideas of a universal, racially neutral Britishness or Englishness, and which has filtered through into the popular consciousness through television programmes like *Goodness, Gracious Me!* is, none the less, a rather specific new kind of racialising discourse that makes particular sense only in the British context.

The critique of British racism, therefore, involves exposing the particularistic underpinnings of a supposedly racially neutral/universal Britishness.

The close links between such universalising narratives of civilisation and naturalistic understandings of human difference is once again manifest. Richard Dyer, for example, points specifically to the ways unstated assumptions about whiteness function in western art and photography. Here white is constituted as the universal condition, while the non-white is inevitably seen as exceptional. In this way a civilisational narrative serves continually to particularise and racialise non-whites, while denying the racially specific foundations of its own universal ideals. There is, writes Dyer,

> no more powerful position than that of being 'just' human. The claim to power is the claim to speak for the commonality of humanity. Raced people can't do that – they can only speak for their race. (Dyer, 1997: 2)

In these recent British discussions of race, there is very little sense that Caribbean immigrants should be seen as bearers or creators of their own distinctive cultural traditions. Or put another way, even among the current British intellectual *avant garde* of intellectuals and artists, including such prominent spokespersons on race as Stuart Hall, Paul Gilroy and Homi Bhabha, there is significant hostility to what they take to be cultural essentialism, hence to 'American-style' multicultural challenges to dominant modernist paradigms. Consider the words of Paul Gilroy in his extremely influential critique of the anti-racist movement of the 1980s:

> At the end of the day, an absolute commitment to cultural insiderism is as bad as an absolute commitment to biological insiderism. I think we need to be theoretically and politically clear that no single culture is hermetically sealed off from others. There can be no neat and tidy pluralistic separation of racial groups in this country. It is time to dispute with those positions which, when taken to conclusions, say there is no possibility of shared history and no human empathy. We must beware of the use of ethnicity to wrap a spurious cloak of legitimacy around the speaker who invokes it. Culture, even the culture which defines the groups we know as races, is never fixed, finished or final. It is fluid, it is actively and continually made and re-made. (Gilroy, 1993: 57)

In their different ways Stuart Hall and Homi Bhabha have also expressed their concern with the essentialising of racial (and cultural) identities, mobilising notions like hybridity to break down the impression that identities are fixed, discrete and immovable. It remains to be seen whether this particular response, one be it said that still bears the imprint of an individualistic liberalism and its commitment to a kind of racial 'main-streaming' that radical multiculturalism rejects, will ultimately fulfil its aim of generating a British society more inclusive of its racial and cultural minorities. But it is clear that as a result of this conflict, the notion of Britishness has undergone a profound change. At least for an increasing number of Britons, the category 'British' can now easily accommodate 'Black Britons' and at least some Asians as well. There is an increasing tendency now to think of Britishness as once again a racially neutral identity, but this time one that is inclusive of at least certain categories of 'blacks', while English-ness (along with Scottish-ness, Welsh-ness etc.) is now used to describe the culturally or racially particular category. Again *contra* the assertions of certain critics of modernity, here a racially exclusive notion of Britishness has become more inclusive, although doubtless now generating new exclusions (to an extent Muslim Asians, as well as newer refugee groups from other parts of Europe, Africa and the Middle East).

The Postmodernisation of Malay Identity

In his recent and masterful history of Malaysia, the British historian Timothy Harper argues among other things that existing histories have generally failed to appreciate the extent to which political and cultural developments in the late colonial period continued to shape Malaysia's political landscape at the end of the twentieth century. In his overview of the project he writes:

> The anatomy of late colonialism that follows is a contribution to the comparative history of western expansion and retreat. But as I spent more time in Malaysia the book became an exercise in Southeast Asian social history. The achievement of independence is examined, not primarily through the metropolitan mind of colonialism, but through the struggle within Malayan society for its soul. Many of the ideas and forces this brought to prominence still dominated political life in the 1980s and 1990s . . . (Harper, 1999: xi)

This argument, that processes that have their origin in the late colonial period constitute a key formative influence on contemporary cultural politics in Malaysia, is repeated later in the book, when Harper takes others to task for overemphasising the impact of more recent changes in Malaysian society. 'I want to suggest', writes Harper, 'that the kind of politics promoted in the late colonial period had far more influence in shaping the landscape of post-colonial politics than existing accounts have allowed. Its legacy lay not so much in what the British achieved, as in what the British allowed others to accomplish' (1999: 274–275).

This thesis constitutes a useful point of entry into debates over the changing nature of race relations and identity politics in contemporary Malaysia, not just because I am one of those singled out by Harper for overemphasising the effects of more recent social change, but because it throws important questions into relief about the fate of the modern Malay–Islamic imaginary outlined in a previous chapter. Does a vision of Malaya that has its origins in the late colonial period that is Harper's main historical object indeed continue to dominate the cultural and political landscape? And do its silences continue to shape race relations, particularly relations between Chinese and Malay Malaysians at the beginning of the twenty-first century? I have referred to a personal disagreement with Harper here not in order to dismiss his argument out of hand. Indeed I suspect that Harper is right to suggest that a number of observers, including myself, have tended to underplay the continuities in a system of race relations, with which I suspect we both have little sympathy, that has its origins in the colonial period, but which as Harper so rightly maintains, cannot be said merely to have been a colonial construction. At the time of writing there were signs that earlier nationalist appeals to the special rights of Malays were once again again mobilising at least a segment of Malay political opinion.

Perhaps a useful way into the discussion of the extent to which a late colonial discourse on political emancipation, one inflected to a considerable extent by particularist cultural and religious values, persists today is to compare the expression of ideas about race and modernity in popular culture in the late colonial period, such as in the Ramlee films, with those found in more recent popular culture. An interesting point of departure is the rise to popularity of so-called *nasyid* groups that achieved such success especially with the Malay public in the late 1990s. *Nasyid* is a term that describes a particular style of popular music, pioneered by the male singing group Raihan, a name which means heavenly scent in Arabic. *Nasyid* groups were modelled to some extent on British and American boy and girl bands, typically consisting of four performers singing a capella style songs and ballads. The difference is that *nasyid* groups have been given a distinctive Islamic image – adopting a global form of Islamic dress and singing inspirational songs which, at least on the surface, avoid reference to sex and love in favour of positive Islamic sentiments. Lyrics such as 'Let us find a way to know our God, feel the tortures of hell fire' are typical of Raihan songs.[4] Lisa Muhamad, a member of Huda, an all-female *nasyid* group also produced by Warner, told a journalist: 'Basically, the message is to love Allah and instil good values in our children so they will be good citizens.'[5]

Raihan enjoyed significant commercial success after being signed and promoted by Warner Records in 1997. Their first album sold 600,000 copies in Malaysia, and over a million copies when overseas sales are taken into account.[6] According to some, the profits generated by Raihan and Huda rescued Warner Music in Malaysia, which had been hit badly by the 1997 financial crisis. In 1999 Raihan won the industry prize for best vocal group in Malaysia, as well as an award in the specially created category of Islamic music. The success of Raihan and Huda prompted most record labels in Malaysia to create their own *nasyid* groups in the late 1990s.

There are similarities between the music, performative styles and images of late 1990s *nasyid* groups, and those of P. Ramlee. Doubtless both appeal primarily to an ethnically Malay audience, their lyrics are mainly sung in Malay (although in the case of *nasyid* music with a liberal admixture of Arabic words and phrases). The lyrics of the songs, and the video clips that accompany them, are addressed exclusively to Muslim themes. Like the Ramlee films, *nasyid* is completely silent on the fact of Malaysian racial, cultural and religious diversity. There are also musical similarities and parallels in instrumentation. Although his music was in no sense purely indigenous to Malaya, as we have seen Ramlee was heavily influenced by Latin and American jazz; none the less the addition of elements from Middle Eastern, Indian and Malay-Indonesian musical traditions makes

Ramlee's music recognisably Malaysian.[7] *Nasyid*, like other Malaysian popular musical forms, draws on elements that have come to constitute Malay pop, many of which were laid down by an earlier generation of popular musicians in Malaysia.

There are also differences that one might argue are relatively insignificant as far as our theme is concerned, being due less to any significant transformation in the racial dimensions of popular culture, and more to changes in taste, and developments in music production and consumption. For example, while Ramlee's music, as opposed to his films, was probably mainly designed to be listened to on the radio or the gramophone, Raihan's performances are clearly designed to be seen (on television, or in popular video cd and karaoke format).[8] Audiences in the late colonial period would also have had ample opportunity to watch Ramlee's musical performances because most of his films contained musical interludes, the difference here lying in the collective nature of audience behaviour for Ramlee's music as opposed to the much more privatised ways in which audiences nowadays consume television, compact discs and music videos.

There are also potentially rather significant differences between Ramlee and the *nasyid* groups which testify to a hardening of the group boundaries established in earlier popular musical forms. The most striking of these is the centrality of Islamic imagery in the whole *nasyid* phenomenon. It would be wrong to suggest that Islam was not also a significant part of the Ramlee image. We have already had occasion to note the importance of attitudes and behaviours deemed Islamic in Ramlee's films. But here religious ideas seem to be inextricably bound up with symbols of Malayness, a good example being in dress. There is no mistaking the fact that Ramlee is, in most of his films, a Malay, because he is wearing clothing that clearly signals this fact. Raihan and Huda, on the other hand, wear clothes that would simply never have been seen in Malay villages in Ramlee's time. Their clothing styles are instead at least read in contemporary Malaysia as Islamic or even Middle Eastern, not Malay.

Similarly, in late twentieth century Malaysia, most assume that Islam encourages sexual segregation, and that it is this (rather than the influence of all girl and boy bands in the West) that determines that *nasyid* groups are always single sex. By contrast, most of Ramlee's musical performances involved males and females, as singers and dancers. Dancing, particularly women performing what Malay Muslims now think of as provocative dances, is completely absent from the *nasyid* clips. Once again this may be due at least in part to the styles of Western a capella groups. But in Malaysia, this absence of dance is read as Islamic.

A third example of differences between Ramlee and *nasyid* performance is in their respective landscaping. Ramlee almost always performs, particularly in his films, against the background of the Malay *kampong*, its presence signalled by Malay houses, rice fields, tropical vegetation and the like. Such an identifiably Malay landscape is rarely present in *nasyid* clips. Instead, when there is a landscape portrayed, it is more often an Islamic one, by which I mean that scenes of desert and barren hills that most Malaysian viewers would identify as Middle Eastern are projected behind the singers.

One might want to argue that this Islamisation of Malay popular cultural forms has little implication for Malaysian race relations, or that it has even served to accentuate existing racial divisions. Although Malays are not the only Muslims in Malaysia, Islam has none the less always been a major factor distinguishing Malays and non-Malays. Indeed, adherence to the Islamic faith is part of the constitutional definition of Malayness. The perception, one incidentally that is shared by many Malaysians and outside observers of the Malaysian social landscape, that the nation has become more Islamic since the revivalist *dakwah* movements of the 1970s, signifies for some a hardening of the line between Malays and non-Malays. And given that this is a view expressed by some non-Malays, who see in the rise of Islamism, whether among government supporters or adherents of the most successful opposition party, an even greater threat to their rights as citizens in the future, then there is at least support at the phenomenological level for the argument that the system of antagonistic race relations forged in the late colonial period continued to plague Malaysian society at the end of the twentieth century.

One could certainly not argue that the *nasyid* phenomenon testifies to the rise in the popular imagination of a liberal or civil society, or of the notion of a pan-Malaysian citizenry (*bangsa Malaysia*) so fondly hoped for by at least some members of the political elite. On the contrary, the Islamisation of popular subjectivity, and of the political process in general, appears to violate principles basic to both Western liberal and republican traditions Yet in spite of the continuities in the popular constructions of Malayness in the examples discussed here, it is also possible to see through the example of *nasyid* music evidence of a significant change in popular racial imaginaries in contemporary Malaysia.

First, we could say that the Islamic subject constructed in and through cultural phenomena like *nasyid* differs from Ramlee's Malay subject not so much because one is more or less Islamic than the other, but because the former is primarily an urban and middle class subject, while the latter is a member of a, subaltern, peasantry. In the Ramlee films the individual hero, and the *kampong* republic as collective hero, is mostly a salt of the earth peasant, a poor but honest man who battles against his physical urges, untamed nature, aristocratic privilege and the like to win through in the name of Malay virtue. The heroes and heroines of *nasyid* epitomised in the images projected by the singers, are clean-cut, expensively dressed (if in Islamic rather than Western designer labels), educated, modern urbanites, members of the Malay middle classes resisting the (western-style) temptations of urban life (sex, alcohol, drugs) through self-control and adherence to their religious faith, providing advice to a target audience composed of young people facing the classical dilemmas of the young urban middle classes. Indeed, although audience research is difficult to come by, it is likely that this indeed describes the social profile of the large majority of the consumers of *nasyid* music, just as it describes the main consumers of popular music more generally.

From this perspective the culture of a *nasyid* performance is just as exclusive as that of a Ramlee production. The two are completely silent about their others. But it would be a mistake to treat *nasyid* as though it were an isolated musical style dominating the market for popular entertainment in the same way as Ramlee did in the late colonial period. *Nasyid* music is instead part of a much larger market for popular music that, by contrast with that for Malay films in the 1950s, is also characterised by significant diversity. It is diverse over time in the sense that popular musical styles change as fast in Malaysia as they do anywhere else. The rise of *nasyid* to the top of the pop charts followed on from a succession of other diverse musical styles – ethnic music, global music, heavy metal, Cantonese pop, Indian film music, local rap and hip hop groups, dance music etc., and its dominance of the market will doubtless be as short-lived as these others.[9] *Nasyid*, even at the height of its popularity, moreover, was merely one of a multitude of style niches in the popular music scene, each with its own dedicated band of followers. In one sense tribalistic, modern popular music also forces fans of particular genres into an acknowledgement that they are part of a wider if fragmented audience for popular music. Indeed fans of each particular construct style themselves precisely in opposition to others. There is therefore a shared sense among fans of popular music that in spite of the diversity of genres and associated styles – both over time, and at any point in time – that they are also members of a more inclusive group of young urbanites with a taste for popular culture. There is evidence in contemporary Malaysia that especially the middle class urban youth identify themselves through popular music as a group distinct from others – older people, consumers of high culture, villagers, traditionalists (such as fans of Chinese opera or traditional Malay music and dance) and the like. In other words, although it may not always be expressly acknowledged, there is a growing sense of a generalised youth culture particularly in Malaysian cities that may be segmented according to the diverse and changing tastes in particular musical styles, but which as a whole differs in important ways from other cultures that tend to be portrayed as rather old fashioned, wedded to rural traditions, the tastes of an older generation etc. There is a sense, therefore, in which fans of *nasyid* music, provided they are members of this generation, will not be seen in exclusivist terms, since they are also part of this more general category of young, urban Malaysians into modern popular music with all its diversity of styles, a sensibility catered to by the popular culture industries through the sale of recordings, but also youth fashion, magazines, television shows and the like.

The signs are that the formation of this intensely commercialised Malaysian youth culture draws on somewhat earlier traditions of youth alienation and protest.[10] This underground still exists to a certain extent, but it has been largely harnessed and repackaged by commercial publishers, record companies and so on in ways entirely familiar to observers of the late twentieth century popular music scene in the West.

The nature of this youth market is, perhaps, thrown into relief by the growth of a nostalgic market for Ramlee films and music videos. These too are freely available in music shops throughout Malaysia. They have reached a fairly large audience, and Ramlee has been promoted by the government, eager, as we have seen, for icons of Malay excellence. Yet young urbanites, including young Malays, are not particularly interested in the Ramlee revival, associating it with the interests of an older generation. A number of people told me that Ramlee's appeal was limited to members of the older generation nostalgic for the old days, a time when it is supposed Malays led a simple village life, when the demands of religious leaders were less harsh, and when, one might surmise, the majority of Chinese Malaysians were forced to take a back seat in the political arena and in the creation of a national culture.

The growth in the generalised idea of a Malaysian urban youth culture, which at least for a time includes the *nasyid* phenomenon, therefore implies a subtle but none the less significant shift in the patterns of racialisation in popular Malaysian discourse. *Nasyid* music and performances, in other words, may manifest the same silences about the racial and cultural diversity found in Ramlee's work. But Malaysian youth culture, of which it forms a part, certainly does not. To hold a concept of youth culture is inevitably to acknowledge diversity within it, and hence explicitly to recognise that Malaysia is a multiracial society. This is more generally true of the Islamic, as opposed to the Malay, understanding of identity in contemporary Malaysia. As a number of observers have pointed out, adherence to Islam under current circumstances in fact implies a recognition of the existence of non-Muslims. It can even be argued that Islam provides a model for co-existence among peoples of different religious faiths that is lacking in other universalist religions (see Hussin Mutalib, 1993). Certainly part of the Islamic revival in Malaysia has involved attention to the terms under which non-Muslims should be accommodated within the political process: through the promotion by influential Islamist intellectuals of so-called civilisational dialogues; to attempts (so far not terribly successful) to forge alliances between Muslim and non-Muslim opposition parties; to the working through of the implications of the imposition of Islamic law in the northeastern states governed by the opposition Islamic party, PAS. It is not possible to argue in all this that formulae wholly satisfactory to Muslims and non-Muslims have been worked out yet, but it also has to be pointed out that the problem of the diversity of Malaysia's citizens is increasingly on the agenda, and that the complete silence about non-Malays manifest in expressions of Malay cultural nationalism from the late colonial period is perhaps gone forever.

As one might expect, there is also a global dimension to *nasyid* music, and to middle class Islamic culture more generally that is absent in the

Ramlee phenomenon. Recognition of the globality of particular musical genres further contributes to the opening up of popular tastes to the possibility of diversity. The ways in which the image of *nasyid* groups is constructed, and the ways in which that image is interpreted as we have seen implies identification with modern Muslims throughout the world. The contrast with Ramlee here is very striking. Ramlee films and songs are explicitly addressed to nation, the audience being reminded of the importance of loyalty to God, country and nation (*Tuhan, Negara, Bangsa*). By contrast, reference to the nation is almost entirely absent in *nasyid*, the listening and viewing subject of *nasyid* performance always being first and foremost a member of a non-national, hence global, Muslim community.

But the global dimensions go further, since at least the producers of *nasyid* music are seeking to go global by marketing the music in other Islamic countries, and producing musical collaborations between groups like Raihan and what they see to be similar performers elsewhere. Tony Fernandes, vice-president of Warner Music Southeast Asia for example, plans to combine Raihan with Take Six, Boyz 2 Men or Stevie Wonder in the United States, while others have attempted to promote links between *nasyid* and American gospel groups (see Cheah, 2000).

The important changes in ideas about cultural and racial diversity constructed in the Malaysian popular imagination become clearly manifest once *nasyid* is examined in the context of an emerging Malaysian, and global, youth culture. There is no doubt that the work of exposing the silences about racial diversity manifest in the earlier work of someone like Ramlee has been carried out mainly by multinational capital through the increasingly globalised culture industries. But the effect has been the rise of a new generation of Malaysians who are at least far more predisposed than were their elders to engage with the racially and culturally diverse nature of their own society and of the new global order. Whether or not this also generates a predisposition among young Malaysians towards a greater tolerance of otherness remains to be seen, although there is a good deal of impressionistic evidence to suggest both that common participation in this global youth culture is increasing the levels of interracial interaction in Malaysian cities,[11] and that it has facilitated interracial cooperation in the movement for reform that is currently focused on the conflict between the Prime Minister and his former deputy, Anwar Ibrahim, jailed on trumped up charges of sexual and financial misconduct. Many have commented on the fact that the rallies supporting Anwar, as well as the Keadilian party headed by his wife, were composed overwhelmingly of young people from all of Malaysia's racial groups, raising the very real possibility for the first time in Malaysia's history of a serious challenge to a political system shaped entirely by considerations of race.

There is also evidence, however, of the opposite tendency, that is of the continued salience of the exclusionary discourses of Malay nationalism. Most recently, partly as a result of splits in the Malay vote in the 1999 election, Malay leaders, including the Prime Minister, seem to be appealing again to the Malays not to forget their heritage, and the goals of Malay nationalism. One observer has spoken of a re-communalisation of Malaysian politics after a decade when it appeared that communal rhetoric seemed to have gone into decline.[12] It remains to be seen whether the strategy will be an effective one, or whether the new social and cultural circumstances manifest in the growth of an urban 'youth culture' will mean appeals based on the older vision of Malay nationalism fall increasingly on deaf ears.

Three quite different, if interlinked, modernities, three different critical takes on the modern condition, three modernisms. Each is exclusive, even racist, although not in the same way.

To borrow a term from Uday Mehta, each 'effects' its exclusions in a particular way: one by a notion of the history of the mastery of nature; one through a notion of the other as irreducibly alien by dint of language, religion and cultural insiderism; one through its absolute silences about the diverse make-up of the nation.

Each of these three narratives has had its own history, a result of particular political contests and economic processes. In Britain, primitive-mania set in train a debate within British culture over the pros and cons of civilisation which shaped subsequent debates over immigration. And it took this encounter to expose the racial particularism of deep-seated assumptions about the universality of British values. In America republicanism generated a politics of recognition, in turn leading to the idea of a 'multicultural' nation – a conflict that took place initially in any case through the fight to control America's cities. A Malay–Islamic nationalism came under attack first from other ethnic nationalisms – Chinese and Indian. But in part as a consequence of the deepening of a global market cultural, and even religious identity became a matter of lifestyle choice as much as an undying political attachment to God, country and nation. The conflict over whether identity should be the basis for political commitment or simply one of many niches in a global consumer market continues to this day as Malay political elites strive to recommunalise a society already intimately linked into a global cultural economy.

Popular modernisms have in each case been transformed in the process. Many Americans who once would have demonised new immigrants as culturally unassimilable now recognise the rights of cultural groups at least to take part in a multicultural conflict over the right to their own cultural heritage. Many Britons are now prepared to admit that the public arena should be open to blacks as well as whites. A growing number of, particularly young, Malaysians are willing to accept that the nation contains within it a diversity of urban lifestyles. In none of these cases has modernity been immune to the demands of its others to be included, the result in each case being new understandings of human nature and human diversity, and a general shift away from the search for abstract universal principles and towards more contingent and embedded notions of what makes us modern.

But this is not to say that modernisation inevitably conquers racism. Along with earlier forms of racial and cultural exclusion, new kinds of exclusion are effected. African Americans as a group continue to be marginalised. The rules of the game of multiculturalism are in some ways just as restrictive as those of an earlier republicanism. In Britain there may be a growing recognition that the categories of nation and race are problematic, and that a hybrid 'Britishness' should open up public life to all citizens. Yet the public sphere in Britain, and more so elsewhere in western Europe, still remains very white, and fears about refugees and new immigrants from eastern Europe and the Muslim world, can still reach fever pitch. And postmodern identities generated through the market in global lifestyles everywhere remains fragile precisely because not everyone enters the market on an equal footing. For those who 'fail', representing an increasing proportion of humanity, cultural nationalism retains its appeal.

And finally the conflicts over race, culture and identity appear to be globalised in a wholly new sense. The end of the Cold War seems to have breathed new life into the project of universalising American values not just across the nation, but throughout the globe. America, Britain and their allies at times see themselves as the world's policemen, bringing the 'benefits' of their own modern achievements to the victims of non-modern 'despots' and 'tyrants' in Africa, Asia and the former communist world. This in turn generates the grounds for a counter-imperial rhetoric elsewhere, where politicians and religious leaders call attention to the 'colonial' implications of this renewed threat to their hard-won national sovereignty. It may be that we are reliving conflicts at the global level that were once more restricted in scope. But it is equally certain that no solutions will emerge until it is understood that there has never been, and can never be, a single, abstract and homogenising 'project of modernity' without a continuation of the racial and cultural exclusions that left their mark on the twentieth century.

Notes

1 The biography of Justice Seabury, one of La Guardia's major supporters, traces this split between liberal reformers – sympathetic to immigrants and labour and promoters of welfare – and upstate New York republicans (see Mitgang, 1963).

2 *Rising Damp* was written by Eric Chappel. Twenty-eight episodes were produced for Yorkshire television between 1974 and 1978.

3 I would like to thank Atticus Narrain for helping me appreciate the innovative nature of the racial comedy in *Goodness, Gracious Me!*

4 Lyrics for some of Raihan's songs can be found at http://pages.whowhere.lycos.com/internet/imnogman/Raihan.html

5 Quoted in Harrison, 1999, from which the information on Huda was largely obtained.

6 Some of the information on Raihan comes from an article in Malaysia's *New Straits Times* (see Cheah, 2000). I am also indebted to Kean Wong in Kuala Lumpur who was a wonderful source of information on Malaysian popular music.

7 I have been assured by some Malaysian musical experts that there is absolutely nothing distinctive about Malaysian popular music. They argue that the western influence is so

pervasive that only non-musical markers, such as the dress of performers, or the use of Malay lyrics, serve to give it a Malaysian feel. As a non-expert, I find it difficult to assess this judgement. Without wishing to disagree that at a purely musical level Malay pop music is almost entirely derivative, particularly of whatever is currently popular in the West, I would still argue that a style of popular singing and performance has been created that, however derivative, is none the less almost always recognisable as Malaysian for whatever reason.

8 Although there are now quite a number of films of Ramlee musical performances recently released on video cd as well.

9 For summaries of changing tastes in popular music in Malaysia, both written before the rising popularity of *nasyid*, see Lockard, 1998 and Zawawi Ibrahim, 1995.

10 In Malaysia at least a subaltern youth culture of protest is generally traced to the 1980s with the emergence of local metal bands, supported by an underground music press of crudely produced fanzines (see Kean Wong, 1995).

11 Changes in patterns of social interaction among, particularly, Chinese and Malays is treated in greater depth in a forthcoming book on Malaysian modernity that I am currently writing with Maila Stivens. Here we also examine the ways in which patterns of urbanisation and the formation of new middle classes, as well as changes in electoral patterns, are contributing to the possibility of a less racialised social order in contemporary Malaysia.

12 I first heard the term 'recommunalisation' used by the leader of the opposition Democratic Action Party, Lim Kit Siang, at a talk given at Monash University in May 2000.

REFERENCES

Appadurai, A. (1993) 'Patriotism and its Futures', *Public Culture*, 5 (3): 411–429.

Arnason, Johann P. (1987) 'The modern constellation and the Japanese enigma'. Part I, *Thesis Eleven* 17, 1987. pp. 4–39; Part II, *Thesis Eleven* 18/19, 1987. pp. 56–84.

Arnason, Johann P. (2000) 'Communism and Modernity', *Daedalus*, 129 (1): 61–90.

Asma Abdullah (1993) 'Oh, to be a global and local Melayu', *New Straits Times*, 23 December, p. 30.

Assayag, Jackie, Lardinois, Roland and Vidal, Denis (1997) *Orientalism and Anthropology: From Max Müller to Louis Dumont*. Pondichéry: All India Press (Pondy Papers in Social Sciences, 24).

Attfield, John (1981) *With Light of Knowledge, A Hundred Years of Education in the Royal Arsenal Co-operative Society, 1877–1977*. London and West Nyack: RACS/Journeyman Press.

Bailey, Peter (1998) *Popular Culture and Performance in the Victorian City*. Cambridge: Cambridge University Press.

Baker, Lee D. (1998) *From Savage to Negro: Anthropology and the Construction of Race, 1896–1954*. Berkeley, Los Angeles and London: University of California Press.

Bannister, Robert C. (ed.) (1992) *On Liberty, Society, and Politics: The Essential Essays of William Graham Sumner*. Indianapolis: Liberty Fund.

Barrow, Logie (1986) *Independent Spirits: Spiritualism and English Plebians, 1850–1910*. London and New York: Routledge (History Workshop Series).

Barrow, Logie and Bullock, Ian (1996) *Democratic Ideas and the British Labour Movement, 1880–1914*. Cambridge: Cambridge University Press.

Bauman, Zygmunt (1989) *Modernity and the Holocaust*. Cambridge: Polity.

Bauman, Zygmunt (1991) *Modernity and Ambivalence*. Cambridge: Polity.

Baumann, Gerd (1996) *Contesting Culture: Discourses of Identity in Multi-Ethnic London*. Cambridge: Cambridge University Press.

Bierley, Paul E. (1973) *John Philip Sousa, American Phenomenon*. Columbus, OH: Integrity Press.

Boas, Franz (1940) *Encyclopedia of the Social Sciences*. Vol. 13. 25–36. New York: Macmillan.

Breisach, Ernst A. (1993) *American Progressive History: An Experiment in Modernization*. Chicago and London: Chicago University Press.

Broesamle, John J. (1990) *Reform and Reaction in Twentieth Century American Politics*. New York: Greenwood Press.

Buenker, John D. (1973) *Urban Liberalism and Progressive Reform*. New York: Charles Scribner's Sons.

Burrow, J. (1966) *Evolution and Society: A Study of Victorian Social Theory*. Cambridge: Cambridge University Press.

Carter, Bob, Harris, Clive and Joshi, Shirley ([1993] 2000) 'The 1951–1955 Conservative government and the racialization of Black immigration'. Reprinted in Kwesi Owusu (ed.) *Black British Culture and Society*. London: Routledge.

Castoriadis, Cornelius (1991) *Philosophy, Politics, Autonomy* (edited by David Ames Curtis). New York and Oxford: Oxford University Press.

Chatterjee, Partha (1986) *Nationalist Thought and the Colonial World: A Derivative Discourse?* London: Zed Books.

Cheah, Julian (2000) 'Warner's man with the music instincts', *New Straits Times*, Life Is. . . Section, 31 January, pp. 6–7.

Clifford, Hugh (1993) *At the Court of Pelusu and other Malayan Stories* (selected and introduced by William R. Roff). Kuala Lumpur: Oxford University Press.

Clodd, Edward (1895) *The Story of 'Primitive' Man*. London: George Newnes Ltd.

Crunden, Robert M. (1982) *Ministers of Reform: The Progressive's Achievement in American Civilization, 1889–1920*. New York: Basic Books.

Curry, Patrick (1992) *A Confusion of Prophets: Victorian and Edwardian Astrology*. London: Collins & Brown.

Czitrom, Daniel (1991) 'Underworlds and Underdogs: Big Tim Sullivan and Metropolitan Politics in New York, 1889–1913', *Journal of American History*, September: 536–558.

Daedalus (2000) *Multiple Modernities*. Special issue, 129 (1), Winter 2000.

Dinnage, Rosemary (1986) *Annie Besant*. Harmondsworth: Penguin (Lives of Modern Women series).

Drakeford, Mark (1997) *Social Movements and their Supporters: The Greenshirts in England*. Houndmills, Basingstoke: Macmillan.

Dyer, Richard (1997) *White*. London and New York: Routledge.

Eisenstadt, S.N. (2000) 'Multiple Modernities', *Daedalus*, 129 (1): 1–29.

Erie, Steven P. (1988) *Rainbow's End: Irish-Americans and the Dilemmas of Urban Machine Politics, 1840–1985*. Berkeley, Los Angeles and London: University of California Press.

Fabian, Johannes (1983) *Time and the Other: How Anthropology Makes its Object*. New York: Columbia University Press.

Featherstone, Mike, Lash, Scott and Robertson, Roland (eds) (1995) *Global Modernities*. London: Sage Publications.

Fiamingo (1898) 'The Conflict of Races, Classes and Societies', *The Monist*, 17: 380–414.

Fisher, Sidney (1896) 'Immigration and Crime', *Popular Science Monthly*, 49: 625–630.

Fraser, Robert (ed.) (1990) *Sir James Frazer and the Literary Imagination: Essays in Affinity and Influence*. Houndmills, Basingstoke: Macmillan.

Frazer, J.G. (1908) *The Scope of Social Anthropology*. London: Macmillan and Co.

Gates, Henry Louis Jr (2000) 'A Reporter at Large: Black London'. Reprinted in Kwesi Owusu (ed.), *Black British Culture and Society*. London: Routledge.

Giddens, Anthony (1992) *The Transformation of Intimacy: Sexuality, Love and Eroticism in Modern Societies*. Cambridge: Polity Press.

Gilroy, Paul (1993) 'The End of Antiracism'. Reprinted in James Donald and Ali Rattansi (eds), *'Race', Culture and Difference*. London: Sage Publications in association with The Open University.

Gordon, Milton M. (1964) *Assimilation in American Life: The Role of Race, Religion and National Origins*. New York: Oxford University Press.

Guillaumin, Colette (1991) 'Race and Discourse', in Maxim Silverman (ed.), *Race, Discourse and Power in France*. Aldershot: Avebury.

Habermas, Jürgen (1995) 'Citizenship and National Identity: Some Reflections on the Future of Europe', in O. Dalibour and M.R. Ishay (eds), *The Nationalism Reader*. Atlantic Highlands, NJ: Humanities Press.

Hargrave, John ('White Fox') (1916) *Wigwam Papers*. London: C. Arthur Pearson.

Hargrave, John ('White Fox') (1918) *The Totem Talks*. London: C. Arthur Pearson.

Hargrave, John ('White Fox') (1919a) *Tribal Training*. London: C. Arthur Pearson.

Hargrave, John ('White Fox') (1919b) *The Great War Brings it Home: The Natural Reconstruction of an Unnatural Existence*. London: Constable and Company.

Harper, Timothy (1996) 'New Malays, New Malaysians: Nationalism, Society and History', *Southeast Asian Affiars*, pp. 238–255.

Harper, Timothy (1997) 'The Politics of the Forest in Colonial Malaya', *Modern Asian Studies*, 31 (1): 1–29.

Harper, Timothy (1999) *The End of Empire and the Making of Malaya*. Cambridge: Cambridge University Press.

Harris, Neil (1983) 'Nineteenth Century American March Music and John Philip Sousa', in

Jon Newsom (ed.), *Perspectives on John Philip Sousa*. Washington, DC: Library of Congress.

Harrison, Frances (1999) 'Women's Band Sing Pop for Allah', *Guardian*, 27 May, p. 14.

Hawkins, Mike (1997) *Social Darwinism in European and American Thought, 1860–1945*. Cambridge, New York: Cambridge University Press.

Hawthorn, Geoffrey (1976) *Enlightenment and Despair: A History of Sociology*. Cambridge: Cambridge University Press.

Heller, Agnes (1990) *Can Modernity Survive?* Berkeley: University of California Press.

Herzfeld, Michael (1985) *The Poetics of Manhood Contest and Identity in a Cretan Mountain Village*. Princeton, NJ: Princeton University Press.

Hirschfeld, Lawrence A. (1998) 'Natural Assumptions: Race, Essence, and Taxonomies of Human Kinds', *Social Research*, 62 (2): 331–439.

Hooker, Virginia M. (2000) *Writing a New Society: Social Change through the Novel in Malaysia*. Sydney: Allen and Unwin.

Horsman, Reginald (1981) *Race and Manifest Destiny: The Origins of American Anglo-Saxonism*. Cambridge, MA and London: Harvard University Press.

Hull, David L. (1998) 'Species, Subspecies, and Races', *Social Research*, 62 (2): 351–367.

Hussin Mutalib (1993) *Islam in Malaysia: From Revivalism to Islamic State*. Singapore: Singapore University Press.

Hyde, Arthur H. (1898) 'The Foreign Element in American Civilization', *Popular Science Monthly*, 52: 307–400.

Jacques, T. Carlos (1997) 'From Savages and Barbarians to Primitives', *History and Theory*, 36 (2): 190–215.

JanMohammed, Abdul R. (1985) 'The Economy of Manichean Allegory: The Function of Racial Differentiation in Colonial Literature', *Critical Inquiry*, 12 (1): 59–87.

Jefferson, Thomas ([1787] 1954) *Notes on the State of Virginia*, edited with an Introduction and Notes by William Peden. Chapel Hill, NC: University of North Carolina Press.

Kahn, Joel S. (1990) 'Towards a History of the Critique of Economism: the 19th Century German Origins of the Ethnographer's Dilemma', *Man* (N.S.), 25: 108–128.

Kahn, Joel S. (1993) *Constituting the Minangkabau: Peasants, Culture and Modernity in Colonial Indonesia*. Oxford and Providence: Berg.

Kahn, Joel S. (1994) 'Subalternity and the Construction of Malay Identity', in Alberto Gomes (ed.), *Modernity and Identity: Asian Illustrations*. Bundoora, Vic: La Trobe University Press.

Kahn, Joel S. (1995) *Culture, Multiculture, Postculture*. London: Sage.

Kahn, Joel S. (1996) 'Growth, Economic Change, Culture and the Middle Classes in Malaysia', in Richard Robison and David S.G. Goodman (eds), *The New Rich in Asia*. London: Routledge.

Kean Wong (1995) 'Metallic Gleam', in Hanif Kureishi and Jon Savage (eds), *The Faber Book of Pop*. London: Faber and Faber.

Kessler, Clive (1978) *Islam and Politics in a Malay State: Kelantan 1839–1969*. Ithaca, NY: Cornell University Press.

Kögler, Hans Herbert (1996) 'The Self-Empowered Subject: Habermas, Foucault and Hermeneutic Reflexivity', *Philosophy and Social Criticism*, 22 (4): 13–44.

Kramer, Paul (1999) 'Making Concessions: Race and Empire Revisited at the Philippine Exposition, St Louis, 1901–1905', *Radical History Review*, 73: 74–114.

Kratoska, Paul and Ben Batson (1992) 'Nationalism and Modernist Reform', in Nicholas Tarling (ed.), *The Cambridge History of Southeast Asia*, volume 2. Cambridge: Cambridge University Press. pp. 249–324.

Kuper, Adam (1988) *The Invention of Primitive Society, Transformations on an Illusion*. London and New York: Routledge.

Lash, Scott (1990) 'Postmodernism as Humanism? Urban Space in Social Theory', in Bryan S. Turner (ed.), *Theories of Modernity and Postmodernity*. London: Sage.

Lears, T.J. Jackson (1981) *No Place of Grace: Antimodernism and the Transformation of American Culture, 1880–1920*. New York: Pantheon Books.

Lebovics, Herman (1992) *True France: The Wars over Cultural Identity, 1900–1945*. Ithaca, NY and London: Cornell University Press.

Llobera, J.R. (1996) 'The French Ideology? Louis Dumont and the German Conception of the Nation', *Nations and Nationalism*, 2 (2): 193–211.

Lockard, Craig A. (1998) *Dance of Life: Popular Music and Politics in Southeast Asia*. Honolulu: University of Hawaii Press.

Luhmann, Niklas (1982) *The Differentiation of Society*. Translated by Stephen Holmes and Charles Larmore. New York: Columbia University Press.

Luker, Ralph E. (1991) *The Social Gospel in Black and White: American Racial Reform, 1885–1912*. Chapel Hill, NC and London: The University of North Carolina Press.

McGrane, Bernard (1989) *Beyond Anthropology: Society and the Other*. New York: Columbia University Press.

McNickle, Chris (1993) *To Be Mayor of New York*. New York: Columbia University Press.

Mahathir Mohamed (1970) *The Malay Dilemma*. Singapore: Donald Moore Press.

Marsden, George M. (1980) *Fundamentalism and American Culture: The Shaping of Twentieth-Century Evangelicalism, 1870–1925*. New York/Oxford: Oxford University Press.

Massa, Mark S. (1990) *Charles Augustus Briggs and the Crisis of Historical Criticism*. Minneapolis: Fortress Press.

May, Henry F. (1976) *The Enlightenment in America*. New York: Oxford University Press.

May, Henry F. (1991) *The Divided Heart: Essays on Protestantism and the Enlightenment in America*. New York and Oxford: Oxford University Press.

Mehta, Uday ([1990] 1997) 'Liberal Strategies of Exclusion', reprinted in Frederick Cooper and Ann Stoler (eds), *Tensions of Empire: Colonial Cultures in a Bourgeois World*. Berkeley, CA: University of California Press.

Milner, Anthony (1982) *Kerajaan: Malay Political Culture on the Eve of Colonial Rule*. Tucson, AZ: University of Arizona Press.

Milner, Anthony (1995) *The Invention of Politics in Colonial Malaya: Contesting Nationalism and the Expansion of the Public Sphere*. Cambridge: Cambridge University Press.

Mitgang, Herbert (1963) *The Man who Rode the Tiger: The Life and Times of Judge Samuel Seabury*. Philadelphia and New York: J.B. Lippincott and Co.

Morris, Ronald L. (1980) *Wait Until Dark: Jazz and the Underworld, 1880–1940*. Bowling Green, OH: Bowling Green University Popular Press.

Nonini, Donald M. (1992) *British Colonial Rule and the Resistance of the Malay Peasantry, 1900–1957*. New Haven, CT: Yale University Southeast Asian Studies, Monograph Series 38.

Norton, Pauline (1983) 'Nineteenth Century American March Music and John Philip Sousa', in Jon Newsom (ed.), *Perspectives on John Philip Sousa*. Washington, DC: Library of Congress.

Paul, Leslie A. [Little Otter] (1929) *The Folk Trail. An Outline of the Philosophy and Activities of Woodcraft Fellowships*. London: Noel.

Peterson, Virgil W. (1952) *Barbarians in our Midst: A History of Chicago Crime and Politics*. Boston, MA: Little, Brown and Company.

Pippin, Robert B. (1991) *Modernism as a Philosophical Problem, On the Dissatisfactions of European High Culture*. Oxford: Basil Blackwell.

Pocock, J.G.A. (1975) *The Machiavellian Moment: Florentine Political Thought and the Atlantic Republican Tradition*. Princeton, NJ: Princeton University Press.

PuruShotam, Nirmala (1998) 'Disciplining Difference: "Race" in Singapore', in Joel S. Kahn (ed.), *Southeast Asian Identities: Culture and the Politics of Representation in Indonesia, Malaysia, Singapore and Thailand*. Singapore: Institute of Southeast Asian Studies.

Reiss, Steven A. (1995) *Sport in Industrial America, 1850–1920*. Wheeling, IL: Harlan Davidson Inc.

Riis, Jacob A. (1901) *The Making of an American*. New York and London: Macmillan.

Riis, Jacob A. ([1890] 1962) *How the Other Half Lives, Studies among the Tenements of New York*, with an Introduction by Donald N. Bigelow. New York: Hill and Wang.

Robinson, James Harvey (1912) *The New History: Essays Illustrating the Modern Historical Outlook*. New York: Macmillan.

Ross, Dorothy (1979) 'The Liberal Tradition Revisited and the Republican Tradition Addressed', in John Higham and Paul Conkin (eds), *New Directions in American Intellectual History*. Baltimore, MD: Johns Hopkins University Press.

Rundell, John and Mennell, Stephen (eds) (1998) *Classical Readings in Culture and Civilization*. London: Routledge.

Rushdie, Salman (1998) 'Comment: it's human nature', *Guardian*, 3 December, p. 24.

Rustam A. Sani (1993) *Melayu Baru dan Bangsa Malaysia: Tradisi Cendekia dan Krisis Budaya* (New Malays and the Malay Nation: Intellectual Tradition and Cultural Crisis). Kuala Lumpur: Utusan Publications and Distributors.

Said, Edward (1978) *Orientalism*. New York: Pantheon.

Scott, James (1985) *Weapons of the Weak: Everyday Forms of Peasant Resistance*. New Haven, CT and London: Yale University Press.

Seton, Ernest Thompson (1912) *The Book of Woodcraft and Indian Lore*. London: Constable and Co.

Seymour-Smith, Charlotte (1985) *Dictionary of Anthropology*. Boston, MA: G.K. Hall.

Schefter, Martin (1989) 'Political Incorporation and Containment: Regime Transformation in New York City', in John Hull Mollenkopf (ed.), *Power, Culture and Place: Essays on New York City*. New York: Russell Sage Foundation.

Shahnon Ahmad (1977) *Kemulut* (Crisis). Kuala Lumpur: Utusan Publications.

Siegel, James T. (1969) *The Rope of God*. Berkeley, CA: University of California Press.

Sivaramakrishnan, K. (1995) 'Situating the Subaltern: History and Anthropology in the Subaltern Studies Project', *Journal of Historical Sociology*, 8 (4): 395–429.

Smart, Barry (1990) 'Modernity, Postmodernity and the Present', in Bryan S. Turner (ed.), *Theories of Modernity and Postmodernity*. London: Sage.

Smith, Chris Judge (1995) 'John Hargrave – "White Fox", A Biographical Note'. Posted on the website of The Woodcraft Folk.

Solomos, John (1989) *Race and Racism in Contemporary Britain*. London: Macmillan.

Sousa, John Philip ([1896] 1994) *El Capitan*, Music by John Philip Sousa, Libretto by Charles Klein. Edited by Paul E. Bierly, in Deane L. Root (General Editor), *Nineteenth-Century American Musical Theatre*, Volume 14. New York and London: Garland Publishing Inc.

Sousa, John Philip (1928) *Marching Along: Recollections of Men, Women, and Music*. Boston: Hale, Cushman & Flint.

Sousa, John Philip (n.d.) *Pipetown Sandy*. Indianapolis: The Bobbs Merrill Company.

Stocking, George W. Jr (1987) *Victorian Anthropology*. New York: Free Press.

Stocking, George W. Jr (1995) *After Tylor, British Social Anthropology 1888–1951*. Madison, WI: University of Wisconsin Press.

Stolcke, Verena (1995) 'Talking Culture: New Boundaries, New Rhetorics of Exclusion in Europe', *Current Anthropology*, 36 (1): 1–24.

Strathern, Marilyn (1990) 'Out of Context: The Persuasive Fictions of Anthropology', in Marc Manganaro (ed.), *Modernist Anthropology: From Fieldwork to Text*. Princeton, NJ: Princeton University Press.

Syed Husin Alatas (1977) *The Myth of the Lazy Native: A Study of the Image of the Malays, Filipinos and Javanese from the 16th to the 20th Century*. London: Cass.

Syed Husin Ali (1981) *The Malays: Their Problems and Future*. Kuala Lumpur: Heinemann Asia.

Symposium (1994) *Symposium on Islam and the Challenge of Modernity: Historical and Contemporary Contexts*. Kuala Lumpur: International Institute of Islamic Thought and Civilization.

Taguieff, Pierre-André (ed.) (1992) *Face au racisme*. Volume II: *Analyses, hypothèses, perspectives*. Paris: La Découverte.

Tanner, Duncan (1990) *Political Change and the Labour Party, 1900–1918*. Cambridge: Cambridge University Press.

Taylor, Charles (1975) *Hegel*. Cambridge, New York: Cambridge University Press.

Trautmann, Thomas R. (1997) *Aryans and British India*. Berkeley, CA: University of California Press.

Turner, Bryan S. (1990) 'Periodization and politics in the postmodern', in Bryan S. Turner (ed.), *Theories of Modernity and Postmodernity*. London: Sage.

Turner, Frederick Jackson ([1924] 1950) 'Since the Foundation [of Clark University, 1889]', in F. Turner (ed.), *The Significance of Sections in American History*. Gloucester, MA: Peter Smith.

Turner, Terence (1997) 'Human Rights, Human Difference', in Terence Turner and Carole Nagengast (eds), *Universal Human Rights versus Cultural Relativity*. Special Issue of *Journal of Anthropological Research*, 53 (3): 273–291.

Tygiel, Jules (1957) *Baseball's Great Experiment*. New York: Random House.

Wade, P. (1993) 'Race, Nature and Culture', *Man*, 21 (1): 17–34.

Wagner, David (1997) *The New Temperance: The American Obsession with Sin and Vice*. Boulder, CO: Westview Press.

Wagner, Peter (1999) 'The Resistance that Modernity Constantly Provokes: Europe, America and Social Theory', *Thesis Eleven*, 58: 35–58.

Walsh, George Ethelbert (1890) 'Immigrants and the Sweating System', *The Chautauquan*, 18: 74.

Ward, J.S.M. (1917) *Gone West. Three Narratives of After-Death Experiences*. London: William Rider and Son Ltd.

Ward, J.S.M. (1921) *Freemasonry and the Ancient Gods*. London: Simpton, Marshall, Hamilton, Kent and Co.Ltd.

Ward, J.S.M. and Stirling, W.G. (1925–6) *The Hung Society or the Society of Heaven and Earth*, 3 volumes. London: The Baskerville Press Ltd.

Warren, Allen (1987) 'Popular Manliness: Baden-Powell, Scouting and the Development of Manly Character', in J.A. Mangan and James Walvin (eds), *Manliness and Morality: Middle-Class Masculinity in Britain and America*. Manchester: Manchester University Press.

Wazir Jahan Karim (1990) 'Prelude to Madness: The Language of Emotion in Courtship and Early Marriage', in Wazir Jahan Karim (ed.), *Emotionss of Culture: A Malay Perspective*. Singapore: Oxford University Press.

Weber, Eugen (1976) *Peasants into Frenchmen: The Modernisation of Rural France, 1870–1914*. Stanford, CA: Stanford University Press.

Weyant, R.G. (1973) 'Helvetius and Jefferson. Studies on Human Nature and Government in the 18th Century', *Journal of the History of Behavioral Sciences*, 9: 29–41.

Wheeler, Richard A. (1928) *The Modern Malay*. London: George Allen & Unwin.

Williams, Raymond (1983) *Keywords: A Vocabulary of Culture and Society*. London: Fontana.

Wittrock, Björn (2000) 'Modernity: One, None or Many? European Origins and Modernity as a Global Condition', *Daedalus*, 129 (1): 31–60.

Wolf, Eric (1994) 'Perilous Ideas: Race, Culture, People', *Current Anthropology*, 35 (1): 1–12.

Wolfe, Patrick (1991) 'On Being Woken Up: The Dreamtime in Anthropology and in Australian Settler Culture', *Comparative Studies in Society and History*, 33: 197–224.

Woodiwiss, Anthony (1998) *Globalisation, Human Rights and Labour Law in Pacific Asia*. Cambridge: Cambridge University Press.

Yoshino, Kosaku (ed.) (1999) *Consuming Ethnicity and Nationalism: Asian Experiences*. Richmond, Surrey: Curzon Press.

Zawawi Ibrahim (1995) *Popular Culture at the Crossroads: Malay Contemporary Music*. Kuala Lumpur: Akademi Pengaji Melayu.

Zechenter, Elizabeth M. (1997) 'In the Name of Culture: Cultural Relativism and the Abuse of the Individual', in Terence Turner and Carole Nagengast (eds), *Universal Human Rights versus Cultural Relativity*, Special Issue of *Journal of Anthropological Research*, 53 (3): 319–347.

INDEX